CoreEmpathy

NCTE Editorial Board

CoreEmpathy

*Literacy Instruction with
a Greater Purpose*

Christie McLean Kesler
Western Washington University

and

Mary Knight
Carnegie Center for Literacy and Learning

NATIONAL COUNCIL OF TEACHERS OF ENGLISH
340 N. NEIL ST., SUITE #104, CHAMPAIGN, ILLINOIS 61820
WWW.NCTE.ORG

Staff Editor: Bonny Graham
Manuscript Editor: The Charlesworth Group
Interior Design: Jenny Jensen Greenleaf
Cover Design: Pat Mayer
Cover Image: iStock/Biljana Cvetanovic

NCTE Stock Number: 08680; eStock Number: 08697
ISBN 978-0-8141-0868-0; eISBN 978-0-8141-0869-7

Library of Congress Cataloging-in-Publication Data
Names: Kesler, Christie McLean, 1965- author. | Knight, Mary, 1953- author.
Title: CoreEmpathy : literacy instruction with a greater purpose / Christie McLean Kesler, Mary Knight.
Other titles: Core empathy
Description: Champaign, Illinois : National Council of Teachers of English, 2021. | Includes bibliographical references and index. | Summary: "Provides teachers a practical and powerful way to connect academics with social emotional learning using classroom anecdotes combined with anchor charts and student writing"—Provided by publisher.
Identifiers: LCCN 2021003052 (print) | LCCN 2021003053 (ebook) | ISBN 9780814108680 (trade paperback) | ISBN 9780814108697 (adobe pdf)
Subjects: LCSH: Language arts. | English language—Composition and exercises—Study and teaching. | Affective education. | Empathy. | Teacher-student relationships.
Classification: LCC LB1576 .K455 2021 (print) | LCC LB1576 (ebook) | DDC 372.6—dc23
LC record available at https://lccn.loc.gov/2021003052
LC ebook record available at https://lccn.loc.gov/2021003053

Empathy is really important.... Only when our clever brain and our human heart work together in harmony can we achieve our full potential.
—Jane Goodall

Contents

Acknowledgments

First and foremost, we'd like to thank the teachers who worked in partnership with us in implementing CoreEmpathy in their classrooms: Michelle Aras, Jenny Bornemann, Heather Coutts, Daina Hunter, Kendal Maxwell, Jordan Nova, Josh Nova, Laura O'Rourke, Tiffany Pace, Linda Peters, Shannon Holman Ramirez, Amy Rounds, Karen Sellers, and Jennifer Tait. Simply put, without your hard work, input, and feedback, this book would not be. Thank you also for your steadfast belief in us. You provided the wind for our sails.

Thank you to Pam Pottle, school principal, for her time and school leadership perspective.

Also integral to our book's existence, we'd like to thank our editors Kurt Austin for his easygoing diligence—apparently never doubting that we were on the right track—and Bonny Graham for her clear and professional guidance, as well as all the professionals at NCTE who helped birth *CoreEmpathy* into the world. A special thanks to The Charlesworth Group for their copyediting expertise.

We are grateful for all the much-needed technical help along the way, notably from Connie Moore, who designed our website; Erin Barnhill, for a brainstorming chart that helped guide our course; Tara Kambou, for artistic guidance; and Jim O'Rourke, for visual layout and art. We are also thankful to Reverend Soni Cantrell-Smith for prayer support and to Carol Jago for consulting with us at a pivotal point in our process.

Because we live 2,500 miles apart, our creative sessions have most often occurred at each other's homes, where we have appreciated the nourishment and support from our families. However, we'd also like to offer our heartfelt gratitude to Brie Bergman (whom we miss terribly) and her husband Bill Lennon, who provided us with such a beautiful space in their home on Whidbey Island to nurture the first seeds of *CoreEmpathy* into being.

A Message from Christie

For Rae, the very first to read this manuscript—you are a beacon of light in this world and in my heart. For Dav—you teach me about words and life. I just can't believe my incredible fortune to have you as my children. My love is yours, unconditionally.

To my mom and extended family—I am so grateful for your generous support and curiosity. You kept moving obstacles out of my way.

And to my CSALTTs, Sarah and Lola, Tam and Tara—you've been there all along.

To my Western Washington University students, past and present, who tried lessons, explained your thinking, and were so generous with your encouragement.

And to Mary—your art expressed in this world is love and strength intertwined. You teach me. You inspire me. In that deep place in my heart, I am grateful for you.

A Message from Mary

In addition to all the educators who have invited me into their classrooms, I want to thank my writing students and readers throughout the decades who have taught me so much about writing and how to teach it. You've kept my passion for the craft alive.

I'm also grateful to Spalding University's MFA in Writing program for giving me the tools to jump-start this next phase of my career, and to the Carnegie Center for Literacy and Learning for the breadth of your support in ways too numerous to count.

Deep gratitude to my writing colleague and friend Margo Buchanan for her unending moral support, and to my friends and family who are always standing by, cheering me on. I'd especially like to thank my son, Zach, my grandchildren, Milo and Zora, who are a constant source of inspiration in all that I do, Michael and Rose, Richard, Kurt, soul sisters Susan and Kate, and Carol Bischoff, who continues to send me links to all-things-empathy.

And then, there's Christie—*wow*. Who knew our wanting to work together someday would lead to this? There are simply no words to express the depth of my gratitude for you. I am not only a better writer and teacher because of you, I'm a better person, too.

A Message from Both of Us

And then there's *you*—our new teacher-reader friend—the one who now holds this book in your hands. Your hard work and dedication to this field is evident in that you are exploring this approach outside of your incredibly busy workday. We are grateful in advance for your time with us and for bringing an open mind. We also appreciate that you bring a wealth of real-world classroom knowledge to the CoreEmpathy approach. We hope you'll be in touch with us (www.Core Empathy.com) to share the fruits of your experience. Thanks in advance for that, too. You see, you are already our partner. We've been holding you in mind and heart all along.

Authors' Note

We have used pseudonyms in place of student names to protect their anonymity—with the exception of Nina and Madison, whose writing appears in Chapters 5 and 7.

Our book represents our combined scholarship, enhanced by a partnership in which empathy has always led the way. In other words, each of us has had a hand in every chapter, page, and word. Therefore, we've chosen to use the pronoun *we* throughout the text to represent our shared voice. Only when we are telling a personal story does the narrative shift to the "I" point of view, where we indicate by name which one of us is speaking.

Introduction: A Greater Purpose

In our darkening and dividing world, empathy is a beacon of hope.
—*Miranda McKearney, cofounder of EmpathyLab*

We can't think of a time when teaching hasn't been crazy. Sometimes it's been a little crazy, sometimes a lot. Like you, we've experienced strikes, reforms, pressures, crises, movements, changing standards, a devastating lack of resources, national debates, and a pandemic. While we enter the profession with a love for children, big hearts, and a deep calling to make a difference in children's lives, the reality is that much of our time is spent doing what is needed, rather than what our heart wants. Too much of our energy goes to solving the craziness.

We want to show you that there is a beacon of hope and light for our classrooms. It doesn't need a debate or a strike. It won't leave you feeling pressure or disappointment. In fact, it will do the opposite. It will leave you feeling energized and inspired. And it will do that for your students, too. As if that's not beautiful enough, it will bring these feelings while simultaneously deepening the academic learning in your classroom.

It's empathy.

Why empathy? Empathy is the gateway to mutual understanding and caring. It helps create learning environments in which everyone knows they belong. Literacy learning with empathy opens minds and hearts to a deeper understanding of story, which, in turn, leads to greater academic success. Empathy is the foundation of a literacy classroom in which everyone feels safe to explore and express who they truly are.

CoreEmpathy is an approach to teaching literacy that views reading and writing through an empathy lens. Its application will bring new life not only to your literacy classroom, but also to you. We've created reading and writing lessons out of this approach, but the real joy comes when you apply CoreEmpathy to an existing curriculum and to stories that you already have and love.

CoreEmpathy is unique because it combines the social–emotional empathy learning with academics. Therefore, it will deepen your student's literacy learning while cultivating empathy in your classroom, making it a safe and vibrant place to be. Indeed, *both* will happen. Learning will deepen and empathy will bloom.

We'll be providing a plethora of articles, research studies, quotes from expert voices, and classroom evidence that show just how significant empathy is to academic and career success. For instance, the Momentous Institute, a Dallas-based organization dedicated to providing therapeutic services within an educational setting to kids, explains higher empathy in elementary age kids correlated in higher reading and math scores (Thierry, 2014). And the *American Journal of Public Health* published a longitudinal study that followed 800 kindergartners for more than nineteen years—until they were well into their twenties—that showed that those individuals who demonstrated social–emotional skills such as empathy in kindergarten were also the ones most likely to enjoy later college and career success (Jones et al., 2015).

These findings are exciting, and we have more to offer in the ensuing pages, but what we're most interested in sharing with you here is the quality of the teaching and learning experience that's possible when you choose empathy as your greater purpose. All it takes is a simple shift in your focus for empathy to begin working in your classroom.

At a Title I school in rural West Virginia, Tiffany teaches a second-/third-grade classroom in which all her students but one live in families below the poverty line. Tiffany is always looking for something new to ignite her students' learning, which is why she enthusiastically said "yes" to using the CoreEmpathy approach to literacy in her classroom. It begins with an introduction to empathy—what it is and what it looks like in the students' lives (see a description of the Empathy First lesson in Chapter 3.)

Adjusting to what her students need, Tiffany augmented the lesson with a video discussing how our five senses can help us empathize. She was anticipating the class read of the book by Patricia MacLachlan (1980), *Through Grandpa's Eyes*, which relies heavily on sensory details to inspire the main character to empathize with his blind grandfather by "stepping into his grandpa's shoes" (we've provided lessons for this book in Chapter 6). Where this class conversation about empathy went, however, took Tiffany completely by surprise.

She began with the senses of *seeing* and *hearing*. A week before, one of her students had broken his arm on the playground. Tiffany asked her students how what they saw and what they heard helped them imagine what the boy was feeling when he broke his arm, as well as how witnessing the event had made *them* feel.

The next sense she brought up was *taste*, and she asked her students for examples from their own lives of how taste might help them empathize. Her students responded by sharing anecdotes about their living conditions that, rather than *demonstrating* empathy, *evoked* empathy in their classmates. Says Tiffany, "This is when my heart began to break."

The first student shared: "I wish people would show me empathy when my belly hurts 'cause we don't have food." This one revelation unleashed a cascade of empathic responses, like the student who said, "I know what you mean. I try not to be grumpy, but, when we run out of food stamps, we don't have anything to eat and that makes me angry."

Next, the discussion moved to *touch* or *feeling*. One student said he hated it when winter came because his family didn't have money and he was always cold. When Tiffany asked him to clarify, he said his family couldn't pay the electric bill, so they had to use a tiny heater that you "pour stuff into." Another student responded with, "Don't worry. I know how you feel. Last winter, we couldn't pay for the stuff for the heater either and we had to use blankets." *Smell* elicited a personal story from a boy who sometimes can't take a bath when the family runs out of hot water. This led to his classmates' conclusion that "we shouldn't make fun of someone's stinky or dirty clothes because their parents might not be able to afford the water bill."

Later that afternoon, when Tiffany told her class it was time to go outside for recess, they all just sat in their seats staring at her. "When I asked what was wrong," Tiffany relates, "one student said he would rather stay in and play because, that way, the student with the broken arm could play too."

Clearly, empathy had been unleashed in Tiffany's classroom. In just one simple empathy lesson, everyone felt safer and, consequently, more open to learning about one another. Now, not only have her students become more engaged readers and writers, Tiffany says, but she and her assistant have noticed how much kinder her students are, reaching out to others in distress on the playground and generally getting along better.

Time and again, we've heard stories like these from teachers like Tiffany who say they see immediate results after adopting the CoreEmpathy approach. This is the greater purpose that teaching literacy through an empathy lens inspires: more safety, more belonging, more joy in both teaching and learning.

And, wow, couldn't we all use a little more of *that*?

Like a drop of food dye dispersing in a cup of water, all it takes is a drop of empathy into the heart of your classroom for change to start taking place.

All it takes is a drop of empathy into the heart of your class- room for change to start taking place.

And the change isn't only in the way students treat one another. It's in the learning, too. As empathy is prac- ticed, academic learning is simultaneously deepened.

That's what Laura, a teacher from Seattle, discovered in her first-grade class. Have you ever finished teach- ing a lesson and thought, "Yes, my students learned the targets, but the learning still feels superficial?" That's how Laura often felt until she began teaching literacy through an empathy lens. She was surprised by how "alive" her students became during their reading and writing lesson time. "The learning just kept getting deeper and more interesting to them. They were *living* the books," she said. "I was originally attracted to this approach for the empathy alone, but I quickly realized this was the best thing I could have done for my students to teach them to become stronger readers and writers."

Linda, a third-grade teacher in a south Seattle school, says that CoreEm- pathy lessons have taught her students to imagine how another person is feel- ing and the language to talk about their own feelings. Teaching in a classroom where English language learners constitute the majority, Linda says that reading with an empathy lens has "unlocked the value of story" in her students' lives.

Fourth-grade teacher Josh was also impressed with the effect of empathy on his students' learning—particularly on reading standards they often found chal- lenging. Recognizing an author's purpose, for instance, became easier and more meaningful as his students "stepped into the author's shoes."

Similarly, after facilitating writing workshops in sixth-grade classrooms, Mary suddenly realized the unexpected impact writing with empathy was hav- ing on voice—a craft element that can be elusive to teach. Attention to craft ele- ments that inspire a reader's empathy seemed to allow the expression of each writer's unique presence to shine through their words. Likewise, after Christie taught using CoreEmpathy with a class of kindergartners, their teacher Heather remarked: "This is the best writing I've seen my students do all year."

We'll take a closer look into these classrooms in later chapters, but, for now, we're anticipating your questions:

- How do I do this?

- How much time will it take?

- Why is empathy so important?

- What do you mean by *empathy* anyway?

- Can it really be taught?

- What is the connection between empathy and literacy learning?

- And, oh, by the way, did you hear me when I asked, "How much time will it take?" *I have too much to teach in my day already!*

Yes, we hear you!

We will answer all of these questions and more within the pages of this book, but first—the time factor. After all, this is a teacher's most cherished commodity, so let us set your mind at ease right now.

The CoreEmpathy approach is not something you need to squeeze into an already-packed instructional day. Nor does it require you to replace the literacy curriculum you already use. Indeed, it enriches it. It elevates it. CoreEmpathy is easily implemented within existing curricula, books, and practices, allowing you to teach to literacy standards while *simultaneously* cultivating empathy in your classroom. Craziness ebbs, the reason you teach flows.

Reading this book will deepen your understanding of empathy and its transformative role in your literacy classroom, while also helping you gain confidence in creating and facilitating your own empathy-rich lessons. Here is what you will find:

- Chapter 1, "Why Empathy Is Core," tells you about empathy—what it is and what it is not. It also explains how we have come to our definition of empathy and how to use it with learners in kindergarten on up.

- Chapter 2 describes what is fundamental to CoreEmpathy.

- Chapter 3 gets you started teaching literacy through an empathy lens, with tips on such things as how to choose an empathy-rich story to center your literacy and empathy teaching.

- Chapter 4, "Empathy-Infused Reading," walks you through the steps of empathy-infused reading instruction with plentiful classroom examples.

- Chapter 5, "Empathy-Infused Writing," brings you back to your literacy instruction by explaining how to extend and incorporate the empathy knowledge students received in reading into their writing.

- Chapter 6 offers reading and writing lessons inspired by empathy-rich stories.

- Chapter 7, "The CoreEmpathy Classroom," describes ways to let empathy guide your classroom culture.

- And finally, Chapter 8, "CoreEmpathy for You," focuses on how self-empathy is essential to living your greater purpose.

A great deal of your learning and eventual mastery, of course, will happen in the classroom itself, as you and your students view reading and writing through an empathy lens. Indeed, the main requirement will be a simple shift in focus. It's the empathy lens that makes all the difference. And we can't wait to show you how and why it works.

The Difference an Empathy Lens Can Make

We've been researching and studying empathy and its relevance to literacy learning for more than seven years now, developing a K–6 curriculum and inviting teachers like yourself to try out the CoreEmpathy approach in many elementary school classrooms. These learning environments reflect a wide range of demographics, cultures, structures, and challenges.

View these classrooms through an empathy lens, however, and you'll see that the students and teachers within them have far more in common than what sets them apart. In every learning community across the country, there are children who long to be seen, valued, and understood being taught by teachers who long to feel the joy of teaching while making a difference in their students' lives.

And everyone wants to know they belong.

We bring you CoreEmpathy.

Why Empathy Is Core

> When you start to develop your powers of empathy and imagination, the whole world opens up to you.
>
> —*Susan Sarandon, American actor*

Something wonderful happens in your life when you ground yourself in empathy—that is, when you begin to see life through an empathy lens. That's what we've been doing over these years of developing this approach to literacy. We thought we were creating an approach that just might revolutionize literacy learning—and, yes, we realize that's a lofty goal in and of itself—but what caught us by surprise was how this focus on empathy deepened not just our relationship, but *all* of our relationships. Not only that, we began to see how empathy might be an answer to many of our world's problems, if only people would take a moment to step into each other's shoes. What we began to witness in our personal and professional lives was what Helen Riess (2018) calls "the empathy effect." Everything changes—what we see, what we believe, and how we experience life—when viewed through an empathy lens.

For this reason, we believe it's important for you, the teacher-reader, to become grounded in empathy first—understanding what it is and why it's core—before delving into the more tangible matters of teaching reading and writing according to the CoreEmpathy approach. We know you're eager to get started, to hit the ground running, and get out there and teach. We love your enthusiasm and we know it well because it also dwells in us!

But here's the thing: grounding yourself in empathy first—that is, learning specifically what it is and why it's core to both learning and life—is essential to your success in implementing the CoreEmpathy approach in your classroom. It's also essential to getting in touch with your greater purpose, that reason you got into teaching in the first place.

Hopefully, this new and deeper understanding of empathy discussed in this preliminary chapter will become your inspiration, the very power center out of which your teaching will blossom in many seemingly miraculous ways. Not only that, we believe you'll see the results immediately too—not just in each individual student's increased academic success, but also in the environment of your classroom. But understanding empathy at its core and *as* core comes first.

How Empathy Is Core to Our Lives

During our very first creative retreat years ago, when the idea of writing a book about empathy-infused literacy instruction was just a seed of an idea, we began brainstorming our title, lightly, playfully. Often a title doesn't become clear until near the end of a book, but, in this case, the vision that was forming between us was so exciting we wanted to call it something. After all, coming up with a title is part of the fun of beginning a project—like naming a band!

As we bantered back and forth discussing key concepts, the term *CoreEmpathy* leapt into the space between us, and we immediately knew it was right. Although the subtitle has morphed over time, CoreEmpathy has steadfastly remained as exactly the right name for not just this book, but also our work overall.

Quite simply, CoreEmpathy bloomed from the seed of the idea that a focus on academic standards *alone* was not enough for the kind of inspired learning experience we knew was possible in the classroom. There was something else that needed to be at the *core* of the learning. And that something else, we believed, was empathy.

> *When you cast the seeds of empathy in your classroom, everything grows.*

Since that moment of conception, our understanding of the rightness of the name CoreEmpathy has deepened. *Core* at its simplest means "a central and often foundational part of something" (Merriam-Webster, n.d.-a), but a secondary meaning from Google involves "the tough central part of various fruits, containing the seeds" (Lexico, n.d.-a), as in the core of an apple. This meaning offers an intriguing metaphor, for, as we've discovered in CoreEmpathy teaching, when you cast the seeds of empathy in your classroom, everything grows—learning, understanding, relationships, cooperation, and joy, to name just a few of those "various fruits."

When we first began envisioning what literacy learning would look like through an empathy lens, the implementation of Common Core State Standards (CCSS) was becoming a hot topic around the country. That conversation continues, of course, and includes discussions around assessment, the value of national standards, and "teaching to the test." Because you can use the CoreEmpathy approach with the curriculum you already have, you can certainly use it with the standards you have as well—the Common Core and others. For us, the discussion is centered on deepening literacy learning, period.

This idea of certain standards being core to our students' success, however, led us to ask if the practice and cultivation of empathy might also be core, not only to a student's learning but to their lives as well. What began as an intuitive belief soon began to acquire real-world proof. Not only were we seeing positive results from our own field-testing and teachers' testimonials, but we were also finding reports from experts in other disciplines of how core empathy is to all our lives. Here are just a few examples:

- Roman Krznaric, a founding faculty member of the School of Life in London, leading authority on empathy, and author of *Empathy: Why It Matters and How to Get It*, speaks of empathy as "the heart of who we are." "Ultimately, the best reason to develop the habit of empathizing is that empathy can create the human bonds that make life worth living," he advises (2014, p. xxii).

- "The ability to understand what other people are thinking and feeling is key to our species survival. . . . [Empathy is] the glue that holds communities together": this is how a group of professors of social work from Arizona State University describe empathy in their groundbreaking book, *Assessing Empathy* (Segal et al., 2017, pp. 1, 7).

- Jeremy Rifkin, author of *The Empathic Civilization*, argues that empathy lies at the very core of human existence: "The ability to recognize oneself in the other and the other in oneself is a deeply democratizing experience. Empathy is the soul of democracy" (2009, p. 161).

- Cambridge psychologist Simon Baron-Cohen (2012) conjectures, in his book *The Science of Evil*, that evil is the absence of empathy, or, as he calls it, "zero degrees of empathy," as demonstrated by psychopaths.

- Stephen R. Covey (1989), in *The 7 Habits of Highly Effective People*, recommends that empathetic communication is one of the keys to improving interpersonal relations, and that empathetic listening is crucial to cooperation and teamwork.

- In an interview on shame and empathy, Dr. Brené Brown, professor of social work at the University of Houston and a leading researcher on vulnerability and shame, says that empathy is the very thing that moves us into deeper and more meaningful relationships—that, according to our neurobiology, it is "why we are here." Furthermore, she says empathy is what enables our sense of connection with each other, the very essence of our human experience (Murphy, 2019).

- Bill Drayton, often referred to as the "father of social entrepreneurship," claims that empathy is the number one skill for career success in the twenty-first century. "In this team-of-teams world . . . people need different skills," he says. "They must master empathy, teamwork, the new leadership, and changemaking first. Only then will they be able to put their knowledge to work. The most important of these skills is empathy. It is the foundation for everything else" (2012, para. 11).

- From the medical field, Helen Riess, Harvard educator and founder of the Empathy and Relational Science Program at Massachusetts General Hospital, developed a brief empathy skills training program for doctors, who, after they received the training, received significantly higher ratings from their patients than those doctors who weren't trained. Riess (2018) writes, "We know that when patients are treated with greater empathy and respect, they have a better experience and as a result are more likely to trust their doctor, stick to medical recommendations, and have better health outcomes" (p. 4).

- And, finally, Mary Gordon—one of the pioneers of empathy education and the author of *Roots of Empathy* (2009)—describes a broader vision for empathy beyond its importance for a child's well-being. "During the Nuremberg Trials," she points out, "one of the judges described the war crimes as a failure of empathy. Empathy is integral to solving conflict in the family, schoolyard, boardroom, and war room. The ability to take the perspective of another person, to identify commonalities through our shared feelings, is the best peace pill we have" (cited in Krznaric, 2014, p. 31).

If empathy is considered core to our lives by so many experts and therefore core to our classrooms, then what exactly *is* this mysterious benefactor? In the remainder of this chapter, we'll explore what empathy is and is not, why it is needed now more than ever, the science of how it works, if it can be taught, how it develops, and, finally, how empathy is core to academic success and the literacy classroom itself.

But, first, let's clarify what we mean by empathy and how the word came to be.

What Empathy Is ... and Isn't

As literacy teachers, we love words. After all, words are the building blocks of what we teach, and we love the search they send us on—the search for meaning. So, what does the word *empathy* mean?

We recommended that our CoreEmpathy teachers ask their students "What is empathy?" before they began their Empathy First lesson (for further details on how to teach this lesson, see Chapter 3). This is something you might want to do as well before trying out the CoreEmpathy approach. We wanted to see if the word *empathy* had come into the students' awareness yet, and we also wanted to provide a baseline for teachers to see how their students' understanding of empathy would change as a result of their new learning.

About half of the students surveyed answered, "I don't know" or "not sure." Many guessed it was a feeling. Still others gave answers like "It's when you feel sorry for someone" or "It's kind of like pity for someone," definitions more closely resembling "sympathy" than empathy with a world of difference in between (more on that soon). One of our favorite answers came from a second-grade girl who asked, "Is it a pizza topping?" Oh, that we lived in a world in which empathy was served as regularly as America's favorite meal!

In the midst of these I-don't-knows and misconceptions, a few students got very close to what empathy is all about. One answer—"Loving someone"—suggests that empathy might inspire love or even be a result of it. Another answer— "Being a good friend, and it might not be someone you know"—starts to get at how empathy doesn't discriminate, how it can inspire us to reach out and act with compassion even to a stranger.

And then there were the very few who had obviously heard about empathy before, like this fifth-grade girl, Paityn:

> I think empathy means putting yourself in someone else's shoes. Someone might be having a really bad day and you might have just not got picked to play the game you want, so you put yourself in someone else's shoes. They are probably having a harder day.

By the time we're adults, most of us have heard that phrase "putting yourself in someone else's shoes," but Paityn seems to intuit that empathy has the capacity to take us outside of ourselves, to see that the other's circumstance may be more difficult than our own.

Turning to Merriam-Webster's (n.d.-b) online dictionary, *empathy* is defined as follows:

The action of understanding, being aware of, being sensitive to, and vicariously experiencing the feelings, thoughts, and experience of another of either the past or present without having the feelings, thoughts, and experience fully communicated in an objectively explicit manner; *also* : the capacity for this.

If you are wondering how your students will grasp this definition, we had the same thought. We want empathy to be accessible to even our youngest learners. We address this in Chapter 3, with the Empathy First lesson, in a more classroom-friendly manner.

The *Oxford English Dictionary* defines it more simply as "the ability to understand and share the feelings of another" (Lexico, n.d.-b). This comes closer to something we will use. Notice that neither of these dictionary definitions says that empathy is only about understanding sad or painful feelings, as the definition of sympathy, for instance, implies. "Feelings" is used generically and implies the broad range of all feelings. We like this inclusion, and you'll find that we use this broader treatment of feelings in the approach to defining empathy we eventually adopted.

Like most words, the definition of the word *empathy* has evolved over time. According to Helen Riess (2018), in her book *The Empathy Effect*, the concept of empathy was derived from the German term *Einfühlung*, which means "feeling into" and refers to "the emotional experience that was evoked in an observer by viewing a work of art" (p. 12). It was later expanded again by the Germans to "describe the process by which a person comes to know how another person thinks and feels" (p. 127). Borrowing from this meaning and the Greek word *empatheia* (from *em*, which translates to "in," and *pathos*, "feeling"), Edward Titchener, a British American philosopher in the early 1900s, coined the term *empathy* to differentiate it from *sympathy*. The latter is the experience we have when we feel bad for someone else's suffering, whereas the former is what we experience when we enter into the emotional state of another person *as if* it were our own. In other words:

> **Sympathy means feeling sorry *for* the other.**
> **Empathy means feeling *with* another.**
> **And the prepositions make all the difference!**

Roman Krznaric (2014), a leading authority on empathy whom we discussed earlier, defines it this way: "Empathy is the art of stepping imaginatively into the shoes of another person, understanding their feelings and perspectives, and using that understanding to guide your actions" (p. 11). We like this definition a lot, particularly for its relevance in the educational setting.

First, Krznaric's definition includes the two types of empathy we are using in our approach: *affective empathy*, which relates to feelings ("I can imagine what another person is feeling"), and *cognitive empathy*, which relates to perspective-taking ("I can imagine what another person is seeing or thinking"). His definition also puts the imagination front and center as the channel for empathy's expression. The imagining process implies that we are taking a leap in thought to understand another person while not actually taking on their experience. According to the authors of *Assessing Empathy*, this differentiation is crucial. It's so important, in fact, that they view the ability to tell that our feelings are separate from another's feelings as imperative (Segal et al., 2017).

This distinction also feels important to us, as there is an experience called *empathy overload* or *empathy burnout* that can happen to the most emotionally sensitive—or, rather, attuned—students in our classrooms. According to Judith Orloff (2018), author of *The Empath's Survival Guide*, some people are more susceptible than others to absorbing people's emotions and need good boundaries to keep them from becoming emotionally drained or exhausted. So, rather than saying that empathy is "*feeling* what another feels," we say empathy is "*imagining* what another feels." The word *imagining* is the healthy boundary that still allows for an empathetic connection to be made. We also want to emphasize that empathy is more than imagining another person's pain or sadness. We can empathize with another's joy, too—and every feeling in between.

Our CoreEmpathy Definition

It is with deep exploration that we've arrived at a working definition of empathy for literacy teachers to share with their students. We believe the one we've developed encompasses many of the above considerations, while still being accessible for early elementary students to understand. Here's how we define it:

Empathy

Empathy is imagining what another's life is like.

It is seeking to understand what another sees, thinks, and feels.

When I empathize, I act with kindness and compassion.

Again, the word and activity of *imagining* as well as the phrase "seeking to understand" both draw the empathizer toward the other, while also providing an important buffer zone that says, "Although I'm experiencing this important connection, I am not the other."

Even though empathy itself technically encompasses the first two sentences, we believe the concept strongly suggests a call to action—that is, a compulsion to act compassionately as a result of empathizing. This action component feels important enough that we've included it in our definition.

A New Term: Eco-Empathy

As you will note above, we use the word *another* in our empathy definition, rather than *another person*, because some books you choose for the CoreEmpathy approach will explore empathy with another living being such as a plant or animal. In the book *Fireflies!* by Julie Brinckloe (1986), for instance, a young boy eventually empathizes with the fireflies he has trapped inside a jar. (See Chapter 6 for sample lessons using this book.) We call this *eco-empathy*—that is, experiencing empathy with another living being in the natural world. Like empathy among humans, we believe that eco-empathy is crucial for our planet's survival.

> *We call this eco-empathy—that is, experiencing empathy with another living being in the natural world.*

The term and how it's used in our approach are best explained through that foundational empathy practice of finding common ground—that is, finding what we have in common with another living being—and how that knowledge then influences how we behave. We asked Raelani Kesler—an organic farmer, educator, and soil scientist—to read our definition and expand on it. Her expert voice in the field combined with a love of the earth since childhood focuses our purpose for including eco-empathy as an essential element of CoreEmpathy. She explains:

> Eco-empathy is a way for children to begin to understand how they are part of the living ecosystem of our planet and the way in which they're connected to the world around them physically and emotionally. We tend to be kinder to those we feel connected to. I hope that, as connections are established between children and nature, empathetic inspired actions follow.

Ultimately, she says, eco-empathy within the stories we read can give children the words to express that connection.

Raelani sees herself as just another living being and ultimately wants our children to see themselves that way also:

My existence depends on the sun and water just as the lives of plants, fungi, and other animals do. It was formative for me to realize that our fates are intertwined. Cultivating reverence for the natural world by developing language around empathy toward nature helps us steward the environment.

We hear the commitment to caring for our planet and couldn't agree more.

The great primatologist Jane Goodall echoes Kesler's passion when she discusses empathy in her work with primates. In an interview with Krista Tippett (2020), producer of the podcast *On Being*, Goodall discussed the integral role she believes empathy has played in her work: "I was told at Cambridge that you have to be absolutely objective, and you must not have empathy with your subject." She goes on to talk about an experience she had observing a chimpanzee family, and how empathy helped her find common ground, imagining why a young chimp might be acting a certain way, as well as how such a process can give you a platform from which you can then examine it scientifically. She concluded, "It's that intuition, that aha moment, which you wouldn't get if you didn't have empathy" (Tippett, 2020).

Whether it inspires a pathway to stewardship, an integral approach within the scientific method, a call to environmental activism, or simply a new respect for and understanding of other living beings, we believe eco-empathy is a crucial practice that will benefit our students and their world.

Why Empathy Is Needed Now More Than Ever

When we first began to develop the CoreEmpathy approach to teaching literacy back in 2013, the word *empathy* was rated as the eleventh most looked-up word in Merriam-Webster's online dictionary. That seemed impressive enough to us, but, years later as we go to press, its ranking has risen to seventh and it seems like we're hearing about empathy everywhere. Regardless of where we see it mentioned—whether it's in a book, article, blog, podcast, or news report—empathy, or its lack, is often at the core of the story.

A study out of the University of Michigan, for instance, found that college students today are 40 percent less empathetic than they were in 1979, with the steepest decline coming in the last ten years (O'Brien, 2010). One has to wonder if this decline in empathy has something to do with the rise of the digital age.

Technology comes with a lot of benefits for the learner, of course, but there can be losses, too. Too much screen time, for instance, at home and at school can be a detriment to the development of social–emotional skills such as empathy.

According to Sherry Turkle (2016), a professor at MIT and the author of *Reclaiming Conversation: The Power of Talk in a Digital Age*:

> We are being silenced by our technologies—in a way, "cured of talking." These silences—often in the presence of our children—have led to a crisis of empathy that has diminished us at home, at work, and in public life. (p. 9)

And in her book *The Empathy Effect*, Helen Riess (2018) writes, "Screens can be a barrier to empathy because they take away opportunities to notice how other people respond and feel" (p. 82).

One doesn't need a study to know that an empathy deficit exists within the realm of American politics often exhibited by our leaders themselves, while, in television and social media, many young people seem to thrive on how mean they can be to each other. What's a teacher to do?

Teachers see the effects of this lack of empathy every day—on the playground or even in our classroom—when someone makes fun of another person they consider different or "other." It's painful to watch and we're often called to facilitate apologies or dispense discipline. And yet the behavior persists, perhaps with a different perpetrator or a different victim. It's like that Whac-A-Mole game. Squash one incident and the behavior pops up somewhere else. For far too long, bullying has been considered an inevitable reality in our schools.

A family resource coordinator we interviewed a few years ago commented that the bullies in her school district seem to be getting bolder. In one of her city's middle schools, for instance, a bully group has formed calling themselves the "Redneck Mafia." Their mission is to terrorize students of races and religions different from their own. Recent studies around bullying are plentiful and show that this experience is happening nationwide, expressing in a multitude of ways, all of them detrimental to our children's well-being. A study completed by www.stopbullying.gov, for instance, reported that "about 49 percent of children in grades 4–12 reported being bullied by other students at school at least once during the past month, whereas 30.8 percent reported bullying others during that time" (Lessne & Harmalkar, 2013). The www.stopbullying.gov website goes on to advise:

> Solutions to bullying are not simple. Bullying prevention approaches that show the most promise confront the problem from many angles. They involve the entire school community—students, families, administrators, teachers, and staff such as bus drivers, nurses, cafeteria and front office staff—in creating a culture of respect. (US Department of Health and Human Services, 2020)

We would add that this culture of respect begins with empathy, the perfect antidote to the bullying epidemic.

What we are suggesting is a complete and total integration of empathy into a school's culture, something that is being increasingly recognized as an antidote to school dropout rates and as a crucial factor in students' academic and future career success. According to *How Learning Happens: Supporting Students' Social, Emotional, and Academic Development*, published by the Aspen Institute National Commission on Social, Emotional, and Academic Development (2018), "Effectively weaving social, emotional, and academic components into the fabric of a school helps students remain motivated to develop skills to navigate and succeed within their learning communities and to serve as responsible, contributing members of society" (p. 3). Although this report refers to the benefits of social, emotional, and academic learning in general, we believe that, when empathy is at the core of that learning, students thrive.

How Empathy Works in the Classroom

We all want our children to feel safe in their learning environments, because, first and foremost, we want them to be happy. But feeling safe is also a prerequisite to being open to learn. Common sense tells us that academics will inevitably suffer in classrooms where students feel closed off from one another, unsure of their belonging, and not understood. Empathy can help with that. A lot.

Research has shown that, when schools adopt social–emotional programs such as those cultivating empathy, academics flourish. For instance, Durlak et al.'s (2011) study from Loyola University Chicago reported an 11 percent rise in grade and test achievement as well as reductions in school dropout and absentee rates in schools where socioemotional programming existed. *InformED*, an online resource serving teachers in the twenty-first century, states it clearly. In the article "How Empathy Affects Learning, and How to Cultivate It in Your Students," Saga Briggs, managing editor of the blog, writes, "Empathy and academic outcomes research show a remarkable correlation between students' empathetic understanding and their academic performance" (Briggs, 2014, para. 17).

There it is. Empathy and successful learning. We've developed the CoreEmpathy approach so that this successful learning can become a reality in every literacy classroom. In fact, educators are already asking for something like CoreEmpathy. The report by the Aspen Institute National Commission on Social, Emotional, and Academic Development (2018) we discussed earlier calls for an "integrated approach," explaining its importance as follows:

We are drawing from scientific evidence that social, emotional, and cognitive capabilities are fundamentally intertwined during the learning process. We're also listening to a growing chorus of voices—students, educators, parents, community leaders, researchers, and policymakers—to make the case that students are most successful when they're given the opportunity to learn in environments that recognize that these skills are mutually reinforcing and are central to learning. We know that, when done well, an integrated approach to social, emotional, and academic development benefits each and every child and can be part of achieving a more equitable society. (p. 1)

Truly, we think we're on to something . . . and plenty of people before us have been blazing the way.

CoreEmpathy's Roots

CoreEmpathy grows from the roots of empathy-based programs that have come before it, such as Ashoka's Start Empathy (www.startempathy.org) and Mary Gordon's groundbreaking Roots of Empathy (www.rootsofempathy.org). In *Empathy: Why It Matters, and How to Get It*, Roman Krznaric (2014) discusses Mary Gordon's work. Founded in 1996, Roots of Empathy has engaged over half a million children ages five to twelve in classrooms worldwide. In a Roots of Empathy classroom, the class "adopts" a baby who, along with one or both parents, visits the classroom over the course of the school year. Students watch the baby's unfolding development and practice taking the baby's perspective. Empathy-based art activities encourage students to apply what they've learned about empathy in their relationships with classmates and in the wider community (Krznaric, 2014).

The impact of Roots of Empathy on student academic success has been well documented. Kimberly Schonert-Reichl, a psychology professor at the University of British Columbia, has been studying Mary Gordon's work for almost twenty years, and, for her, the evidence is clear: kids do better academically in schools where the Roots of Empathy program exists (Schonert-Reichl et al., 2012).

In addition to empathy-based social–emotional programs that support children's academic success, there are a host of anti-bullying books and programs that recognize empathy as an important aspect of their solutions. One book in this genre particularly stands out for us as a forerunner of the CoreEmpathy approach. Lester Laminack and Reba Wadsworth's (2012) professional development book for teachers, *Bullying Hurts: Teaching Kindness through Read Alouds and Guided Conversations*, reveals the power of a shared story to illuminate our shared humanity, thus neutralizing bullying behaviors. The authors' read-aloud and guided conversation strategies offer multiple benefits, not the least of which is developing literacy skills while attending to a student's social–emotional wellbeing.

All of these established efforts that have preceded us offer a wonderful foundation to CoreEmpathy, an approach that extends what we know about the empathy effect and incorporates it into the very fabric of existing curricula, specifically, literacy learning. This is exactly the systemic approach the government website www.stopbullying.gov and the Aspen Institute are advocating. And, since studies show that most bullying occurs in the middle grades, why not begin this cultivation of empathy in the elementary grades *before* students get to middle school? CoreEmpathy is designed to do just that.

The CoreEmpathy approach encourages students to practice empathy through literacy learning, thus building a safe and supportive learning culture while deepening academic learning.

The CoreEmpathy approach encourages students to practice empathy through literacy learning, thus building a safe and supportive learning culture while deepening academic learning. It's a constructive response to the empathy deficit. We've seen it work, and we believe you will, too.

But how long will it work? Does the empathy effect last? Most studies that have researched the effects of empathy programming on student success have focused on a relatively short time period. However, a longitudinal study published in the *American Journal of Public Health* gives us encouraging insight as to how students receiving the CoreEmpathy approach might fare into adulthood. We discussed it before, but, with regard to the longevity of empathy, it carries a big message. Damon Jones and his team began with 800 kindergartners and measured their empathy capacity along with other social–emotional skills. Almost twenty years later, they reconnected with these young people to see how they were faring. Turns out that those who, early on, had related well to their peers, handled their emotions better, displayed empathy, and were good at resolving problems went on to enjoy more successful lives—doing things like attending college, staying away from crime and drugs, and obtaining full-time jobs (Jones et al., 2015).

So, here's the deal: when empathy is present in the learning environment, a student's test scores can be improved (*Yes!*), learning is richer (*Hurray!*), grades go up (*Always a good thing . . .*), relationships are better (*Beautiful!*), and a career is in their future (*Yippee!*).

What's not to love about all of that?

But Wait . . . Can Empathy Really Be Taught?

A few years ago, we had an editor of another publishing house tell us that our CoreEmpathy ideas were great, but that he believed empathy developed as a natural by-product of reading literature, that it didn't need to be taught. Needless to say, we were stunned. We'd already been working on CoreEmpathy for several years and this person in authority was telling us our project was . . . *unnecessary*? What if he was right?

Like this editor, many people hold opinions or beliefs about empathy that, until recently, have had very little science to support them. Many believe, for instance, that empathy is something that some people have in abundance while others have it in short supply, often pointing to certain media personalities as evidence of the latter. Still others take it for granted that we're born with the ability to empathize and that it develops naturally, believing that there's very little we can do to move it along.

Science, however, tells us that, except in the case of psychopaths, empathy is a natural ability that comes with being human, and that, indeed, we can impact its development through conscious practice. "Empathy is not a fixed personality trait: it can rise and fall depending on the situation, and we can train ourselves to get better at it" (Krznaric, 2014, p. 33).

Turns out, our brains are wired for empathy. There are these cells called *mirror neurons* that fire up in our brains "both when we experience something (such as pain) and also when we see somebody else going through the same experience" (Krznaric, 2014, p. 21). For instance, when we see someone accidentally hit their thumb with a hammer, we flinch, right? That's because our mirror neurons are firing as if our thumb had been hit, too. Writes Krznaric (2014), "People with lots of mirror cells tend to be more empathetic, especially in terms of sharing emotions" (p. 24). Further research is revealing that mirror neurons are just "one part of a complex 'empathy circuit' comprising at least ten interconnected brain regions" (p. 24).

Now, just because we have the brain circuitry to empathize doesn't mean we automatically develop it. According to Krznaric (2014), almost all of us have the ability to empathize but very few of us ever use our full empathic potential.

The good news is that our brains are malleable and, like our muscles, our neural circuitry can be developed through empathy practice.

Apparently, the key to developing this potential at any age is "to make a conscious effort to focus on the minds of others" (Krznaric, 2014, p. 27). Empathy is like learning how to play a musical instrument. It's best when we start young, but an instrument can be learned at any age "as long as we put in the effort to practice," advises Krznaric (2014, p. 27).

The good news is that our brains are malleable and, like our muscles, our neural circuitry can be developed through empathy practice.

So, can empathy be taught? The short answer is "yes," but the longer answer is that you're not really teaching it. Through the CoreEmpathy approach, you're helping your students develop what is already there. And that development depends upon you helping your students to focus on the cultivation of empathy within them as a conscious activity.

Contrary to those who believe that you don't need to teach it, as you teach reading and writing through an empathy lens, your students' natural ability to empathize will develop as they consciously practice and use their empathy "muscles"—or, in this case, circuitry. "We understand empathy to be a coming together of multiple components, both unconscious and conscious. We consider the practice of bringing the unconscious to a level of consciousness as one that can be developed and taught" (Segal et al., 2017, p. 40).

If empathy can be taught, then what are our students learning? Quite simply, empathy learning is about empathy practice. It's not about memorization, it's about skill building. What's really exciting about the CoreEmpathy approach is that empathy skills are simultaneously developed along with reading and writing skills. We go into a lot more depth about how this happens in the reading and writing chapters of this book (Chapters 4 and 5), but the chart below outlines the core empathy goals, skills, and practices your students will be cultivating as a result of the CoreEmpathy approach.

CoreEmpathy Goals, Skills, and Practices
"I can recognize and express feelings."
Students practice recognizing and identifying feelings in themselves and others. This includes developing a feeling vocabulary, practice in "reading" facial expressions and body language, and practice in asking someone else how they feel, as well as how to express their feelings to others.

"I can listen."
Students practice active listening as a way to honor each other's ideas and to inspire their own. This includes practice in developing eye contact, keeping the body still yet relaxed, and how to listen for the feelings behind the words.

"I can appreciate."
Students practice how to notice and express appreciation for the positive qualities in someone or something else. This practice includes expressing appreciation for their teachers and peers, the stories they read, and what they're learning.

"I can find common ground."
Students discover their similarities with each other and the characters in books as they share their insights and life experiences through noticing, writing, and discourse.

"I can empathize."
Students learn and practice understanding the perspectives and feelings of others through all the above practices. Through this empathy practice, students will become adept at stepping into another's shoes, imagining what another's life might be like, seeing the world through the other's eyes, and imagining what they're thinking and feeling.

"I can act with kindness and compassion."
Inspired by empathy, students practice kindness and compassion, learning appropriate and helpful ways to respond to another's feelings or experiences. Sometimes, this practice looks like an offer to help, words of encouragement or appreciation, simply listening to the other express their feelings, or offering to be *with* the other and not say a word.

As you will notice, practice is a key to cultivating these CoreEmpathy standards. It's embedded in the language. We envision these on classroom walls to be referenced often, perhaps acting as a guide. Furthermore, as students explore empathy in stories, participate in discussions, apply what they discover about empathy and an author's craft to their own writing, and then apply all of this to their lives both inside and outside the classroom, a student's empathy quotient *will* develop as they practice. And, incidentally, the practice never ends.

Finally, now that we've established the overall empathy goals, skills, and practices behind the CoreEmpathy approach, we also wanted to give you a global view of how a CoreEmpathy literacy classroom expresses itself in the world:

In our CoreEmpathy literacy classroom ...
- we read for empathy;
- we write with empathy;
- we support each other through the practice of empathy.

It's as simple as that.

. . . .

So back to that editor who told us that empathy didn't need to be taught. As we recovered from our initial shock, we picked ourselves up by our bootstraps and said to each other, "Wait . . . It's one thing for something to develop within us unawares, and quite another thing for us to consciously develop an ability that we knowingly choose to use—not just in the activity of reading and writing, but in the activity of living as well." As the science now suggests, it's the conscious choice to practice, develop, and then apply empathy to any given situation with any given individual or living being that makes all the difference.

Indeed, empathy is a practice that is already changing the world—one child, one relationship, one classroom at a time. When you first stepped into teaching, wasn't *this* your greater purpose?

2

The Fundamentals

....

Learning is a result of listening, which in turn leads to even better listening and attentiveness to the other person. In other words, to learn from the child, we must have empathy, and empathy grows as we learn.

—Alice Miller, Swiss psychoanalyst

Vision or pipe dream? "Can this really be my classroom?" you may be asking. Or perhaps more important, "How do I make this vision a reality?" As teachers, we may see the value that empathy can bring to our classrooms, but—wow—with all the other teaching demands, how do we get it done?

As described in Chapter 1, CoreEmpathy *combines* literacy learning and the cultivation of empathy. Empathy and literacy. They are irretrievably bound together in a kind of alchemical mix, and, as they interact, each begins to shine— kind of like gold. You don't teach them separately. *You teach them together.* And, as we've said before, you don't have to add anything to your day. All you need is to put on a different lens. The empathy lens.

In this chapter, we want to show you the fundamentals behind this vision of empathy-rich literacy learning while also giving you concrete examples of how empathy and literacy intermix so beautifully in classrooms like yours. We want you to step into the shoes of children to see how empathy develops, and how each aspect of development is addressed by the CoreEmpathy approach. And we'll discuss the literacy instruction you'll be doing when you teach literacy through an empathy lens, as well as the empathy skills your students will be learning and practicing. But first, getting down to the nitty-gritty, we want to focus on why story is at the very heart of the transformation you'll see unfold in your classroom.

Our Story

We can't think of a better way to show you why story is at the heart of the Core-Empathy approach than to tell you a story. This one's about us.

CoreEmpathy's inception began one morning when we enjoyed a synergistic moment over coffee on Whidbey Island in the state of Washington—a place we had both called home for many years and yet one we'd soon be leaving for new homes over two thousand miles apart. As we shared a review of our lives, careers, and mutual friendship, a moment came over us when we looked at each other and said, "Someday we're going to do something together . . . and it's going to be great."

Each of us strives to create a life in which heart, purpose, and profession are united.

We had no clue what that "something" would be, but it was one of those intuitions we just *knew* would come true.

Each of us strives to create a life in which heart, purpose, and profession are united. Some days are better than others in living that life. Nevertheless, in this moment of parting, we felt assured that an educational pathway would someday be revealed that we would journey together—one that would become part of our greater purpose.

That day would have to wait for a few years down the road, and yet come it did. In the fall of 2012, soon after Sandy Hook's tragic school shooting in Newtown, Connecticut, shocked the world, Mary felt a calling to help. While preparing a graduate lecture on the power of empathy in children's fiction and how to evoke it, she came across Maja Djikic and Keith Oatley's (2013) work from the University of Toronto. Their initial study (later reported in the 2013 article) concluded that reading fiction cultivated a reader's ability to empathize. An idea began to emerge.

After the Newtown tragedy, no one could have predicted the horrors we would see in the future of our schools. Who could even fathom it? Since Newtown, literally tens of thousands of students have witnessed or fallen victim to school shootings, from Sandy Hook to Parkland and beyond. The trauma that has remained from the devastating events needs to be addressed, as does the sad probability that they are not over (Scher, 2019).

In addition to concerns about school violence, there is an expanding awareness of racial and social inequality in education as well—reflective of our society as a whole. Teachers are adding their voices to this important conversation, knowing that their approach to literacy instruction impacts not only classroom inclusivity, but also the very fabric of their learning community. Perhaps at no other time in history have we become more aware of the power of story, as individuals affected by violence, prejudice, and other injustices are telling their stories of what it's like to live in their shoes.

Addressing these issues undoubtedly involves a complicated range of solutions that need to come from many people working together with a lot of big hearts, but, as we've lived our story, it's become clear to us that empathy must be at the core of systemic change. And the experts concur: empathy combats alienation, connects people, and builds understanding. Empathy teaches us relationship. Empathy creates a caring community because it acts as a connector, and it can be a gateway for huge social change (Krznaric, 2014; Segal et al., 2017). As teachers of reading and writing, we've combined the elements of literacy and empathy to encourage the change we want to see.

And so, that's our story. CoreEmpathy is our way of doing that "something great" we envisioned over a decade ago, and now here *you* are, a part of that story, too. You see, when empathy is at its core, the story never ends; it deepens and grows, and there's always more to explore. Join us in its continuing creation by visiting our website, www.CoreEmpathy.com, and share your joys, challenges, and innovations with us, because, after all, it's *you* who will make the empathy real, planting and harvesting its fruits.

But first . . . let's ground ourselves in the power of story.

Story Is Essential

What do we mean by *story*? Story, in its essence, is poetry or prose that contains the elements of character, setting, conflict, and resolution.

You may also recognize it as narrative. You can find it everywhere: in your life, in the events and places you've been, even in the interactions with the children in your classroom. It's found in the books on your classroom shelves and on your nightstand. It can be true (personal narrative, biography, or creative/narrative nonfiction); it can be made up (contemporary, realistic, popular, or literary fiction); or it can be a combination of both (historical fiction.) In any or all cases, it's story that is essential.

Yes, CoreEmpathy transforms literacy teaching by infusing empathy. Yes, it meets literacy skills, strategies, and standards, tends to the heart of the student, and provides an avenue for academic growth—all while helping students appreciate the gift of story, and, in fact, *because* of the gift of story. Story is the vehicle through which all of this happens.

Story is essential to CoreEmpathy because it's essential to empathy itself. Miranda McKearney (n.d.), social justice entrepreneur and one of the founders of EmpathyLab, explains that neuroscience shows us that the emotions we feel for a book's characters prepare our brains to have the same sort of sensitivity toward real people. Moreover, Djikic and Oatley (2013) explain that we, as readers, enter into an imaginary world created by fiction, and, by doing so, we build our ability to empathize and take another person's point of view. Clearly, combining empathy and story is a winning recipe. To capstone this idea, Krznaric (2014) writes, "Empathy is at the heart of storytelling itself" (p. 150).

> *Story is essential to CoreEmpathy because it's essential to empathy itself.*

Indeed, we take this to heart. That's how we have come to pair narrative stories (notice we didn't say "fiction," because narrative stories can exist in poetry, biography, and creative nonfiction as well) with the CoreEmpathy approach . . . because the reading, writing, and sharing of stories quite literally offers practice in empathy as students enter into their virtual world, seeing a different perspective on life through each character's point of view. Because they are young, students in our classrooms can have limited life experiences with emotions. A story's virtual world, however, can offer them vicarious emotional experiences from which they can learn and grow.

Does story help to provide greater purpose? Yes. As a teacher told us, her students were "*living* the books." Maria Nikolajeva (2013), professor of education at University of Cambridge, writes, "Reading fiction is not only beneficial, but indispensable for our cognitive and emotional development. In plain words, reading makes us better human beings, which teachers certainly must seize upon" (p. 254).

We'll go into more detail later, but, first, here is a snapshot of how empathy and literacy support each other through the empathy-rich stories you'll be choosing:

- Reading offers practice in empathy as students enter the imaginative world of a story, seeing a different perspective on life through each character's point of view—particularly that of the protagonist.

- Empathy-rich stories invite readers to learn from characters who model empathy or who perhaps change from less empathetic to more empathetic as they encounter other characters who are very different from themselves.

- Stories from diverse literature with protagonists of races, religions, or ethnicities, or with physical characteristics, abilities, or preferences different from those of many of your student readers can also inspire practice in perspective-taking as students read through an empathy lens.

- It doesn't take much of an imaginative stretch to see how this practice of perspective-taking also might lead to more acceptance of one another's differences in the classroom and in the world at large. The CoreEmpathy approach to literature encourages not just acceptance, but also a deep appreciation of the exquisite diversity empathy-rich stories often express.

- Writing students deepen their empathy practice and vice versa as they model the craft elements the story's author uses to draw readers into the sensory world of the characters. And their writing will grow stronger in the process.

Why Empathy and Literacy Are a Perfect Match

The marriage of empathy and literacy is no accident. Indeed, it's been a long-term relationship. According to some experts, one that has lasted over several thousand years.

Despite current appearances of our society's empathy deficit, the psychologist and linguist Steven Pinker and author James Rifkin both claim that, in the long arc of human history, empathy has *increased* while violence has steadily declined. Both regard literacy as one of the main reasons for empathy's growth, citing the technological advancement of the printing press that made literature more accessible to the masses (Segal et al., 2017). According to Pinker (2012), the greater availability of literature allowed people to engage in perspective-taking through reading—or what, in CoreEmpathy, we might call *empathy practice*:

> Stepping into someone else's vantage point reminds you that the other fellow [*sic*] has a first-person, present-tense, ongoing stream of consciousness that is very much like your own but not the same as your own. It's not a big leap to suppose that the habit of reading other people's words could put one in the habit of entering other people's minds, including their pleasures and pains. (p. 175)

Let's expand on the idea that there is a direct correlation between reading fiction and the cultivation of empathy. Recall the University of Toronto professors who conducted the 2013 study published in *Scientific Study of Literature* that, in many ways, was the seed of CoreEmpathy? In simplest terms, it tells us the more fiction is read, the more empathy one has (Djikic et al., 2013). One of its researchers, Keith Oatley (2008), expands on this point, writing, "We have discovered that fiction at its best isn't just enjoyable. It measurably enhances our abilities to empathize with other people and connect with something larger than ourselves" (para. 3). A series of five follow-up studies published in *Science* confirmed this finding and extended it by focusing this phenomenon to literary fiction as well (Kidd & Castano, 2013).

What each of these studies has in common is the relationship reading has with cultivating empathy, particularly in fiction and narrative-based genres. We learn from them that it has not only been studied, but restudied and confirmed. That's powerful. CoreEmpathy's approach to simultaneous learning of social–emotional skills and literacy takes root.

The more we read *Empathy: What It Is and How to Get It*, the more we recognize it as a capstone book for empathy ideas. This is what author Roman Krznaric (2014) says about the marriage between empathy and reading:

> Empathy is at the heart of storytelling itself. Whether it is through highbrow literature or popular fiction, a fine novelist is an empathic magus who can enable us, if only temporarily, to shed our own skin and step into another way of looking at the world. (p. 150)

Let's return to the classroom. Laura, the first-grade teacher in Seattle we mentioned in our introduction, shows us what combining literacy and empathy looks like through CoreEmpathy. Before students were introduced to CoreEmpathy, reading fluency was valued from the beginning of the school year as Laura often read aloud to her class with an active voice. As her students began to read, fluency was emphasized in her instruction repeatedly as she had students reread to put phrases together or reread with expression. This was all working relatively well, yet she felt something missing.

And then, as Laura began using the CoreEmpathy approach, reading fluency took on a whole new meaning for her budding readers. Now, reading fluently means that words come alive. Understanding fluency is no longer just a voice response, but a body and mind response as well. Her students are reading *as if* they are the characters. This is literacy learning deepening.

Not far from Laura's school in miles, but worlds apart in economics, Linda's inner-city school is surrounded by empty buildings with broken windows and graffiti-filled walls. Most of Linda's third-grade students live in poverty, some with excruciatingly difficult home lives. Many are English language learners whose home language is different from the school's primary language, and yet, when Linda began merging empathy and literacy in her classroom, that language barrier began to melt.

"As a class, we are starting to move from being passive readers to more active, engaged readers," she told us. "The Empathy First lesson kick-starts my students' ability to engage with text. As opposed to watching what the characters are doing, the students are feeling what they (the characters) are feeling. It makes all the difference in the depth of their analysis."

"Students are instinctively citing text evidence as the clues for their inferences," Linda added. A new convert to the empathy–literacy mix, she believes that CoreEmpathy gives her students an added edge, in that it "sets them up to be brilliant"—a greater purpose at work.

Incidentally, the books that Linda used to describe her students' learning were in the curriculum she already has. This is a perfect example of overlaying the empathy lens onto existing stories currently on your shelves or in your curriculum. Further, she did not change her existing curriculum calendar. In other words, the timing of when she was going to use those particular stories didn't alter either. We call this "elevating the existing curriculum," because her students' analysis deepened when the stories were read through an empathy lens. It's the "added edge" that she described wherein her students discussed the stories in ways she hadn't experienced them, or a previous class, doing before.

This greater purpose is also at work in the writing classroom, as empathy and writing are also a perfect match. Writer as "empathic magus," as Krznaric suggests, implies that the cultivation of empathy doesn't just happen in the practice of reading, but in the practice of writing as well. The previously cited University of Toronto professors not only agree with him, but go on to say that writers enter the world of someone else with greater persistence and perseverance than someone reading their story (Djikic et al., 2013). Fiction writers are creators of an imaginary world after all. Although we wholeheartedly agree with Krznaric, Djikic, and colleagues that there's magic in the writing process, as the term *magus* suggests, we also believe there's nothing so special about how a writer applies empathy through storytelling that it can't be taught.

> *Not only does this approach create stronger readers and writers, but it encourages the development of good citizens, too.*

The CoreEmpathy approach to literacy addresses the development of our students as writers in equal measure with reading. In fact, each side of that literacy coin—reading and writing—are designed to support each other. This is the literacy reciprocal effect. The close reading of an empathy-rich story sets up that story to be a mentor text that the writer then models, using craft elements that activate reader empathy. Turns out, engaging reader empathy is a key to powerful writing. That's very good news for literacy learners and teachers alike.

But wait . . . there's *more*. If CoreEmpathy were just about deepening literacy learning and skills, that would be enough, right? But it's not. Not only does this approach create stronger readers and writers, but it encourages the development of good citizens, too. That's the part where empathy itself deepens. This is how emotional and academic learning happen simultaneously.

Take, for instance, a CoreEmpathy lesson that I (Christie) taught in a second-grade classroom in Everett, Washington, in which I invited students to retell a story in partners. A classmate arrived late from a special education classroom, unaware of what had occurred in his absence. Before I could step in and bring the student up to date, two reading partners called him over, invited him to sit between them, and gave him the book. They retold the story to him, as he turned the pages. What an elegant demonstration of empathy, problem-solving, and compassion all happening at once and initiated by the students themselves!

With empathy front and center within literacy learning, a teacher wasn't needed to suggest what might happen or even tell the students how to be empathetic classmates. They figured it out on their own, applying what they learned about empathy in a cooperative manner. The results were instant; reading through an empathy lens had just been introduced that day. What's more, literacy learning continued uninterrupted, and, in fact, deepened, as the inclusive act made reading that much more enjoyable for all three students involved.

When reading in the narrative mode, we immerse ourselves in the lives of the story's characters as we vicariously experience what happens to them from their point of view. This being true, it certainly follows that we are learning to care about other people whose lives may be very different from our own (Nussbaum, 1997, pp. xvi, 10, 66). It isn't a far stretch to imagine that empathy practice through literacy learning inspires readers to be better citizens, thereby making empathetic choices for the common good.

The Developmental Stages of Empathy and the CoreEmpathy Approach

When we began our research into empathy, we asked ourselves, "At what grade level should empathy teaching and practice begin?" In other words, when does empathy first show up in our kids? As parents, we may sometimes wonder if it will ever show up at all. After all, preschoolers are notorious for their selfish, "me first" behavior—"Give me that toy!"—never seeming to think about the other child's feelings and certainly not stepping into their shoes. However, it was during CoreEmpathy's early stages that I (Mary) had a firsthand experience of an empathy sighting in the very young. I was babysitting my eighteen-month-old grandson, Milo, when, with great delight, I witnessed empathy in action.

Milo had just toddled up to the chair where his grandfather was napping and stared at him. I quietly told him, "Grandpa is taking a nap." Milo grinned, walked over to his toy basket, pulled out a teddy bear, and then toddled back to his snoozing grandpa, where he tucked the stuffed animal gently under his arm.

Clearly, I had just witnessed empathy. Milo, at less than two years old, had observed the other, imagined what it was like to be taking a nap (a point of common ground), and then proceeded to let this understanding guide his actions.

> *As early as kindergarten and first grade, our students already have everything they need to begin the practice of empathy.*

Turns out, Milo was right on time in his empathy development. Tonia Caselman, author of *Teaching Children Empathy*, explains that children begin to develop empathetic concern for others between the ages of one and two. By the age of two, a child can recognize another's emotional state. At ages three and four, they are increasing their awareness of feelings and responding to sad ones in soothing ways (Caselman, 2007). And, by five or six, children can begin to engage in *perspective-taking*—or "the mental flexibility to intentionally adopt the perspective of the other" (Decety, 2005, p. 144). This aspect of empathy is more commonly referred to as "walking in another person's shoes," or imagining what another is experiencing.

This is such good news! It tells us that, as early as kindergarten and first grade, our students already have everything they need to begin the practice of empathy. They also have enough experience to understand a definition of empathy such as the one we've designed for our Empathy First lesson (see Chapter 3). Amazingly, their experience by the age of six already includes both *affective empathy* (i.e., imagining what the other feels) and *cognitive empathy* (i.e., taking the other's perspective or imagining what the other sees or thinks).

As with any practice, of course, it's important to begin with the fundamentals, which in the case of empathy, begin with paying attention to feelings. In kindergarten and first grade, the CoreEmpathy approach begins with a focus on these building blocks of empathy: identifying and expressing feelings in ourselves and each other. Many picture books are perfectly suited to this practice, as students look at depictions of characters' facial expressions and body language as well as reading or listening for feeling words. Primary teachers have reminded us that little ones need to grow their emotion vocabulary. Limited feeling words such as *sad, happy,* and *mad* need to develop into more nuanced words such as *frustrated* or *confused, excited* or *delighted, disappointed* or *furious.* Stories that engage this more nuanced vocabulary are perfect for the task.

Expressive photographs or wordless books also can inspire student practice in reading another's expressions and attaching that growing emotion vocabulary to them (Poole et al., 2019). "In order to identify feelings of other people—whether real or fictional—students need to have a well-developed emotion vocabulary," affirms Vicki Zakrzewski (2014, para. 20).

> Being able to recognize and label emotions as they occur within themselves helps students do so in others. Examining how emotions impact fictional characters' lives also provides a non-threatening opportunity for students to reflect how emotions affect their own lives and the people around them. (Zakrzewski, 2014, para. 20)

As we move up the elementary grades with the CoreEmpathy approach, students' emotion vocabulary continues to deepen and grow. Students continue to practice core empathy skills such as reading facial expressions and body language for feelings, establishing eye contact, and practicing empathetic listening skills that support understanding and cooperation in the classroom (Covey, 1989).

Students become increasingly adept at practicing empathy in the upper elementary grades, as stories that are read and modeled in writing become more sophisticated. Older readers apply empathy to the text for more reasons than simply imagining what the characters' lives are like or noticing how they model empathy, but additionally to imagine the author's purpose behind their craft, and, through empathy, to discern possible motivations behind a protagonist's actions. As characters become more complex, empathy helps readers decode them in meaningful ways. When older students read about characters very different from themselves, empathy paves the way for not only acceptance but also a heart-centered understanding of those differences while also acknowledging what we hold in common as human beings.

When entered through the empathy portal, discussions about a book and its characters also deepen with each passing year. Deeper understandings of craft elements such as characterization and an author's purpose, when seen through an empathy lens, benefit the developing writer as they create more complex stories, stepping into the shoes of their characters and seeing their imagined world through their characters' eyes. Add to this an empathy-rich learning environment that fosters curiosity and creative risk-taking, and writing becomes inspired. Student voice shines through.

Perhaps the most significant development in elementary age children affecting the development of empathy is what happens in the social and relational areas of the brain. According to Riess (2018), "These areas are active at all ages, but in the young and evolving brain these areas are particularly busy" (p. 98). This brain activity accounts for the growing importance of friendships as children grow older, until "by the time a child is in middle school, the importance of the peer group soars above all else" (p. 98). What a perfect time for the practice of empathy. And what better motivation for a literacy learner than how empathy creates better friendships.

A plethora of stories in the elementary grades focus on the changing relationships between friends. When read through an empathy lens, these stories provide wonderful models for how empathy works—or doesn't work—in our relationships with others. In a chapter called "The ABCs of Empathy in Education," Riess (2018) advocates for "socially motivated learning techniques" that take advantage of young peoples' socially motivated brains. According to the research, she says, subject matter presented in a relational context allows students to better absorb information into their already-primed empathic brains (p. 99).

The CoreEmpathy approach is all about creating these relational contexts through story. No wonder it inspires so much joy!

CoreEmpathy's Foundational Literacy Elements

Vicki Zakrzewski (2014), in her article "How to Integrate Social–Emotional Learning into the Common Core," challenges the notion that teaching the CCSS keeps teachers too busy to address the social–emotional needs in the classroom. She posits that there are language arts standards that give teachers a prime opportunity to teach both (Zakrzewski, 2014). CoreEmpathy can be useful to any classroom, and we're targeting grades kindergarten through sixth grade for now (with plans to focus on middle and high school later) without it mattering if you use the CCSS or a different set of standards. For us, the argument is not if we can combine CoreEmpathy with the CCSS, but rather that we can combine academic rigor in literacy with empathy.

Literacy is a big world. There's a lot to teach. Even within reading and writing learning, there are many pieces to teach to help our students to become proficient at it. So which ones are foundational to CoreEmpathy? The breadth and depth of the answer are areas we are still discovering. Our approach doesn't touch every aspect of literacy instruction, but it does have a powerful impact on vital ones. As we listen to teachers who have taught with the CoreEmpathy approach, we hear valuable messages.

Teachers tell us that by engaging CoreEmpathy, they've seen deep growth in the following areas:

Reading comprehension: metacognitive processing of students as readers as well as characters within a story and how they operate, making inferences from text, character traits, and how they change throughout a story, setting details, character motivation, connecting reading to self as a reader or the lives of other characters with similar struggles, whole text understanding gained from analyzing, interpreting central message and theme, and applying that message to their own lives

Reading fluency: prosody, dialogue, responding to punctuation, reading in meaningful phrasal units, and using a conversational voice

Writing craft elements: developing voice, building characterization, point of view, showing not telling by using sensory details, being inspired to write (motivation), the inside view of characters, active verbs, plot, conflict, emotional arc, setting, emotional tone

We'll explore these elements in more depth in the reading and writing chapters, Chapters 4 and 5, but this is certainly not an exhaustive list. As you begin to practice the CoreEmpathy approach, you'll discover even more ways your students' literacy learning will deepen when explored through an empathy lens. We can't wait to hear about your discoveries.

> Write us through our website:
> www.CoreEmpathy.com.

Now that we've sharpened the focus of our empathy lens in terms of how empathy deepens literacy learning and why story is at its heart, it's time to bring the CoreEmpathy approach into your classroom. Where does instruction begin? With empathy first, of course.

3

Getting Started:
Engaging CoreEmpathy

. . . .

Face-to-face conversation is the most human—and humanizing—thing we do. Fully present to one another, we learn to listen. It's where we develop the capacity for empathy. It's where we experience the joy of being heard, of being understood.

—*Sherry Turkle, American social scientist and psychologist*

"Empathy first" has become a motto for our work together. We remind each other of it when the work of creating gets muddied with the myriad of decisions and questions that can lead us down different paths. How do we best explain a concept? How do we share what we learned from others? How will the information best flow toward our readers? You may be recognizing yourself in similar questions when you plan lessons. There's not only a lot to teach, but your learners are diverse, complex, multifaceted, beautiful human beings whom you want to reach. Our answer? Empathy first.

We engage empathy first with our work and our friendship. It gives us direction. Just like a map or a compass, it is the reliable "true north" that directs us in the first steps to take. We've seen it happen over and over and we've heard it from teachers: engage empathy and the results can be some of the best work you've seen your students do. It's where greater purpose begins—empathy first.

We wrote an introductory lesson for teachers to use flexibly in their classrooms that teaches empathy before you engage your students in other learning. We call it "Empathy First." Many say that they choose to begin each morning with it; others find it helpful to ignite literacy learning any time they want students to use perspective-taking as a tool; and still others use it as an opening to reading aloud. Whatever the time and purpose, the CoreEmpathy approach first begins with teaching empathy clearly and concisely.

Laura Hay (2018), in her article "A Case for Promoting Empathy in Schools," writes, "Empathy is not something to be learned in a forty-five-minute lecture on the subject: it's something all of us are born with, but it, like any other skill, demands practice" (para. 3). The various uses of the Empathy First lesson are part of the practice she discusses. The more you teach it, the more second nature it becomes for your learners. The more second nature it becomes to your learners, the more places they find to apply it. Rather than practice makes perfect, practice *is* perfect.

The first thing we want to draw your attention to is how much there is to "see" in the lesson. Empathy First has many visuals to anchor your students in the concept. As explained in Chapter 1, empathy is complex and we want to make sure our learners get it right. But, beyond understanding it, we also want them to have the language to apply it to their reading, writing, and relationships later. And we want them to do all of this quickly. The visual document and the hand motions are the answers. They anchor the different parts of empathy's definition and associate it to everyday language in minutes. Students can see empathy as they say it. We suggest displaying the Empathy First visual first, shown below. In Appendix A, there is a one-page enlarged version better suited for classroom use.

Empathy Is ... Imagining What Another's Life Is Like

It is seeking to understand what they ...

   see 👁

   think 🧠

   feel 🤍

  I empathize when ...

    I *notice* by watching and listening.

    I *imagine* what they see, think, feel.

    I *act* with kindness and compassion.

With students looking at the chart, the teacher talks to them using the dialogue below and simultaneously demonstrates the hand motions described in italics.

Empathy First Lesson

As you say the following, point to the part of the definition on the visual and make the movement that corresponds to it. Invite students to read and make the movements with you or after you as an echo.

Teacher: Let's take a look at our Empathy First visual and learn what empathy means: "Empathy is imagining what another's life is like."

HAND MOTIONS: For "empathy," place hand over heart. Use this motion whenever you say the word. For "imagining," place fingers of one hand over forehead (mind) and "release" above. For "another's life is like," place one hand vertically in front of your eyes then rotate the other hand around it.

Putting the hand motions and explanation together, it will look and sound as follows. The teacher puts her hand over her heart and says, "Empathy is," then she taps her forehead with her hand and moves it up and out while saying "imagining"; then, with her left hand vertically in front of her eyes, she rotates her right hand around it while saying "what another's life is like."

TEACHER: It is seeking to understand what they ...

> see (*point to eyes*),
>
> think (*point to head*),
>
> feel (*tap heart*).

Introducing the actions of empathy brings different hand motions to indicate how it is done. The next part of the lesson, below, describes how to put empathy into actionable steps.

TEACHER: I empathize when ...

> I notice ... by watching (*salute*) and listening (*cup ear*).
>
> I imagine (*same as imagining above—tap your forehead with your hand then move it up and out*) ... by what they see (*point to eyes*), think (*point to forehead*), feel (*tap heart*).
>
> I act ... with kindness and compassion (*with hand pausing on the heart, extend it outward*).

The lesson ends with an actual example of empathy, and can be altered to fit the learning by describing a time in your life when you thought empathy was present. You can change your empathy example to fit particular challenges that are happening in your classroom. Other times, you may wish to skip this step because the lesson is in review. Watch for a classroom example when students are practicing empathy right in front of you. Last, you can treat this step flexibly by asking for the example to originate from your students.

TEACHER: Let me give you an example of empathy. (*Feel free to give an example from your own life, making sure to model the above language within your story.*) A friend of mine talks to me about her visit to her grandmother's house, and I can imagine how happy she felt when she was there. In fact, I feel happy, too, just listening to her. That's empathy! I am able to see my friend's grandmother through her eyes. I'm imagining what my friend's experience was like.

How important are the hand motions? You may think to simplify the lesson without them, or think that your students will be embarrassed to do them because they are too old or too cool. We urge you to reconsider. The hand motions are an adaptation from the Total Physical Response (TPR) technique pioneered by James Asher (2009), emeritus professor of psychology, in his book *Learning Another Language through Actions*. It is often used with vocabulary development in language learning because the body movements are used as a conduit between understanding a concept and the language used to describe it. On his website, TPR World (www.tpr-world.com), Dr. Asher calls TPR "the most powerful tool in your linguistic toolbox" because it prepares your students for a successful transition into speaking, reading, and writing. This is a great fit for CoreEmpathy, and we appreciate that it has proven to have staying power as it's been used for over fifty years successfully. In essence, it offers a way for your students to indicate empathy in their body. Their mind *and* their body are learning the CoreEmpathy language.

> *In essence, Empathy First creates the lens, and the lens enriches and elevates literacy learning.*

When is the Empathy First lesson taught and how many times? We recommend it at the beginning of your literacy teaching, when perspective-taking will benefit the learning experience. We prefer it up front and central. Students need to anchor the definition of empathy for other learning to follow. Recall those misconceptions about what empathy really is when we interviewed students. Pizza topping (we know, we're smiling too . . .) or otherwise, it is a complex concept that needs and deserves the clarity and timing that teaching it right away often provides. What empathy is and what empathizing looks like creates the lens in which to do more than view, but to really *see*—the kind of seeing that brings deeper understanding. In essence, Empathy First creates the lens, and the lens enriches and elevates literacy learning.

Is this true for our little ones in kindergarten also? Are they too young to get it? Is the language of the Empathy First lesson too difficult for our youngest learners? Kindergarten teachers tell us they not only use the Empathy First lesson, but they use it as is. From firsthand experience, I (Christie) taught it in Heather's Seattle classroom with great success. Remember, five- and six-year-olds are ready for perspective-taking, as we explained in the development stages of empathy found in Chapter 2. Moreover, the TPR elements help all students access it whether they are young or just new to empathy. Roman Krznaric (2014), our empathy guide, expands on the idea that empathy is not only teachable, but that we can develop it at any time, any age, any grade. He says, "There is overwhelming agreement among the experts that our personal empathy quota is not fixed: we can develop our empathic potential throughout our lives" (p. 27).

In addition to telling you about Empathy First, we'd like to return to Josh's classroom to explain how his students experienced it. Remember, Josh is the fourth-grade teacher in Bellevue. He tells us that he began each morning with it until it was internalized. After he led the students with it a number of times, he eventually handed it over to the students to lead. After the opening business was taken care of, there was a new "empathy leader" to start the day. Let's take a moment to visualize classrooms everywhere where our students are all empathy leaders. "Yes" to *that*. At other times, he used the hand motions as cues. He would make one, ask the students what it meant, and then the students would explain the part of empathy he was referencing. This was particularly effective during read-alouds. Whenever empathy was shown in the story through a character, his students automatically put their hands over their hearts. Sometimes, they would even use this gesture while drawing, obviously unaware they were doing it. This gives Josh formative information in how the understanding of the story is being crafted. And what a beautiful moment to enjoy empathy lingering.

Jennifer, a multiage teacher in an alternative K–8 school, often uses the Empathy First visual as a reference tool to physically point to in literacy. She displays it on her document camera. She goes back and forth to it within a literacy lesson, indicating the corresponding aspect of empathy needed for the moment. If a character is displaying empathy for another, she indicates the "see, feel, imagine" part of the visual. If her readers feel empathy through a reaction to a story, she indicates the "notice, imagine, act" part. When teaching writing, the "see, feel, imagine" element is indicated again to initiate the five senses used in quality writing.

In summary, the Empathy First visual can be used to begin a read-aloud or small-group reading, or even to activate prior knowledge. It can be referenced in reading when it is being shown by a character or in writing when the five senses are being called upon or the writer has evoked reader empathy in another way. The visual is the first step in engaging CoreEmpathy because you will use it to teach empathy's definition, as a way to activate the empathy knowledge you may have already set into motion, or to clarify misconceptions. In other words, the Empathy First visual is what sets the intention for empathy in literacy learning. Acting like a portal, it's the way in and the results are often immediate, whether you are teaching it for the first time or for the tenth time and your students are now leading it with hand motions as a reminder of where you've been.

Essentially, the Empathy First visual and lesson set the lens for students to see through their learning and indeed their lives—a portal into deeper learning, fulfilling relationships, healthy community, and academic and career success. A greater purpose worth striving for.

It Begins with Choosing an Empathy-Rich Story

You'll be surprised at how easy this is. Empathy-rich stories are on your shelf right now, we promise. You need only put on your "empathy reading lenses," and you'll be seeing the potential for empathy-infused reading and writing instruction everywhere.

> In Appendix B, you will find the titles of additional empathy-rich books on our shelves as well as web sources on where to find more.

Generally speaking, you want books that Rudine Sims Bishop (1990) poetically describes as:

> . . . windows, offering views of worlds that may be real or imagined, familiar or strange. These windows are also sliding glass doors, and readers have only to walk through in imagination to become part of whatever world has been created or recreated by the author. (para 1)

This "see through" experience is what happens when you read one of these stories through an empathy lens—not just seeing but also understanding what it's like to be someone living in those worlds. Bishop also talks about those same windows offering us "mirrors," a reflection that helps us see ourselves in the other, an experience of common ground. These are the empathy-rich stories you'll be looking for. For instance, among the CoreEmpathy books you select, you'll want to include stories with characters that reflect the racial and cultural makeup of your classroom.

Because experts tell us that fiction is a promising genre for experiencing empathy, we'd suggest starting to look there. Eventually, you will discover empathy-rich texts in other genres as well, such as personal narrative, narrative nonfiction, and poetry, as we discussed in Chapter 2, because they often share similar craft elements, such as scene, characterization, setting, dialogue, and sensory details. Focusing on fiction first, however, gives you a solid place to begin your selection.

> Include stories with characters that reflect the racial and cultural makeup of your classroom.

With your empathy reading lens on, you are looking for the best book choices that fall into one (or a combination) of the following three categories:

1. *inspiring empathy*—a story written in a way that the reader is inspired to feel empathy for a character in a challenging situation
2. *modeling empathy*—a story with a character who models empathy for another character

3. *eco-empathy*—a story in which the reader empathizes with a living being or element in the natural world or in which a character models empathy for something in the natural world, demonstrating eco-empathy.

Using these categories as your guide, we favor choosing a book that is accessible to as many of your readers as possible considering their reading abilities and the school year calendar. You also want to locate it easily, from a classroom shelf or library nearby. But, most important, you want it to be a book to love. The CoreEmpathy process will inspire deep, close reading. Then your students will read it like a writer modeling writing craft elements from it into their own composing. If we as teachers can't savor it, chances are your students won't either.

With a loved story in hand that falls within one or more of the above three categories, the next step is the discerning process. You want to look for the specific places in the story that empathy occurs—where empathy and the story unite. This step is critical to how you will eventually design your reading and writing lessons. In this step, ask yourself questions such as:

- Where are the moments of empathy in the story? Look for them in a character's decisions or reactions to other characters, or look for moments when you feel empathy within yourself as you read.

- Does this story help a reader understand an element of empathy, such as imagining how someone else feels, seeing the world through a character's viewpoint, or imagining what someone else's life is like? Where in the text is that evident?

- What do I, as the reader, *feel* in the character's shoes or toward the character's situation?

- Are there elements of empathy or acts of compassion implicit through facial expressions in the illustrations or dialogue expressed in the story? Are there explicit moments?

- Are there moments in the story when opportunities for empathy are *not* taken by a character and therefore events go badly?

- Does the story inspire students to explore common ground with each other by presenting a situation that is relevant to their lives, our learning community, or the world today?

- Does the story inspire readers to explore common ground with characters who might appear different from them or who may live in different circumstances?

- Where in the story is eco-empathy being made evident? Does it help to build appreciation of the natural world and our place in it, thus inspiring environmental action?

- Do you love it? If you love the story, your students will love it, too.

This entire selection process doesn't take long. Chances are you'll begin discovering opportunities for empathy learning right from the first page—or you won't—and these questions will become second nature to you. After finding where empathy and the story unite, your reading and writing lessons will unfold by considering how you can guide your students to see it, too.

CoreEmpathy and Diverse Literature

Diverse literature—of which we consider multicultural stories a part—offers unique opportunities for readers to use their empathy lens, as they acknowledge, seek to understand, and celebrate a character's race, ethnicity, beliefs, lifestyle, or capabilities, while also bridging differences through the discovery of common ground. Conversely, students who identify with any of those characteristics will also benefit from seeing themselves on the page. Indeed, diverse stories activate the reader's experience of Rudine Sims Bishop's "windows, mirrors, and doors" into self and others.

These are all great reasons for seeking out diverse literature when choosing books for the CoreEmpathy approach. Empathy is a connector, a relationship builder. Empathy and diverse literature are not only a natural match, but also a vital one in our world today.

Empathy-infused literacy, however, goes beyond being that all-important bridge by also offering students equal access to skill-building and meaningful discourse. It asks every student, regardless of background or ability, to deepen their learning. National education consultant Zaretta Hammond (2020) explains that there are three key components of educational equity—multicultural education, social justice education, and culturally responsive education—all of which apply to literacy instruction.

The main purpose of multicultural education, Hammond (2020, Figure 1) says, "centers around creating positive social interactions across difference"—

> *Empathy is a connector, a relationship builder. Empathy and diverse literature are not only a natural match, but also a vital one in our world today.*

something that empathy-infused literacy does so well. Culturally responsive education's goal, however "centers around the affective and cognitive aspects of teaching and learning" (Hammond, 2020, Figure 1). We particularly love how Hammond differentiates between multicultural education and culturally responsive education as it relates to literacy. Although multicultural literature is an important component in the literacy classroom, and for creating equity in general, she says it by no means replaces the need for culturally responsive instruction—that is, instruction that focuses on improving learning for students who have been marginalized educationally. This is where we need to intentionally concentrate our efforts to accelerate learning (Hammond, 2020).

Empathy-infused literacy instruction supports both of these goals, offering a more impactful way to approach multicultural stories while also offering an instructional approach that deepens literacy skills through empathy regardless of a student's background or ability. By its very nature, the CoreEmpathy approach makes those who have been previously marginalized feel part of the whole. In an empathy-rich learning environment, everyone knows they belong and everyone grows.

CoreEmpathy Anchor Stories

The following are some examples of where empathy and the story unite from our CoreEmpathy practice in both primary and intermediate classrooms. All of them have corresponding CoreEmpathy lessons in Chapter 6, or on our website at www.CoreEmpathy.com. They are sequenced by readability level, with the easiest book first, and then growing in difficulty and complexity.

In Primary Classrooms

Happy by Mies van Hout (2012) artfully expresses a variety of feelings through fish faces and its crayon drawings. It does not have a storyline, but it helps to build the vocabulary of emotions that are needed to use later when characters and the conflicts they encounter appear. Fabulous in kindergarten or whenever that language needs to be developed.

My Friend Is Sad by Mo Willems (2007) is a story about an established friendship between Piggie and Elephant, wherein Piggie notices Elephant is sad and tries to cheer him up. However, Piggie's attempts don't work at first because there's a misunderstanding between the two friends. When Elephant finally tells Piggie what's bothering him, the two clear up their misunderstanding and respond by being fully present with each other.

When we look for where empathy and the story unite, we notice the first step of empathizing is clearly modeled—that is, noticing and imagining how someone else feels. This is quickly followed by the next step, which is to respond in a caring manner. But that's not all. This simple story also reveals a finer point of friendship—that a friend sometimes needs to express not only what they are feeling but also what's causing that feeling for the other to fully empathize. Turns out, empathy is a two-way street. Now that's a book we can work with!

The Day You Begin by Jacqueline Woodson (2018) is a picture book telling a lyrical story for empathy practice, as readers step into the shoes of each character and see themselves. It also introduces the idea of self-empathy—suggesting that there is a "brave self" that is always standing with you, reminding you of your value. We also love this book for the idea that empathy flourishes when people tell their stories, and that empathy is a key to everyone feeling they belong, wherever they are, because, where empathy lives, so does community.

The Stray Dog by Marc Simont (2000) offers a different perspective on empathy. In this story, two children are having a family picnic at a local park when they discover a stray dog. Unfortunately, they are forced to leave him at the park that day. The entire family worries about the dog for the rest of the week until they return the following Saturday, rescue him from a dog catcher, and claim him as their own. It's in the family's concern followed by their caring gestures where empathy and the story unite.

Fireflies! by Julie Brinckloe (1986) introduces the reader to the term we explained as *eco-empathy*, or demonstrating empathy toward life in the natural world. In this story, on a summer evening, a boy catches fireflies with his friends. After bringing the jar home, the boy watches the fireflies dim and slow. This is where eco-empathy and the story begin to unite. As he watches them dying, he empathizes with their plight and decides to let them go, experiencing a mix of loss and wonder. This empathetic thoughtfulness followed by a compassionate act are based on perspective-taking of another living being in the natural world.

In Intermediate Classrooms

Through Grandpa's Eyes by Patricia MacLachlan (1980) gives the reader an example of empathy within the family structure, providing multiple instances in which empathy and the story unite. A young boy named John spends the day at the home of his blind grandfather, where he experiences that world through his grandfather's perspective using four of his five senses. This is the ultimate in empathy: literally and figuratively stepping into the shoes of another person and all within a loving, cross-generational relationship. Grandpa also brilliantly demonstrates how we might invite another to empathize with *us* and experience *our* world.

Sit-In: How Four Friends Stood Up by Sitting Down by Andrea Davis Pinkney (2010) is a creative nonfiction book we love for its treatment of true events and for its dynamic illustrations conveying the energy of the nonviolent aspect of the Civil Rights Movement inspired by Martin Luther King Jr. The story begins with the historic sit-in at the Woolworth's lunch counter in Greensboro, North Carolina, in 1960. Keenly aware of her young audience, Pinkney uses empathy to draw her readers into the story, helping them imagine what it must have been like for those four black college students to be refused service simply because of the color of their skin while putting their lives on the line through peaceful means. We also love this book for its language, particularly Pinkney's use of food and recipes as an extended metaphor for the story's themes of integration, racial equality, and justice for all.

The One and Only Ivan by Katherine Applegate (2012) shows how a complex plot can engage various empathetic elements. A shopping mall gorilla named Ivan evokes reader empathy over his plight, while also modeling empathy as he responds to a baby elephant named Ruby. Ruby opens Ivan's eyes to seeing the abysmal conditions in which he and his animal friends live, further opening Ivan up to empathy. Julia, the girl who provides Ivan with the materials to create his art, further exemplifies empathy and compassion in action. The role of art as a gateway to empathy is also celebrated in this exceptional novel. All of these places where empathy and the story unite are rich with possibilities for a dynamic, empathy-infused reading experience.

In *Saving Wonder* by Mary Knight (2016), readers empathize with the protagonist, Curley Hines, who has lost most of his family to coal mining accidents. A rocky relationship between Curley and the coal boss's son, JD, is eventually transformed through empathy as Curley realizes that JD is "just as much of an orphan as he is." The concept of eco-empathy is also illuminated through Curley's point of view, as he empathizes with the plight of local elk, a sycamore tree sacred to the Cherokee, and, most of all, his beloved mountain. Eventually, this empathy moves Curley into action as he uses the power of his words to inspire others to empathize, too.

So that's how it's done. View stories through an empathy lens, looking for what the narrative has to offer in terms of both empathy and literacy learning. When you begin to see all the ways empathy and the story's literary elements intersect, you'll know you're on the right track. If those opportunities also happen to coexist in a book that you love, then the deal is sealed. You've chosen an empathy-rich book!

Now that the book choice has been made, you're ready to unwrap its gifts.

Empathy-Infused Reading

Good fiction creates empathy. A novel takes you somewhere and asks you to look through the eyes of another person, to live another life.

—*Barbara Kingsolver, American novelist*

Reading is the cornerstone of learning. It permeates every subject our students study. It's a conduit toward information and experiences that might otherwise be impossible to obtain. It's a catalyst for grappling with the complexities of humanity. In short, reading makes the impossible possible, and the everyday a wonderment. And teaching it . . . well, that comes with a gravity of importance that can leave us breathless. We know you feel this as you teach, and that you've pledged to work diligently toward your students not only reading well, but also loving it for a lifetime.

Reading with a Greater Purpose

Empathy-infused reading shares this goal to produce lifelong learners who read to learn about themselves, others, the world, and their glorious place in it. And that's greater purpose enough. We know that what we do in the elementary years has lasting impact toward that end. With this common purpose in mind, then, what does empathy-infused reading bring? How could it possibly offer a purpose greater than what we're already doing?

It's a matter of depth and degree. Empathy-infused reading means that the reading experience is enhanced, both for you and for your growing readers. It's more insightful, inspired, and satisfying. Empathy-infused reading enriches the reading experience and enlightens the reader, and that, in turn, inspires lifelong readers living a greater purpose.

It does this by adding another dimension to the reader. Recall the first graders who were learning to change their voice to read with fluency. With empathy-infused reading, they realized that they could *be* the characters, and this gave them new perspective. Suddenly, they were the characters saying the words. Empathy gave them the way to be *in* the story, providing the insight into each character that informed their fluent reading voice, enriching the reading experience. One dimension of fluency says: "Change your voice to respond to the punctuation and the words you see." Empathy-infused reading adds another dimension: "Be the character and speak the words as if you were imagining their world within the story."

Empathy-infused reading can enlighten the reader because it provides them with understanding and insight as they find common ground with characters. The reader is now aware of characters in surprising and personal ways because they are taking their perspective while in the story, rather than simply reading about them from above the pages. Personal connections in reading are a natural result of this approach because a reader's own life and the character's life are connected. That's what empathy does: it connects.

When the reading experience is enriched and enhanced, the teacher and the reader feel its greater purpose.

What Is Empathy-Infused Reading?

I (Christie) began teaching in 1990 in the middle of the whole language and phonics debate. I look back now and reflect that my teacher preparation program taught me more about the debate than it did the tools to execute effective aspects of both—approaching a text holistically and teaching a reader to learn the parts that make it whole. My woeful lack of skills in the first week of school made their uncomfortable appearance well known. After listening to each student read to me, thinking this formative assessment was going to tell me everything I needed to help them become better readers, I realized I had no idea what to do next (*surprise!*). So, I brought my notes (what did I even write?!) to the teacher next door and sheepishly said, "Um, so . . . I've listened to all of my students read . . . now what?"

Wendy was the gracious teacher next door. I am in gratitude to Wendy for many reasons, but the first is not looking shocked or incredulous. Who would blame her if she were thinking it, however? Instead, she opened the curriculum and gently explained the steps to use it from a reachable starting point. A true, empathetic teacher. She helped me to understand that reading was all about understanding, not about getting the words right. Sure, what we read and how we read it matters, but the core of this fruit is the understanding itself.

From this humble beginning, my journey to becoming a reading specialist began. This led me to being a literacy instructor in a teacher education program, then a literacy professional developer. It is no surprise that the deeper schooling and enriched experiences confirmed that Wendy was right. Reading is about understanding. Every reader I've taught has confirmed it too. They love reaching the core of a text because that's where their heart and mind come together to love reading (Figure 4.1). If "reading is to the mind what exercise is to the body," as the eighteenth-century English writer Joseph Addison observed, then empathy is here to infuse new heights to the mind.

FIGURE 4.1. Christie teaching a CoreEmpathy lesson to second graders using *The Stray Dog.*

The CoreEmpathy approach to reading has understanding at its core. Empathy paves the way to understanding what is being read by igniting discovery, and that, in turn, is at the heart of new understandings. Reading and understanding are like a dancer and the dance—inseparable. They overlap, they move together, they create together. Reading the words and understanding what they mean work together in a similar, synergistic way.

Empathy-infused reading is informed by Louise Rosenblatt and her message in *Literature as Exploration* (1995) and *Making Meaning with Texts* (2005). She teaches us that meaning for the reader emerges as they combine words with their thoughts and experiences. It's an interaction of these elements—the reader and the words on the page—that's key, and inspiring these interactions is a large part of the role of great reading teachers. Kylene Beers and Robert Probst (2013) discuss this in their book *Notice and Note: Strategies for Close Reading*: "The text awakens associations in the reader's mind, and out of the mix, meaning is created" (p. 1). Understanding happens at the intersection of components rather than residing in one or the other, the text or the reader's thinking.

> *The CoreEmpathy approach to reading has understanding at its core.*

We couldn't agree more. Reading is about understanding. And understanding comes from reader and text interactions, just as a performance is seen from the intertwining of the dance and the dancer. So what do we add to this formula?

We want the reader to enrich their understandings with empathy. Empathy shifts a reader's interactions with text—sometimes dramatically, sometimes ever so slightly—resulting in understanding with new perspectives, new insights. CoreEmpathy encourages readers to have more opportunities to let their understandings emerge—in fact *deepen*—as they interact with the story. Readers who more deeply understand taking perspectives more deeply understand text.

> *Readers who more deeply understand taking perspectives more deeply understand text.*

It's this depth and degree of understanding that connects us to greater purpose. And the vital energy that fuels the understanding process is one you may know: close reading.

What Is Close Reading within Empathy-Infused Reading?

This is a great question as the definition of close reading has been changing since the adoption of the CCSS and the encouragement of "rigor." The CCSS define *close reading* as "attentive reading" and encourage readers to carefully consider what the author presents to them, then derive understandings from analyzing it (National Governors Association & Council Chief State School Officers, 2010). There appears to be limitations to this, however. For example, it discourages a reader from inputting too much of themselves or wandering too far from what the author writes by requiring responses to have evidence from the original text to be correct (Beers & Probst, 2013). It wants a reader to stay close to the page.

Wanting to expand close reading's initial limits, many are broadening its definition by including more elements. Close reading's evolved definition implies the reader and the text be close together in a more interactive way. Rather than the text being static and the reader approaching it, the expanded meaning of close reading invites the reader to meaningfully interact with the text, bringing their experiences, thoughts, and memories into the mix. Their schema, then, interacts by playing, dancing, challenging, questioning, and relating to the text for meaning to emerge. Influenced by Rosenblatt and her work, Beers and Probst (2013) put it this way:

> Close reading should suggest close attention to the text; close attention to the relevant experience, thought, and memory of the reader; close attention to the responses and interpretations of other readers; and close attention to the interactions among those elements. (p. 37)

Quite naturally, respecting the original text and how the author wrote it is a shared value between close reading's original definition and the CoreEmpathy approach. We want readers to pay close attention to the author's words, noticing elements that they think are relevant, surprising, enterprising, and worth pondering. We also want readers to know where in the text those thoughts occurred and to be considerate and knowledgeable about the author's original words. So we're into that, but we're not limited by it either.

Close reading's new definition of respecting and valuing the words on the page with the inclusion of the reader's schema, thoughts, and reactions is more closely aligned with what our approach calls *empathy-infused reading*. The understandings resulting from close reading become the content for meaningful discourse. Rosenblatt (1995, 2005) and Beers and Probst (2013) inform us that meaning-making requires all of these elements in interaction. It's meaning-making, after all, not meaning *collecting*. And this requires the reader to touch the words with their whole selves. That's empathy's gift.

Once the whole self is in, the love of reading, its greater purpose, is felt. Close, empathy-infused reading is the deepening process of reading a page, thinking about what is said, and then allowing empathy to open an even deeper way into it. It inspires the reader to walk in a character's shoes, quite literally experiencing life as they are experiencing it. The reader sees what the character sees, and vicariously feels what

> *Close, empathy-infused reading is the deepening process of reading a page, thinking about what is said, and then allowing empathy to open an even deeper way into it.*

the character feels. Our limitless approach wants to take a reader as their whole self even closer in and to intensify the interactions between them and the text. In fact, we want the reader to be so close to the page, they feel in it. For the reader, that's making real time and page time the same.

Literary Elements and Reading Goals That Lend Themselves to Empathy-Infused Reading

In Chapter 2, we introduced you to the areas of literacy learning that empathy seems to sensitize, activate, and accentuate—reading comprehension and fluency, and certain writing craft elements. We will examine the reading areas more closely here, while writing craft elements will be explained next, in Chapter 5. Reading areas enhanced by CoreEmpathy include:

- metacognition
- characterization
- setting
- connecting to prior experience
- author's purpose
- inferring and predicting
- central message
- theme
- reading fluency
- reading community

Reading Comprehension

There's no better place to start than with reading comprehension, because it's at the heart of every reading experience. We brought you the great news that empathy-infused reading ultimately leads to deeper comprehension. The areas in relation to which you and your students will actualize this understanding is with the overall text, the characters within it, key details in the text, and the themes and central messages the author wants us to explore. This is done primarily because metacognition (thinking about one's own thinking) is a stepping-stone toward thinking about another's thinking—an aspect of empathy. They are linked. And it's the combination of the two ways of thinking that propels readers to truly powerful, even profound comprehension (Vega, 2016).

Greater purpose is at work when we infuse empathy into the study of characterization. Readers not only understand who a character is more deeply, but they feel a deeper emotional connection with them. This happens because empathy is, in large part, a cognitive process, as discussed in Chapter 1. It activates the part of the brain that we use to imagine.

Through empathy-infused reading, our students' thinking is guided to imagine what a character might be seeing, feeling, and thinking. The affective part of empathy causes an individual to closely notice a person's emotional state, maybe even feel what they are feeling. What is activated in empathy-infused reading, then, is a reader's imagination focused on another person's life, which results in deeper understanding of character. As literacy teachers, we know that narrative stories are primarily told through character; who a character is, what a character wants, and how a character changes over time. When your students' imagination is keenly focused on those aspects of characterization, insights abound.

Imagining what is being seen, heard, and felt also helps a reader to notice the details in the setting. As we ask readers to imagine what a character sees, or what life might be like for a character, the view is emphasized. What is this character looking at? What surrounds them to create the life they have? These questions lead students to be able to see details in the setting—first in their mind's eye, then later in discussion or reader response.

We've described empathy as a connector between people with a shared experience, which in turn becomes the glue adhering common ground. Even if someone has not had the same experience as another, they are able to understand the other's feelings because they can relate through a similar experience. In empathy-infused close reading, we want readers to bring their prior experiences into the stories they read. When they do, they connect themselves with the book, its plot and characters, finding common ground. In other words, empathy activates the connections a reader makes between their experiences and what is happening in the story. This common ground enhances close reading, and here we are at greater purpose once again.

Remember Josh, the fourth-grade teacher in Bellevue? In the introduction, we told you how the empathy practice of "stepping into the author's shoes" made it easier for his students to discover and describe an author's purpose. Through this application of empathy, the author's perspective became synonymous with the author's purpose, making it easier to access. Josh also noticed how the imaginary exercise of perspective-taking expanded his learners' capacity to "see" with the mind's eye, making them better at predicting and inferring.

Predicting and inferring—or drawing conclusions and asking questions in combination with relevant thinking while reading—is often difficult to teach because it requires the reader to move their attention away from words on the page. Empathy acts as a guide for the movement from what is literally read to making meaningful inferences about it. It also prevents the reader from straying too far from the text at the same time. The reader's traveling thoughts remain relevant to comprehending the reading, because what the reader "sees" in their mind's eye is taken from being *in* the text—a state that empathy-infused reading inspires.

Empathy acts as a guide for the movement from what is literally read to making meaningful inferences about it.

Two related core literary elements of a story—central message and theme— are also impacted by empathy-infused reading. Arguably, this is our approach's most powerful impact. A story's central message and theme are often elusive to teach because they can appear ephemeral to a reader. Found after the reading experience, hints and clues swirled all around the story during the reading process. It's challenging for a reader to interpret the swirl into a cohesive message. When empathy-infused reading is used, the unobtainable becomes obtainable. What makes these elements easier through empathy-infused reading can be found within the definition of what they are and how a reader discovers them. Let's take a closer look.

The *central message* of a story is a big idea a writer wants to convey. It's usually a statement about life or how the world works, and how a person can apply it to themselves. Themes can be derived from central messages. Examples of messages are "overcoming difficulty can make us a better person" or "acceptance and love conquer obstacles." The themes derived from these messages could be "resilience" and "perseverance." A reader explores these by paying close attention to a character's actions, key plot details, and how conflict is faced by characters. That's the part that can feel like it's swirling. They then interpret those and, through analysis (CoreEmpathy's close reading) discover new layers of meaning. Recall empathy's influence with characterization through imagining what one sees, thinks, and feels. Empathy also has an insightful impact on an author's perspective. Add in a rich discussion at empathy-laden moments in the story and the result is inspired analysis, enriched close reading. Through these, a reader arrives at relevant themes.

Reading Fluency

Empathy also has a powerful effect on reading fluency. Reading fluently requires a reader to use altering voice qualities in order to read with meaning, pragmatics, syntax, and accuracy. It can be described as "reading like you are talking." Fluent reading can appear inattentive, as if the reader isn't intentionally tending to each word, because the words naturally flow as if in conversation. But underneath the natural speech is a myriad of cognitive language and meaning processing to achieve those results. It's the moment when a professional dancer executes a step so automatically it looks effortless, yet we know it has come with hours of rehearsal, even years of training. When elementary students begin to learn to read or when the text is difficult, the efforts of reading supersede fluency. Empathy makes fluency approachable, however, because a reader is taking the perspective of a character and acting *as if* they are talking just as the character would.

Reading and Writing Taught Together

Let's take a moment to recognize the reciprocal literacy learning effect with many of these literacy areas. Although mentioned earlier, we'd like to explain what we mean here. Instruction in empathy-infused reading deepens a writer, while instructing empathy-infused writing deepens a reader. When we look at areas of literacy through reading and writing with an empathy lens, we see characterization becoming more meaningful, dialogue written with a character's desires in mind, plot being examined more closely for its impact on characters, and places noticed where we care about and empathize with the main character.

This identifying process through an empathy lens offers more meaning than just "what this is"; instead, students are invited to notice "why this element is so important." This in turn leads a reader to start thinking like a writer, creating a bridge between these two areas of literacy. Literacy enjoyment and practice result, holistically arriving at greater purpose.

A Reading Community

In addition to enhancing key literacy areas, there are other benefits of CoreEmpathy to the literacy classroom. One of these benefits is that your learning environment will change. Reading on our own is valuable, of course—vital even—but sharing it brings us together. Reading as a social act is part of its core. Beers and Probst (2013) informed us of this earlier when they described close attention to the responses and interpretations of other readers as an important part of reading interactions. An individual's reading responses are meant to meet another's reading responses. This creates meaning-making discourse. With its empathy-laden discourse, a reading community is created naturally, where the heart of one reader meets the heart of another.

With its empathy-laden discourse, a reading community is created naturally, where the heart of one reader meets the heart of another.

We'd like to show you how.

Preparing to Teach Empathy-Infused Reading

In Chapter 3, we discussed how to choose an empathy-rich story. As we suggested, it can be one that we are anchoring in our explanations, a "loved" story off your classroom shelves, or one from the curriculum you use. No matter where it comes from, you'll want the empathy within it to shine. To prepare to read infused with empathy, let's quickly review our criteria for choosing a story. You want it to be a book you can savor, written in narrative mode, that embodies empathy in at least one of the following categories:

Inspires empathy—a story written in a way that the reader is inspired to feel empathy for a character in a challenging situation. Remember, readers will enter this story's world, real or imagined, and see it through the life of the characters. Their challenges become the reader's challenges.

Models empathy—a story with a character who models empathy. Readers can learn from characters who model empathy by learning how it is expressed, how it can change them, and how it can connect them to others who may seem different from themselves.

> Many of the stories used as examples in this chapter have corresponding sample lessons offered in Chapter 6. You will also find sample lessons on our website: www.CoreEmpathy .com.

Eco-empathy—a story in which the reader empathizes with a living being or element in the natural world, or in which a character models empathy for something in the natural world.

Designing Connecting Questions

Learning how to connect the questions we ask our readers to probe understanding with empathy elements is a foundational concept to the CoreEmpathy approach to literacy learning. In fact, we can't tell you enough how important it is. It's where we unwrap the story's gifts and it sets the stage for so much goodness to come—the deepening reading and writing processes, the rich discussion around text, and the warm community you will all feel in your classroom. Asking *connecting questions* is where we bridge the Empathy First lesson to the stories, helping our students see how empathy will be their portal to deeper understanding and satisfaction in reading and writing.

Identifying the places where shimmering moments of empathy happen in the story is your initial designing step. As discussed, ask yourself questions such as:

- Which pages demonstrate the intersections of empathy and the story most vividly?
- How is it being shown? Is it through the text itself or through facial expressions, actions, or details in the illustrations?
- How can I highlight these in discussion?

These questions will lead you to the specific moments in the story where the possibility for the intersection between empathy and your students' thinking may happen through classroom discourse. Insert a connecting question right there—in those moments where empathy shimmers.

Connecting questions—questions that drape empathy over the story and, vice versa, the story over empathy—promote thoughtful discussion. They are designed to do this in two ways: (1) by including empathy in their wording and (2) by inviting the reader to explore the intersection of their understanding and empathy. We know you'd love examples right now.

Using our anchor books introduced in Chapter 3, we provide examples of the connecting questions we would ask at the moments at which empathy and the story intersect. You will find one example for each category of empathy, with an addition of a foundational book to help students develop an emotion or feeling vocabulary to use later when answering the connecting questions. As you read, notice that the questions combine the story's key elements *and* empathy, and neither component is asked at the expense of or without knowledge of the other. That's the reciprocity of connecting questions. The questions take what you know about asking great comprehension questions while reading and bond empathy to them. You can connect the comprehension questions already in your curriculum to empathy with this strategy and notice elevated conversations through insights and increased engagement. Following our examples, you will find guidelines for writing your own connecting questions on the books in your classroom.

A Book That Establishes a Feeling Vocabulary

Happy by Mies van Hout (2012) is a book that depicts feelings through artful crayon drawings of a fish. Why did we choose it? Rather than a book that fits into one of the three empathy categories, it provides a foundational feeling vocabulary students will need later as they discuss empathy-rich stories.

A feeling vocabulary can also play a key role in students finding common ground with others, or discovering similarities between themselves. That first step into finding common ground occurs when students share the same feeling—"happy," for example—even though the experiences that led them there may be very different. We see a clear place for *Happy* in a kindergarten classroom, but it can certainly be read at any time when increasing a feeling vocabulary might enhance discussions—particularly those centered on perspective-taking. The following are examples of connecting questions that could be asked when reading *Happy*:

- After labeling a feeling on any page—for example, "I see that this fish is happy"—ask, Do you agree? Why do you think so? What about the fish tells you he is happy?
- Are feelings on the inside of us or the outside?
- Have you ever felt like this fish? What was happening when you did?
- Do all feelings feel good?
- Has everyone felt the feeling the fish is feeling? What was happening for you when you felt a similar feeling?
- What happens to feelings?
- Can you show me your "happy" face? (Or insert here any of the feelings expressed by the fish illustrations.) What would your body look like if you were "happy"?

A Book That Inspires Empathy

Sit-In: How Four Friends Stood Up by Sitting Down by Andrea Davis Pinkney (2010) is a creative nonfiction story that, through its treatment of true events, conveys the energy of the nonviolent aspect of the Civil Rights Movement inspired by Martin Luther King Jr. As mentioned earlier, we chose this story because Pinkney masterfully draws the reader into the story as it begins with the historic sit-in at the Woolworth's lunch counter in Greensboro, North Carolina, in 1960. The reader is inspired to feel empathy for the students, imagining what it must have been like for those four black college students to be refused service simply because of the color of their skin while putting their lives on the line through peaceful means. We also love this book for its language, particularly Pinkney's use of food and recipes as an extended metaphor for the story's themes of integration, racial equality, and justice for all.

Sit-In's illustrations also inspire us as readers to go back in time to empathize with the students at the lunch counter by illuminating perspective changes as we view them from the front, back, close up, and in the distance. Further, Brian Pinkney's spirited artwork sometimes has us view the students close to the horizon line or above it, looking down. This facilitates the perspective-taking already inherent in empathizing. We see it vividly on the page and in our mind's eye. The illustrations are yet another opportunity for the reader to feel empathy with the characters in a significant and challenging setting.

Let's take a look at what empathy-rich connecting questions you might ask at the beginning, middle, and end of the story. Again, notice the empathy language combined with the story's events and structure.

At the beginning of the story, we might ask:

- Looking at this picture of four young college students at a lunch counter, what do you imagine they're waiting for? What do the words say they were feeling? What do *you* imagine they were feeling?

- The author uses something everyone in the world understands—food and recipes—to talk about big ideas. Why do you think she does this? Let's watch for every time she uses a cooking term, food, or a recipe to talk about a big idea.

- What must it feel like to be treated like "the hole in a doughnut?"

- Putting yourself in their shoes, what do you imagine the four friends were thinking as they sat there?

In the middle of the story, we can ask:

- What kept those four friends strong in their conviction to "ignore the law" of "whites only" and "refuse to leave?" What inspired them?

- The author uses bold words throughout her story, such as "Be loving enough to absorb evil." Why do you imagine she does this? What changes in you when you see/read them?

- What could you imagine their evening was like when they got home after the first day?

- After reading about what the sit-in students often did at the counter (read schoolbooks, finished homework . . .), ask: What things do you have in common with these students back in the 1960s?

- As the students get treated poorly, they continue to sit in what the author describes as "practicing peace." What can you imagine was happening inside of them? What did "practicing peace" mean to them?

Toward the end of the story, even once the book is finished, we ask questions that guide a reader toward discovering the theme using empathy to fuel their ideas. Here are possible examples for the end of *Sit-In*:

- How would you feel if you were sitting there with them? (*Encourage the expression of all feelings, including strong, or hopeful, or bored.*)

- Where in the story could empathy have been useful or needed?

- Stepping into the shoes of the people who treated these students so poorly, why would they do this? What were they feeling, do you imagine?

- What part did empathy play in helping people to join the students in their work for integration and equality?

A Book That Models Empathy

My Friend Is Sad by Mo Willems (2007) is a fictional story about the friendship between Piggie and Elephant. It falls in the category of empathy-rich books that have a character who models empathy. Piggie notices Elephant's sadness and imagines how he feels. *My Friend Is Sad* also tells a story of empathy in action, as it shows characters who respond in a caring way. Let's take a close look at how you could move your class discussion into the story with empathy.

We want our students to notice the pages at the beginning of the story where Piggie says in a dialogue bubble, "My friend is sad." As he expresses this, his facial expression matches his feeling of concern. Connecting questions that could be asked to enrich understanding of the characters might be:

- How is Piggie showing Elephant empathy here?
- What does his face tell you about how he feels? (You may need to cue the students to his facial expression.)
- Which part of our empathy definition is Piggie showing?

Notice that these questions help a reader "see" who a character is.

In the middle of the story, Piggie disguises himself as characters he knows Elephant likes. This is a great example of perspective-taking, because Piggie is imagining what Elephant likes, not what Piggie likes. In order for readers to understand the characters' motivations and actions, we could ask:

- Noticing how Elephant feels, what has Piggie decided to do?
- How is that demonstrating empathy? Or, in what way could this be empathy?

Toward the end of the story, Elephant is sad because Piggie was not there to share each of these experiences. Piggie has a moment when his face changes into a smile and he exclaims, "I am here NOW!" He's learning to be with his friend. This is a moment where empathy shines. Remember, empathy does not talk down to a person, something "sympathy" implies. Empathy is when someone is beside the person who is expressing their feelings. To understand the story's central message, empathy-infused questions could be:

- What has Piggie realized or learned after trying on different disguises?

- Why do you think that?
- How did empathy help Piggie learn that?

A Book That Models Eco-Empathy

Fireflies! by Julie Brinckloe (1986) is a book in the realistic fiction genre about a boy who catches fireflies on a summer evening and brings them home in a jar. Later, he watches as their lights dim and their movements slow. Feeling sad, he makes the decision to let them go. We chose this book because the richness of the language inspired us to savor it. It contains a character who models empathy toward a living being in the natural world, which demonstrates eco-empathy. Moreover, it gives us a main character that models an important empathy skill— watching and listening. Finally, we chose the book because Brinckloe crafts the illustrations so beautifully with close-ups of the boy's facial expressions and how they change as he watches the fireflies' light begin to dim. We, as readers, empathize with his anguish as he releases them, and yet we also empathize with his joy and wonderment of the natural world when he sees their lights brighten as they pour out into the night.

At the beginning of the story, we want to ask questions that allow a reader to get to know the characters, utilizing empathy once again. In the beginning of *Fireflies!*, the boy eats dinner listening to the fireflies outside. He excitedly finishes dinner and then prepares a jar with air holes in the lid to capture them. Connecting questions to ask to get to know the character could be:

- What is the main character about to do? How do you know? What information from the setting helps you to decide what he is about to do?
- Why is he poking holes in the lid of the jar? Is he being empathetic to the fireflies by doing this? Why? (Label this as a character using empathy to decide.)
- What can you imagine he is feeling? (Label this as a reader using empathy.)

In the middle of the story, the boy brings the fireflies home in the jar and goes to bed. He sits and watches them in their new jar "home" over a series of five pages. He sees that they fall to the bottom and lie there. Their lights dim. He is facing the problem. Connecting questions to ask for understanding character motivation and actions could be:

- Which step in empathizing is the main character showing us?
- What is he noticing that is happening?

- What does his face tell you he is feeling? (You may do this over many pages.)
- How is this using empathy?
- What would you describe the fireflies' life to be like?

At the end of the story, the boy makes the decision to release the fireflies. He is sad and yet there is a sense of wonderment also. Example questions to ask that connect empathy with the central message are:

- Which step in empathizing does he do by releasing the fireflies?
- Why do you suppose he chose what he did?
- As you empathize with the fireflies, what would you have done?
- Do you feel empathy toward him or the fireflies or both?

Books That Combine the Categories

There are stories that combine the categories, and, when you find them, the empathy potential abounds. Chapter books tend to have all three categories as their complex plots allow, and this is no exception for the chapter books we have chosen as our anchors. Suited for a more sophisticated reader, they have moments of empathy woven into their plot, accentuating their complexities because of empathy. They are also stories to love, with words and characters that linger in our memories, of course, and connecting questions can accentuate this far beyond the last page. In other words, follow the same process with books that have more than one approach to empathy—that is, find the glistening empathy moments within the text and design a connecting question to invite thoughtful discussion.

Connecting Question Guidelines

For all of our books and yours, questioning principles emerge whether they are picture books or chapter books. The following are guidelines we use when forming connecting questions using short or long texts.

Connecting questions:

- are asked at moments in the story when empathy shines brightest, connecting story elements with that moment of empathy
- draw a reader into the main characters' personalities and the setting details within the first quarter of the story
- require a reader to notice character motivations and their connected actions in the middle of the story and how these relate to empathy

- invite ideas connecting empathy with the central message or theme toward the end of the story

- usually include the word *empathy* or *empathizing* and inspire a reader to explore a story for deeper meaning

- invite thinking around common ground where readers notice similarities between themselves and the characters

- often begin with "why" and "how" to invite interpretation, open responses, and interconnected meaning

- focus on a character's feelings or probe our own feelings as a reader

- refer reader responses to the different elements of empathy in the Empathy First lesson and visual

The Learning Flow of Empathy-Infused Reading

Once you've chosen an empathy-rich story and have planned the connecting questions, it's time to share it with your students through an empathy lens. It's time to unlock and unfold the mysteries it holds together.

Empathy-infused reading has a *flow* to the learning, rather than a set or series of lessons. You can explore the story through an interactive read-aloud using the connecting questions as a catalyst for discovery in discourse. That's Phase One of the flow and you can complete the CoreEmpathy experience right there. Or you can continue the flow of learning to deeper analysis: Phase Two. In other words, it can be as simple as one reading experience; and it can go deeper, with many connected reading lessons. The amount of lessons—one experience as a read-aloud with connecting questions or many experiences as deep understanding through analysis—is up to you. Do what is right for your classroom depending on your reading goals, curriculum, students' literacy abilities, learning stamina, length of text, and the time you can devote.

CoreEmpathy's approach to empathy-infused reading produces results in each phase and step of the flow, which is why its effectiveness is versatile. Because Phase One is short and straightforward, you can do it as many times as you'd like, letting empathy reside in your reading community anytime you read. Phase Two is more involved as you analyze the story with empathy guiding your way deeper in it. This takes more time involving a series of lessons. The time is well spent, however, because Phase Two yields deeper empathy-inspired understandings of the story and each other.

We chose the word *flow* because the learning is like a wave, fluidly moving. In other words, a core understanding of empathy enhances the core learning of the story, while both contribute to deeper meaning-making and reading experiences. They build together and that makes reading meaningful—a joy in greater purpose. They share the same core. The same heart.

Learning Flow of Empathy-Infused Reading

Phase One: Connect

1. Teach Empathy First.

2. Read the story using connecting questions inviting discourse.

Phase Two: Deepen

1. Chart the story's core.

2. Engage the story's central message or theme.

3. Revisit the text for literary elements and reading goals.

4. Make the empathy learning real.

Phase One: Connect

Teach Empathy First

Remember the Empathy First lesson and its corresponding visual aid with hand motions we described in Chapter 3? That's your first step. Teach Empathy First. Using the Empathy First lesson, plant the seed in relation to which reading and thinking will grow, anchored in the definition of empathy. Do this at the beginning of each lesson, even if you are rereading. Keep the visual where your students can see it during the story discourse, too. This will make referencing it easy.

Read the Story with Connecting Questions in Discourse

We love to begin with the invitation, "Let's enter the story world together." These words suggest something special is about to happen—and it is. Together, you and your students will be using your imaginations to put yourselves in the characters' shoes, to see through their eyes and feel what they feel. The author's words will transport you and your students to another time and place where you'll meet interesting characters who are daring limits and confronting obstacles.

There are many ways for you and your students to read the story, and your usual classroom practices are welcome. However, it *is* important that everyone reads the same story for the first read, preferably as a read-aloud (Figure 4.2), or at least for portions of it. Chapter books offer a great example of books to read aloud in their entirety or in the empathy key moments. The empathy-rich story can be read in one sitting or over many days, but there is substantial evidence that supports reading aloud to students of all ages and stages as being beneficial, even critical, to their literacy development in many areas. Donalyn Miller (2009), in her book *The Book Whisperer*, expresses it holistically: "Not only is being read to highly engaging for students, but research has demonstrated how reading aloud can promote language and literacy development through interaction among students and teachers about texts" (p. 183). Her emphasis on the interactions that happen between students and their teacher highlights the important discourse that we, too, have found highly valuable.

That's not a surprise to Shelby Barrentine and Lawrence Sipe, leading authors and researchers who have supported reading aloud for many years (e.g., Barrentine, 1996; Sipe, 2000). They have found it strengthens a student's lis-

FIGURE 4.2. Christie leading a read-aloud using connecting questions in a kindergarten classroom.

tening and speaking abilities as well as enhancing their language development (cited in Morrison & Wlodarczyk, 2009). Perhaps you want to consider your usual read-aloud classroom time to be empathy focused? Then you could add empathy practice into your learning day without adjusting a minute.

After the invitation to enter the story world, set the reading purpose to look for how empathy works within the story. It can be as simple as, "We've been learning what empathy is. Empathy can help us understand a story more deeply. Let's read today looking for how empathy is working within [*story's title and author*]." Setting the purpose can also include the story's main idea; for example, "When we read today, you will meet a girl who finds a stray dog. *Stray* means 'not belonging, wandering.' Let's read for where empathy is happening in this story keeping that in our minds."

Then savor the words of your stories out loud, especially where empathy really shines in the plot. Read fluently and with fervor. Give this time to create a place for empathy and stories to live in your classroom. Where you notice empathy shining, pause the reading to ask your connecting questions—let the discourse flow.

Initially, the discourse is led by you. It takes time for your students to be good at noticing where empathy resides in a story, but it's our hope they will do so on their own eventually. Then small-group discussions can follow, as students might create their own empathy-inspired questions and thoughts at important parts of a story. Until then, you don't want readers to miss the key places where empathy exists because of reading too casually or quickly, or simply being unaware of what those moments look like. For now, you are leading them to notice empathy within the text first, then talking about their thinking as the story and the empathy-inspired interactions happen.

Empathy-rich discourse follows. This is critical not only because it's where a reader creates the transactions between themselves, the story, and empathy, but also because the conversation helps join everyone together. It's where meaning is made and community is created simultaneously.

The remainder of this section presents helpful guidelines for encouraging discourse that inspire the simultaneous meaning construction mentioned above. They allow empathy-driven close reading to fuel the classroom conversation while promoting a thriving reading community.

Discussion Guidelines

Staying close to the page doesn't mean staying on the same page.
Although you are pausing at empathy-shimmering moments, you and your students may not stay at that moment if the responses invite travel elsewhere in the story. Reader responses from open-ended questions can go in a variety of directions by their nature. For example, you can reread previous parts of the story, examine events that lead a character to their present place, or study pages that foreshadow a scene.

Refocus the discussion with empathy when needed.
Response can also take the discussion further away from the character's position or present feeling. You'll know when this happens because the discussion takes everyone away from the page, and the absence of being "in" the page will be felt. If that happens, let empathy-inspired connecting questions bring you back—perhaps using a question with perspective-taking while inside a scene. For example, if a student talks about a time when they played in their yard, in response to the character in the

story doing that, you might refocus the discourse by asking a question such as, "This common experience can help you understand the main character's life. Entering the character's view on this page, what can you imagine she sees?"

Invite discovery into the discussion.
We don't want you or your students to be put in an uncomfortable place where the teacher holds the "empathy key" to the answers. We want you to think of yourself as leading your students on a path where they notice flowers blooming, bees buzzing, and the sweet smell of the story-garden because empathy's in the air, and not because you're having an "ask and answer" session. A common reason for this to happen is asking questions that begin with "what," "which," or "where." These tend to ask for a correct answer rather than an interpreted answer. Questions that begin with "how" or "why" frequently ask for an interpretation or an answer that is unique to a reader's thinking. For example, "What part of this illustration shows us where empathy is happening?" has a right or wrong answer. However, "How is empathy being expressed in this illustration?" gives readers an opportunity to construct an answer from their personal understanding. If you feel yourself dragging students to answers, relook at the questions for individual expression.

Give students feedback about their answers by bringing the discussion back to empathy.
"You just found common ground with the main character by . . ." or "That's talking about the first step in empathizing, noticing and listening, because . . ." or "You talked about how the character sees their world by . . ." are all ways to affirm how empathy is playing an important part of the discussion.

Encourage your students to elaborate on their answers, particularly with infusing empathy into their responses.
Often a reader will explain a thought without knowing why they thought it or where in the story it germinated. Let empathy invite elaboration or invite the expansion of an idea in community by inviting responses from classmates. For instance, expansion of the idea "He looks sad when he looks at the jar" can be encouraged through "What tells you he is sad?" or "As you imagine what he is feeling, what can you imagine he is seeing also?" Including a classmate into the discussion might sound like, "Where might empathy be alive in so-and-so's response?"

Encourage your students to use the vocabulary of feelings and empathy.
When your students respond with a comment driven by empathy but don't seem to realize it, call it to their attention. Questions such as "Which part of empathy did you just use?" or "How is that empathizing?" or "How might the character feel about what is happening to him?" are ways to both model the language of empathy and invite your students to use it in combination with feelings. These questions help students become more conscious of how empathy works both in stories and in their lives.

You and your students will reread passages and reread the books.
Trust us, your students will reread the books on their own. Your students will *want* to because they will be inspired by their deep understandings. We've seen it happen even with students who have limited word knowledge. Rereading most frequently happens when we have a purpose or a question in mind or with a hypothesis that we want to confirm. This will happen when discovery and interactions are playful in discussions. But we've also seen students savor the author's language and return to the reading to hear it again. Be ready; have the stories easily accessible.

Classroom Idea: Independent Reading and an Empathy Book Basket
In *How Reading Changed My Life*, Anna Quindlen (1998) observes, "Books are the plane, and the train, and the road. They are the destination and the journey. They are home" (p. 74). Make a basket that is home where the stories with empathy live. A place where you and your students, grade-level team members, or librarians can add empathy-rich books for all to read during choice time. The books you have closely read through empathy-infused reading will be books that your students will revisit and revisit. Here they can be at home for access and for sharing with others.

Phase Two: Deepen

Chart the Story's Core

Anchor charts have been used as an instructional tool to "make thinking visible" in lessons for many years. They help teachers and students see the lesson's learning in an organized way because they visually highlight targeted teaching goals while providing space for student responses. Perhaps their most useful benefit is that they are engaging. Students are offered the opportunity to interact with the learning and respond with their own ideas . . . and they seem to count. We use anchor charts for these same reasons, but we call them *story charts*, because, in the CoreEmpathy approach to literacy learning, empathy thinking is anchored in story.

There are aspects of anchor charts that are the same in story charts. They are simple to make with materials that are already in your classroom—chart paper and markers. Or they can be electronic on the promethean board or a slide in an electronic presentation. The latter may be appealing particularly for intermediate students. Another similarity is that an instructional goal is apparent in its construction and organization. For instance, if we want students to capture how a character felt in the beginning, middle, and end of a story, we want the subheadings to highlight those parts.

Story charts are also interactive and engaging, so that your students see their words in a collective place. Remember how important discourse is to the CoreEmpathy approach involving deep discussion about the stories? A story chart is a place to let those ideas live. Finally, we love them for posting on classroom walls or resurfaced electronically to be used in review, to let the story's learning linger, and to provide connections for future stories and the writing craft lessons that follow.

We began our reading experience by focusing on where the story and empathy unite, while also discovering the story's key ideas using connecting questions. The story chart acts as a note-taking device and a visual representation for those elements and their interconnections. That's the big difference. Empathy's role in the book plays an important part on the story chart. While acting as the "voice" of your students' collective thinking and reactions, the story chart enriches them through highlighting the story's empathy. It can also help to activate background knowledge in future lessons. Empathy often happens at subtle moments in a story, and you will want to capture those fleeting moments in writing so that they can be revisited in subsequent lessons. We will see that close reading doesn't happen in one sitting with a story, because it takes time to let the layers of meaning develop.

Begin the story chart with a vision for subheadings and questions that guide students in the practice of both reading standards and empathy—but, from there, the chart's creation is always interactive. Here are questions to guide planning the design of a story chart:

- What key literary elements from the story do you want students to notice?

- What parts of the story will help your students make connections between empathy and the story, and what might the connections look like?

- How can you organize the story chart so that information can be easily retrieved for future learning?

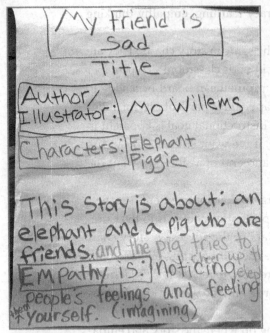

FIGURE 4.3. Story chart demonstrating the link between story structures and empathy.

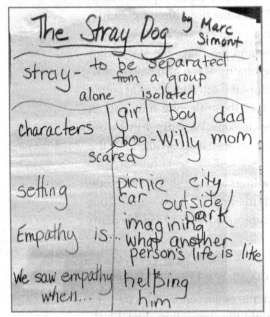

FIGURE 4.4. Student comments are collected from the structure elements and empathy on the same story chart.

Here following are a few examples of story charts we've used with the books that have been anchoring our ideas. We've included photos to give you a better idea of their overall look (Figures 4.3–4.6). Remember: there is no right or wrong way to create a story chart. It is simply there to serve you and your students, to organize the learning while engaging empathy and the story.

In *My Friend Is Sad*, there are two key characters telling the story, so that's a literary element we want students to notice right away. Essentially, it is about the interactions they have and how they demonstrate and define their friendship. This summary may also go on the story chart, accentuating it in our discussion (see Figure 4.3). Under the title, the author and characters are written on the left as a subheading to leave room for students' thinking on the right, varying the use of color for ease of future retrieval. Cueing summary, we write, "This story is about," to allow for multiple interpretations. Last, we want to highlight empathy, so we write, "Empathy in our story is." This initializes the story's overall connection to the practice of empathy.

Now, let's look at another story for a possible story chart design. In *The Stray Dog*, events unfold one day at a time throughout the week. Although using this one-day-at-a-time structure for our story chart makes sense for retelling the story in subsequent lessons, the story's summary needs to be highlighted first. Deciding to focus on both character and setting for the initial understanding of the story, the teacher created this story chart with a left-hand column that reads "Characters" and, under it, "Setting" (see Figure 4.4). As the story is read, the students' responses on both the characters and the different settings are captured on the chart. Color is used to differentiate the subheadings so the information can be easily retrieved later. Notice that empathy is also visible. We want to continually connect the story elements with empathy, so, on the bottom half of the chart, the heading is "Empathy is . . ." and "We saw empathy in the story when . . ." Again, the story chart is a place where your students' ideas can reside.

For *The One and Only Ivan* by Katherine Applegate (2012), Josh's fourth-grade class created three story charts representative of the story and how many times empathy entered its complex plot. As shown in Figures 4.5 to 4.7, each chart demonstrates how empathy is used to deepen understanding about Ivan himself and the life he has. The story charts then progress, inviting the reader's empathy toward Ivan.

The first two story charts, which begin with "What new information did you learn about Ivan's life?" (Figure 4.5a) and "What do you imagine it is like to be Ivan?" (Figure 4.5b), use connecting questions to initiate thinking focused on combining empathy with characterization and setting. Readers know that perspective-taking will help them understand Ivan and his life from the outset. In

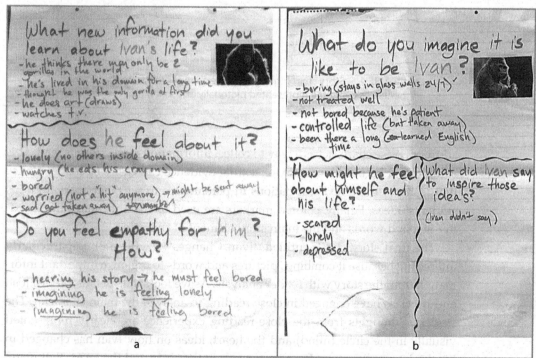

FIGURE 4.5. Color is used to indicate empathy words and character embedded in the questions. Consider these same questions for reading response journals.

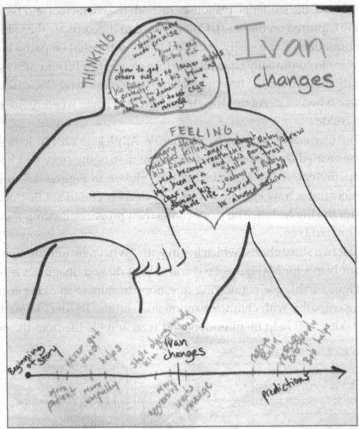

FIGURE 4.6. Story chart highlighting the changes the main character experiences over time represented pictorially and in writing.

addition, these charts act as a way to collect information as the story is read. This is important because locations for textual evidence can easily be made. Notice that Josh put these text associations in parentheses to set them apart from his students' ideas. Finally, colored markers are used to cue a reader to the empathy-inspired words and the main story element of character.

The final story chart, entitled "Ivan Changes" (Figure 4.6), is particularly interesting because it combines pictures and words to organize important information from the story with reader analysis. As we look at its details, we see Josh and his class have engaged in close reading to analyze the main character. The students' thoughts from the close-reading experience are clearly represented visually in the circle (mind) and the heart, ideas on how Ivan has changed in his thinking and feeling. We also can see, in the circle and the heart, that many children contributed ideas about those changes. In addition, Josh added a timeline of the events in the plot in relation to the distinct parts of the book. What a beautiful way to capture his students' thorough analysis.

Last, let's notice the similarities among these three story charts and the most important ideas in creating them, such as:

- The charts recorded what Josh wanted his students to notice about the story's narrative elements.

- The students had input into their creations by making connections between characters, plot events, and empathy.

- Each chart is simple, clear, and contains student voices.

- The charts have been designed to support reading for understanding and central message.

The most important thing to remember, however, is that there isn't a right or wrong way to design a story chart. They represent what we want our students to notice and discuss from their reading. And it's the collective place where their ideas are held around empathy and story so that we can track, revisit, and enjoy them.

The story chart, then, is a page where the learning community meets, where students get to see how some of their ideas are shared and some are unique. This discovery establishes common ground among your students—a prerequisite for empathy—while also offering them practice in not only accepting but also celebrating their differences. Unique, independent ideas can stretch our thinking and help us see something in the story from a different point of view. The story chart is a place where this kind of unique, independent thinking may be celebrated.

The close reading experience has begun with the story chart and interactive reading, along with a vitally engaged classroom of dynamic learners. Reading is the focus, of course, but the story chart helps deepen the story's meaning in the reader's mind, while also setting their empathy lens to "open."

Reader Response and Reading Journals

The initial reading lessons in intermediate classrooms may span a few days or even a few weeks, depending upon the length of the story, thus making the story chart even more helpful for retaining student thinking from chapter to chapter. Readers' journals can augment this practice by asking students to do their independent thinking about the story in their journals and then transfer those ideas to the story chart, thus recording them as a collective whole. The opposite also works, whereby note-taking from the story chart can inspire journal responses.

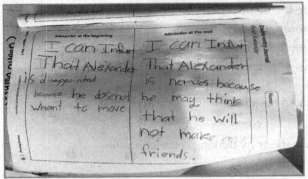

FIGURE 4.7. Reading response journal entry demonstrating comprehension strategy use infused with empathy.

Sometimes, you may want your students to record their thoughts in journals, allowing for the intersection of reading and writing to occur through relevant reader response. This also allows for a reader to indulge in individual quiet thought. We honor this practice in empathy-infused reading, particularly in intermediate classrooms.

Double-entry journals like the one shown in Figure 4.7 are a way to help students see how a character changes over time—in this case, on an individual level. In this journal, a third grader records her thinking at the beginning of a story (*Alexander and the Terrible, Horrible, No Good, Very Bad Day*) and compares it to her thoughts about the main character at the end of the story. Notice the change in her responses from experiencing empathy-infused reading. She's noticing what is happening to the character emotionally, remarking on how the character feels in both parts of the book—disappointed and nervous—rather than only describing events or character traits. Also, there is a level of concern for Alexander at the end of the story in that "he may think that he will not make any friends." This is a demonstration of how we get more deeply involved in the story because we've been empathizing with the characters and caring about them.

In Kendall's fifth-grade classroom in a small school in western Kentucky, students regularly use their readers journals to record their thinking. After reading *Saving Wonder* with her class, Kendall wanted students to notice where in the narrative of the novel the author had inspired readers to care about and empathize with her characters. Kendall began by asking students to simply list all the characters they could recall in their readers journals. Then she asked them to circle the ones they really cared about.

In addition, Kendall asked her students to identify the page number and text that led them to feel empathy for that character (as shown in Figure 4.8), thus offering them practice in referring to a text explicitly when drawing an inference. In addition, the journal offers a place for the reader to explain their thought process from the identified text location to their inference—a thorough reader response.

In Figure 4.8, the reader is detailing her thinking infused with empathy. After referring to page 2 in the novel, where Curley talks about losing most of his family to coal mining accidents, this student writes, "I think it would be very hard for Curley without a Mom or a Dad or even a little brother to play with." In a subsequent writing exercise, this same writer found common ground with Curley by writing about a time she was worried when her mom was in the hospital. Thereby, she empathizes with Curley inspired by events from her own life.

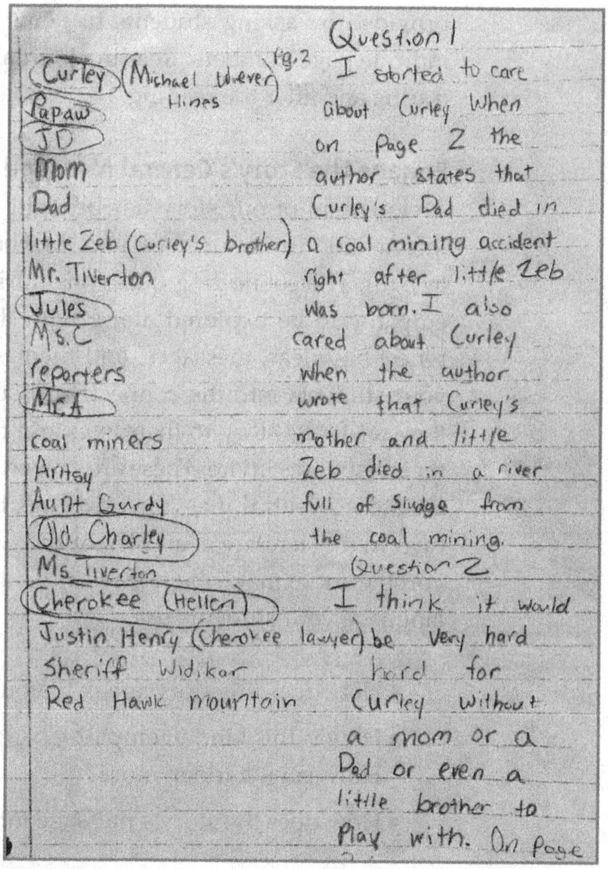
Question 1

Curley (Michael Weaver) Hines
Papaw
JD
Mom
Dad
little Zeb (Curley's brother)
Mr. Tiverton
Jules
Ms. C
reporters
McA
coal miners
Artsy
Aunt Gurdy
Old Charley
Ms Tiverton
Cherokee (Hellen)
Justin Henry (Cherokee lawyer)
Sheriff Widikor
Red Hawk mountain

Pg. 2 I started to care about Curley when on page 2 the author states that Curley's Dad died in a coal mining accident right after little Zeb was born. I also cared about Curley when the author wrote that Curley's mother and little Zeb died in a river full of sludge from the coal mining.

Question 2

I think it would be very hard hard for Curley without a mom or a Dad or even a little brother to play with. On page

FIGURE 4.8. Reading response journal entry infusing empathy with reactions to *Saving Wonder* utilizing textual evidence.

When the class came together to discuss the results of their thinking and caring, another student listed the children's favorite tree, Ol' Charley, as a character she cared about in the novel. What a unique idea: a tree as a character. And yet, this student was also showing her appreciation for the empathy modeled by the protagonist, Curley Hines, who cared about the tree and his mountain, too—enough to risk his childhood home for them. A perfect example of eco-empathy.

This unique idea led to a vibrant discussion of whether things from nature could be considered characters in a realistic novel. After all, they don't do any of the things we normally associate with characters, such as use dialogue, get into conflicts, overcome obstacles, have feelings . . . or do they? When asked if Ol' Charley could be considered a character, one boy answered decisively, "Yes!" When asked "Why?" he said, "Because the children loved and cherished him."

Although these journal entries came after reading the novel, they could have easily been used in this charting-the-story's core phase *during* the read, where independent thinking could be transferred to a story chart and discussed. If students had read the book, continually searching for where their empathy was being evoked, an even closer read of the story might have ensued, making a conversation about characters and caring all the richer.

Recall how empathy-infused reading creates a reading community that revisits pages in the story naturally during close reading and discussion? This is the time to analyze the small moments the author and/or illustrator have provided by asking students to point to facial expressions, reread quotes, or indicate page numbers. Reading journals can aid in the recording of these ideas during and after the reading.

Engage the Story's Central Message or Theme

A close read of our story has brought us to a place where we have insightful information from our book and the characters that empathy has helped bring to light. The connecting questions during the reading acted as the catalyst for empathy to be explored along with the plot. Now the connecting questions reflect big ideas, messages, and themes that bring the personal experiences of your students into the connective tissue. After reading, we ask students how they relate the story to their lives and then highlight the empathy practice that their responses invite. These are powerful questions that help them not only find the story's central message or theme, but explore how the story informs their own lives. Here are examples of the types of questions you can ask, although you'll want to make them more approachable by framing them in the everyday language your students use.

- How does this story speak to you personally?
- How is this kind of empathy happening in your life, in your experiences? How can it happen more?
- How does the story's message inform your life?

As students answer these questions, they are making connections between the story's theme and their lives, and between themselves and each other. They are finding common ground. Once again, reading's greater purpose makes the classroom come *alive*.

In *My Friend Is Sad*, we might approach common ground this way: "After reading the story, how did Piggie practice empathy toward his friend Elephant?" This may be followed by, "What are some ways we can practice empathy with *our* friends?" The first graders had a wonderful time discussing situations in which our friends need us. One answered, "When someone is hurt, I can get someone to help them." Another responded, "If someone is confused in math, I can tell them to use their number line." And another said, "I have big feelings sometimes like Elephant did. When I do, I want a hug." "I can see when someone is sad and I want to ask them to play with me," said another first grader. We read in their responses how they are applying the theme of friendship to what they see, do, and feel every day. And empathy connected them all.

Another example of engaging the central message came in a second-grade classroom during a discussion following the close read of *Fireflies!* The teacher said, "In *Fireflies!*, the boy in our story notices that the fireflies' lights are dimming and decides to let them go. What did you feel as you read this? How can it help you with a hard decision?" One student answered, "I felt really sad when the fireflies' lights were dimming because I thought they were dying. He helped to save them. I want to help an animal like that."

In *The Stray Dog*, I (Christie) initiated the engagement this way: "I noticed that the family felt concern for Willy for five days. That's a long time to be worried and it tells me how important thinking about a person or animal is to empathy. Who do you show empathy in your life by being concerned about him or her?" A first-grade student answered, "I'm worried about my mom when she has a lot to carry, so I could take some of her things for her."

You can ask more sophisticated or abstract questions of intermediate students as you invite them to stretch their imaginations by putting themselves in someone else's shoes. As you read these connecting questions leading to the central messages of these stories, think about how easy it would be to articulate what the themes are through the possible responses.

After close reading *Through Grandpa's Eyes*, for example, the connecting questions leading to theme might be:

- After reading the story and putting yourself in Grandpa's shoes like John did, what would you say about what it's like to be blind?
- What does the empathy that John showed tell you about how you could live?
- Can you think of someone in your life whom you might be able to understand better if you walked in their shoes?
- Just like John learned so much about his grandfather, what do you think you might learn about that person by empathizing with them?

Or, in relation to *The One and Only Ivan*, a teacher might invite students to engage with the central message this way: "We found ourselves practicing empathy as we read because we learned about Ivan's experiences through Ivan's point of view. The next time you are in a disagreement with someone, think about how *they* are seeing the situation. What new things can you learn from doing that?"

Or, for *Saving Wonder*: "Curley and JD had a rocky start to their friendship, didn't they? How do Curley and JD find common ground with each other? Is there a relationship in your life that feels a little rocky right now? How might you use empathy to make your relationship a little easier?"

It's in these core story discussions that readers can return to the text and find where in the book an idea originates, for example. Or they can revisit a part of the book as a catalyst for finding how the story applies to their own lives. In either case, you'll be inviting your readers to notice within the text, examine what it says, and then apply themes to their lives by practicing empathy informed by it.

Emphasis is placed on the definition of empathy within the big idea conversation by returning to the visual, hand motions, and phrases frequently. We connect these to student responses by using statements such as "When you are feeling sad at this time of the story, you are empathizing with our main character because he is feeling sad on his face, too." And "Now you have something in common with John because that is what he did to act compassionately as well." Or "You have just walked in the shoes of Curley by understanding why his cause is important to him."

We've talked about how empathy is a practice. As you engage the story's central message through connecting questions and the discussions that follow, you'll be setting the foundation for the cultivation and practice of empathy in your students' lives. The actions, ideas, and practical applications that your students engage in through close reading will not demonstrate mastery in empathy by any means. However, the central message of a story will illuminate how empathy might be practiced. It's the practice of empathy inspired by a story's central message that changes people, their relationships, and how they problem-solve with others. This is a story's greater purpose.

Revisit the Text for Literary Elements and Reading Goals

Great stories are not read once. We return to them and return to them. In writing, we "read like a writer" to study the author's craft (more on that in Chapter 5). Studying the author's craft through a reader's eyes also deepens understanding of reading. This understanding can make reading like a writer even more effective. It's the literacy reciprocal effect we discussed earlier. We can visit the text to highlight the literary elements that have been crafted so well by the author and the reading goals that help a reader to grow after the story is read and understood. Unexpected benefits come from this next phase in close reading, where analysis deepens even further—this time directed to a certain craft the author used or a reading goal we want our students to achieve.

Fluent reading is a goal best taught once the story is known. Recall that there are certain reading goals that empathy-infused reading often encourages, one being fluency. When students consciously empathize with a character in a book, or when they practice seeing through the protagonist's point of view, they read the text with more expression. Fluency deepens when the words are fueled by a student's knowledge of empathy.

After empathy-infused reading of *My Friend Is Sad*, Laura, the teacher in northwest Seattle, explains it this way: "I had already taught my students how to read with expression. They knew what an exclamation point was and how to respond to it before the unit began. That learning seemed superficial, something for their voice to do. After empathy-infused reading, our readers theater had depth. They read *as if* they were the character, *as if* they were feeling what the character felt. The empathy made all the difference."

In addition to fluency reading with *My Friend Is Sad*, other books offer reading goals for immersion in empathy as well. For instance, the story *The Stray Dog* progresses through each day of the week as the author describes how family members worry about the dog, Willy, thus offering a perfect organizational structure for a successful retell. "Retell," a critical first-grade reading goal, is listed on the story chart. To offer practice in this goal, the chart is created to assist the retell, so that every student can practice at one time. We begin by listing the seven days of the week in the left-hand column (see Figure 4.9). This draws our students' attention to the story's structure. Next to each day of the week, students compose a short sentence that describes the plot event that happens on that day. Now we have a record that can be used as a scaffold for retelling the story when we're ready. This page also shows how the family cared about Willy each day of the week, so the reading goal of retelling and the empathy action of showing concern are joined.

In Daina's classroom in an inner-city school in the city of Everett, the story chart was reviewed then used to set up the retell practice with her students. In partnerships, they began retelling and rereading the story. Recall the student who entered the room, returning from a learning assistance group, and joined the class halfway through the retell? We watched with fascination as one of the partnerships opened their group to him, explained what they were doing by modeling it, then invited him to do it with them. They were practicing empathy and compassion—without teacher prompting! They

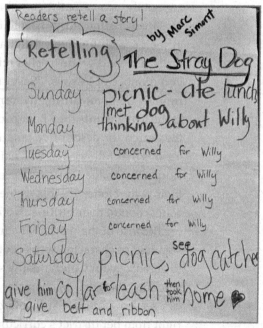

FIGURE 4.9. First graders used this story chart as a scaffold to retell *The Stray Dog* with the sequence of plot mirroring the days of the week.

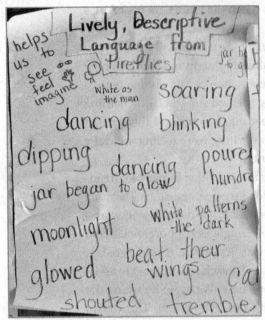

FIGURE 4.10. This story chart is celebrating the vibrant language Julie Brinckloe uses foreshadowing the empathy evoked later in the story *Fireflies!*

demonstrated literacy learning and community building through empathy linked in an inspiring way.

A key literary element accentuated in *Fireflies!* resides in its language and how it evokes vitality, brightness, and movement. With books in hand, the students cocreated a chart (see Figure 4.10) entitled "Lively, Descriptive Language from Fireflies."

As students returned to the story's pages, they found so many examples of lively, descriptive language to add to their chart, the teacher couldn't write fast enough. Their chart was full in minutes. But that's not all. A second page was easily filled. Furthermore, they articulated *why* the language helped them "see, feel, and imagine" in their own words, describing how it helped them "feel the empathy for the fireflies that the boy character in the story is feeling," thus drawing out the eco-empathy component.

"By using the story chart in this manner, my students became more vigilant in their search for lively language, not only in *Fireflies!*, but in other books as well," a second-grade teacher related to us after using empathy-infused reading in a number of lessons. "Several days after studying *Fireflies!*, two boys came running up to me during their independent reading time and pointed excitedly at the lively words they had discovered on their own. The story chart had made the search for descriptive language more conscious, more exciting. In writing lessons that followed, it was natural for me to use *Fireflies!* as a model text. The story chart made that easy." Notice how her students pored over a text all on their own. Notice the playfulness that surrounded the discoveries. Notice the connection to their writing. Notice the greater purpose.

Because of the work that empathy does in deepening your students' understanding of character, webs centering the character's name are a beautiful way to organize your CoreEmpathy story chart. Here is a natural place to record your students' thoughts as character traits are revealed. In Figures 4.11a and b, you can see how Linda's students built character webs from two different stories right from her district's curriculum.

Linda discussed how empathy encouraged insightful responses from her third-grade class such as "excluded," "jealous," "disappointed," "she feels

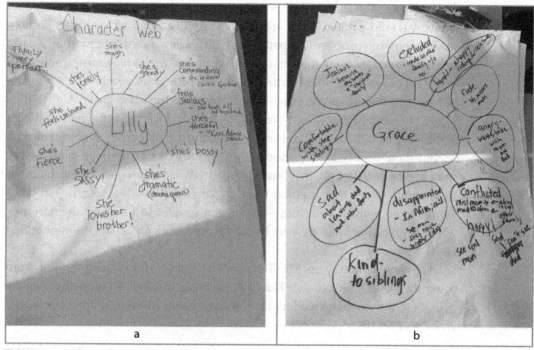

FIGURE 4.11. These character web charts provide a home for your students' empathy-driven understandings of character layered with textual evidence.

unloved," and "conflicted." But that's not all—she explained that the empathy also helped them to connect their insights with reasons for them. It was as if the story, existing in their mind's eye, was imprinted for later retrieval. Powerful. And then she revealed how one of her students who has very little print knowledge was able to add insightful adjectives as an active participant with the entire class as a result of the empathy discourse. That's creating greater purpose.

What is happening? What's causing this excitement . . . this depth of engagement? It's the *empathy*. The classroom has been infused with seeing from another person's point of view and imagining what someone else might feel from the previous learning. They get it. *All* of it.

Identifying a story's point of view and how it influences the unfolding events is an important literary element in intermediate students' reading development. Because a story can be told from different originations; I, you, and he or she, in a limited or omniscient way—each asks the reader to understand the events from a different perspective. Given that a main aspect of empathy is perspective-taking, intermediate readers are successful in identifying a story's point of view with the addition of empathy.

In *Saving Wonder*, the author tells the story through the point of view of twelve-year-old protagonist Curley Hines. As discussed in an earlier section, students have no problems empathizing with Curley and his plight from as early as page 2, but they find other characters, particularly the antagonists, more challenging. For instance, after reading the novel, fifth-grade teacher Tiffany asked her students the provocative question, "Is Mr. Tiverton a bad guy?" At first, they wanted to jump in and shout, "Yes!" After all, Mr. Tiverton is the new coal boss in the story, and the one who wants to blow the top off Curley's mountain.

But then Tiffany saw quizzical, thoughtful looks come over many of her students' faces. After all, they knew empathy was their focus. When she invited students to see the situation through Mr. Tiverton's perspective—in other words, to empathize with him—they began to refer to places in the narrative where he explained exactly why he felt he needed to proceed with mining Red Hawk Mountain.

Applying empathy to Mr. Tiverton's character didn't remove him from being the novel's antagonist. However, reading through an empathy lens *did* help these intermediate readers see the same event through different points of view.

Make the Empathy Learning Real

We love these last moments of empathy-infused reading. It's where school and life lessons intersect. It's when we invite students to bring their valuable indoor learning outside of our classroom walls and not just think about how a book might inform their life, but how empathy can play an active role in it. It's the payoff, or what Beers and Probst (2013) explain in this way: "The most rigorous reading is to find what those words on that page mean in our lives" (p. 42). We would add that greater purpose means we find ways to actualize it, to apply it. Greater purpose informs us that they can take the meaningful parts learned and apply them immediately and every day. It's also where we can inspire readers who later turn to books to learn about themselves and the world around them because they *know* it will inform them wisely.

It's prime time for this to happen. We have the opportunity to touch our students' lives on a stage illuminated by the warm lights of empathy. We are all coming together at a moment when we have experienced empathy and its beauty through story. Now we are prepared, even sensitized, to use empathy in real life (Arizpe et al., 2003; Sipe & Pantaleo, 2008). Let's encourage that dance—it's the dance of greater purpose.

It sounds like . . . "Today we learned a lot about empathy through the characters and the book we read. As you go through your day, notice how someone else might be feeling and act empathetically." Or "Try to imagine how someone else sees a situation and think about how you can act with compassion." Or "As you play at recess, notice how your friend is feeling through their facial expressions, and think about how you can act for both of you to feel happy at play." Or "In our classroom, notice what others might need. Think of a way you can help them as the characters in our book showed us."

At the end of the reading lessons, invitations such as these set the stage for our students to practice empathy in real-life situations. And it's at the right moment when our children's brains have been exercised to feel for a character, to "wire" themselves to feel for real people (McKearney, n.d.). It reinforces the idea that empathy can touch us at any time, any place. When, not if, your students come back to your classroom full of examples of empathy from their own lives, you might consider collecting these moments on a wall or book, reinforcing an empathetic classroom learning environment with your students' lives.

A Review of the Learning Flow of Empathy-Infused Reading

Teaching empathy-infused reading starts with choosing an empathy-rich story and ends with joyful, vibrant readers deeply understanding what they read. You can practice the CoreEmpathy approach to reading by trying out one of our sample lessons in Phases One and Two (see Chapter 6), going to our website (www.CoreEmpathy.com), or designing your own lessons with a much-loved book from your classroom or curriculum. Meanwhile, here's a quick review of the steps to the learning flow (also found in Appendix A).

Phase One: Connect

1. Choose your book: narrative, loved, accessible to your readers, and empathy rich.
2. Peruse it and note the moments of empathy.
3. Design empathy connecting questions to ask at these moments.
4. Engage the Empathy First lesson.
5. Read the story, setting the purpose to look for empathy as you read, and ask connecting questions. Let the empathy-enriched discourse flow.

Phase Two: Deepen

1. Chart the story's core by capturing the book's key ideas and connections to empathy on a visual.
2. Discover the central message and theme while engaging common ground and the story's empathy by asking students a form of the question "How does the story (and its empathy) speak to your life?"

3. Revisit the story for reading goals and key literary elements.
4. Making the empathy learning real by applying empathy responses in your students' lives outside the classroom.
5. Enjoy your classroom's transformation!

Reengaging Greater Purpose: The Transformative Power of Empathy-Infused Reading

Having a wide range of reading abilities within a classroom is one of a literacy teacher's biggest challenges. It tugs at our hearts. How do I reach every reader? How do I stretch every reader from where they are? Linda, the third-grade teacher in the inner-city Seattle school, describes how empathy-infused reading gives access to difficult aspects in reading and makes them obtainable to her struggling readers. She describes it as "transformational" because the emergent readers—students who haven't unlocked the print code yet—do not often participate in discussions regarding a story's message, one of those difficult aspects. They often retell a story because it's a tangible default. This gives them an overall flow of the story, of course, but doesn't deepen their analysis to meaning-making. Empathy-infused reading makes the unobtainable obtainable. Students feel safe to participate in meaning-making discourse because they truly have valuable input, and they know it.

With CoreEmpathy, the analyses of the characters and their actions are accessible because the students see a character in their mind's eye. What they see becomes evidence for analysis. Further, many of the story's clues are within the illustrations. What readers experience from a character's struggle through facial expressions and conflicting actions in the pictures becomes fruit for analysis. All of this helps students understand a story's central message better. Now the struggling reader is offering insightful contributions from their lives to classroom discussion and anchor chart creations that they couldn't before. That's motivating for everyone! That's community building around story. That's deepening and widening literacy learning. In *Culturally Responsive Teaching and the Brain*, Zaretta Hammond (2014) affirms that it's powerfully letting the roots of an individual's culture find common ground—in fact, create common ground—with the group values of the classroom.

Engagement in reading can be transformed also. Motivation is not a struggle with empathy-infused reading; in fact, students are motivated to read and reread. Producing behaviors such as this confirms their lifelong reading trajectory. Further, as empathy draws students deeper into the story and its characters, students read with more fluency and expression. They eagerly choose to read a book for a second and third time over *all* the other free choice activities, to pore back over a text to find "lively" words, and to talk with a partner about the book's characters as if those characters were their friends. The motivation to read with the books that can be deeply discovered comes alive. The engagement in reading is *palpable*.

My (Christie's) college students put voice to what is happening here. Although older and more sophisticated in their reading, the influence that empathy has on their reading experience remains similar. Their sophistication simply offers the words to articulate the deepening process for us to understand what is happening in readers of all ages. After empathy-infused reading of a poem, I asked my class, "How did empathy influence you as a reader?" In their own words, here are their responses:

> "It made my senses spring up to a higher sensitivity."
>
> "Looking at the poem actually became a different experience for me."
>
> "Empathy influenced me as a reader because I imagined myself as the person writing the words."
>
> "Empathy helped me to see through the eyes and the heart of each person experiencing something."
>
> "I thought deeper about my reading because of it."
>
> "I saw the poem through a living lens."
>
> "Empathy let me see what the author saw as they wrote it."
>
> "Empathy allowed me to read the story twice, from two perspectives. The first time from one character's eyes, the second time from another's."

Through empathy-infused learning, these are the readers your students will grow to be—lifelong learners who read and live with greater purpose.

5

Empathy-Infused Writing

When the character's emotions join with the reader's own through shared experience, it brings them closer, bonding them together. Empathy is powerful and, once it grabs hold, it is difficult to break.

—*Angela Ackerman, Canadian writing coach and author*

Christie and I (Mary) have known each other for many years. We met when her children were very young, and now they're in their twenties. I taught her son, Davin, in a Sunday school classroom when he was only four years old. He was an adorable child, friendly with everyone, with a wide grin that would tilt one way or another as he found the humor in something only he understood.

We must have been talking about the wonder of God's creation one month, because one Sunday, Davin shared how much he loved birds. He loved birds so much, he told us, that his parents often read to him from a stack of bird cards instead of a bedtime story. Always trying to capitalize on a student's interests, I invited Davin to choose three of his favorite bird cards to bring in and share with us the following Sunday.

The next Sunday morning as I prepared for church, my home phone rang. It was Christie. In her usual upbeat voice, she said, "Davin is upset about something and would like to talk to you." I couldn't imagine what I'd done to make Davin upset. "Sure," I said. "I'd be glad to." I already felt empathy for this young one who had gathered up enough courage to talk with me.

"Mary," his small voice wavered over the phone line. "You know how you told me to pick my three favorite birds?"

"Yes?"

"Well, I just *can't*!" he blurted out. I could tell he was close to tears.

"Oh, Davin, that's okay, honey. No problem. But can you tell me what's the matter?"

"I can't pick just three . . . because they're *all* my favorites!" he cried as my heart began to melt.

"Oh, Davin, of course. I understand. Forget picking just three. Bring them *all*!"

I'm pretty sure both of us were relieved there was such a simple answer.

I share this story because, as Christie and I approached this empathy-infused writing chapter, we faced a similar dilemma to the one Davin faced. After gathering dozens of student writing samples from a variety of teachers using the CoreEmpathy approach, we had a difficult time choosing which writing samples to share with you, because, well, we love them *all*.

This isn't just because we're saps, which we are. It's because, when you teach empathy-infused writing, your students will show a deeper level of engagement and understanding of the writing process, and their writing will show that depth, too. CoreEmpathy teachers tell us, for instance, that empathy-infused writing instruction inspires student writers to develop their own unique voices. We'll talk more about voice in the Craft Elements That Lend Themselves to Empathy-Infused Writing section later in this chapter, but, suffice it to say, it is one small part of the empathy effect that may be impossible to measure, and yet you know it's there because you see it in your students' work, . . . which is why this chapter comes with a warning: like Davin and his bird cards, as you begin to hear your students' unique voices through their empathy-infused writing, you might just find yourself *loving them all*.

> As you begin to hear your students' unique voices through their empathy-infused writing, you might just find yourself loving them all.

What Is Empathy-Infused Writing?

Empathy-infused writing takes any narrative work—whether it's fiction, nonfiction, or even a narrative in poetic form—to a deeper emotional level. It doesn't just give the reader a sequence of events or merely describe the who, what, and where of the character or narrator's experience. Such a story is dry, void of life—something literacy teachers all too often see. Empathy-infused writing illuminates the underlying thoughts and emotions that drive both the main character and the story forward, as it seeks to inspire an imagined emotional and sensory experience in the reader as well. And it does all this through the employment of writing craft elements particularly suited to help readers step into a character's shoes. Writers can consciously utilize these elements to engage reader empathy.

Many of the stories used as examples for teaching empathy-infused writing in this chapter have corresponding sample lessons offered in Chapter 6. You can also find sample lessons on our website: www.CoreEmpathy.com.

Writing with a Greater Purpose

Before we proceed with a description of what those craft elements are and how to teach empathy-infused writing, we believe it's important to set our purpose for what follows. Specifically, we want to ground ourselves as teachers in the greater purpose of empathy-infused writing. It's what gives us the juice to follow it through.

As teachers, we often limit our discussion of the *why* behind our teaching to correspond with a literacy goal or a genre's specific purpose. For instance, we might say the purpose of informational writing is to discuss a subject with clarity in a well-organized manner, or that the purpose of writing fiction is to tell an imagined story in a way that makes it believable to the reader using elements of plot, setting, and characterization—all worthy and necessary purposes, to be sure. However, just as introducing empathy into the reading goal deepens the reading experience, adding writing with empathy to your students' writing goal deepens their writing. That's your greater purpose in teaching it.

But what might the greater purpose be for your student writers? Why would anyone write with empathy in mind? What is a writer's greater purpose? Empathy-infused writing inspires readers to care. If readers don't care, they don't turn the page. It's as simple as that.

As a children's novelist, I (Mary) have the pleasure of traveling to schools all over the Midwest on author visits, talking about my latest book and offering writing instruction (see Figure 5.1). Always, I lead off the conversation talking about my superpower—you guessed it—empathy. And, of course, I always add, "You have that superpower, too."

As Donald Maass (2016) writes in his book *The Emotional Craft of Fiction*, "Readers fundamentally want to feel something, not about your story but about themselves. . . . They want to feel like they've been through something. They want to connect with your characters and live their fictional experience or believe they have" (p. 25). This connection Maass talks about is achieved through empathy-infused writing, and, as writers,

FIGURE 5.1. Mary Knight during an author visit.

our greater purpose is to inspire our readers to step into our character's (or narrator's) shoes so that they may experience the ups and downs of our characters' emotional lives.

This greater purpose guided by the CoreEmpathy approach applies to all student writers regardless of grade level. For instance, in addition to finding new vocabulary to express their emotions and to use in their writing, kindergartners and first graders can discover that a story is always about a *change*.

Empathy-infused writing inspires readers to care. If readers don't care, they don't turn the page. It's as simple as that.

For example, "Sofia" (a pseudonym), a kindergartner, drew a picture of her classroom on her first day of school. She drew a line from the figure that represented her to the word *nervous* (Figure 5.2). This writing lesson followed the class reading of the book *Happy*, in which colorful illustrations of fish express a wide range of emotions. The book was chosen for the brilliant way it broadens a student's emotional vocabulary.

In the next picture that Sofia drew of her classroom—presumably closer to present day—the figure representing Sofia is almost twice as big, perhaps indicating a growing confidence, and the adult (teacher) looks happy, most likely indicating a positive relationship (Figure 5.3). The conversation that preceded this writing was about how feelings can change. Sofia found an excellent example from her own life about a feeling that changed, and, although she didn't

FIGURE 5.2. Sophia's first drawing with "nervous."

FIGURE 5.3. Sophia's second drawing.

name this final feeling, her picture tells the story. Certainly, this writing exercise—as elemental as it is—has implications for self-understanding, but it also helps anchor one of the main rules of storytelling: *something must change*, not just in the main character's outer world, but in their emotional world as well. Don't think for a minute that kindergartners and first graders can't pick up on this basic tenet.

Many empathy-rich stories are about friendship, another source for writing with a greater purpose. When we read stories about empathy-inspired friendships, we get to see healthy relationship skills in action. When we write empathy-infused stories about friendship—whether it's a narrative from our own life or something imagined—we deepen that understanding while also developing our writing skills. Students in early elementary and intermediate grades, for instance, can see that naming the emotions connected with a personal or character's experience is a skill that can lead to stronger writing *and* stronger friendships.

In a CoreEmpathy writing lesson inspired by the text *Leonardo, the Terrible Monster*, by Mo Willems (2005), second-grade students explored moments when they experienced "really bad days" and a friend or relative stepped in and helped them feel better through empathizing with them. Not only were student writers modeling the text, but they were also modeling the friendship that forms between the characters of Leonardo and Sam, showing how even a bad day can be transformed through one simple act of empathy (see Figures 5.4 and 5.5). When you add empathy to any learning, it deepens the purpose.

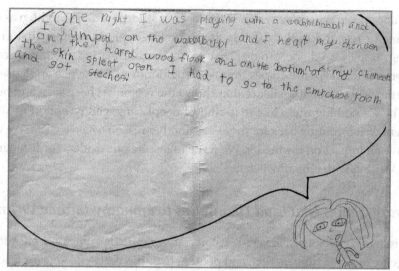

FIGURE 5.4. Student drawing and story: "One night I was playing with a wabblbabbl …"

One night I was playing with a wabblbabbl and I jumped on the wabblbabbl and I heait [hit] my cheneen [chin] on the harrd wood floor and on the botum of my cheneen the skin spleat [split] open. I had to go to the emrchase [emergency] room and got steches [stitches].

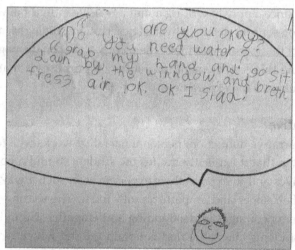

FIGURE 5.5. Second drawing and story: "Are you okay? Do you need water?"

Are you okay? Do you need water? Grab my hand and go sit down by the winndow and breth fress air OK. OK I siad!

Time and again, we've watched the faces of student writers brighten as their classmates respond to their words. It can be as simple as another first grader saying, "I felt scared, too!" in response to a classmate sharing. For older grades, sometimes the response comes through laughter or spontaneous applause and sometimes by a palpable silence that shows the writer has been seen and heard.

There's nothing quite like that kind of deeply engaged reception to keep a student writer coming back for more. It's another reason *why* we write. We write to have an impact on the reader. We write to inspire our readers (or listeners) to care. Writing with empathy is key.

Literary Genres That Lend Themselves to Empathy-Infused Writing

As discussed previously, the genres of narrative nonfiction, personal narrative (a subgenre of nonfiction), fiction, and poetry are particularly effective for teaching empathy-infused reading and writing, as long as there is a narrative flow. We're touching on them here again so that you can view them through a writer's lens and see how you will use them in your classroom to cultivate empathy in your student writers.

Narrative Nonfiction

This genre offers rich opportunities for using empathy-inducing craft elements that are usually considered fictional devices. The same rules for characterization in fiction, for instance, apply to writing about a real-life individual whereby the writer draws upon sensory details, physical descriptions, dialogue, and so on to draw a portrait of that person and make them come to life on the page. The only difference in using this craft element for nonfiction purposes is that the details come from the subject's life experience.

Personal Narrative

A subgenre of narrative nonfiction, personal narrative works well for CoreEmpathy purposes, in that it explicitly invites the student to find a point of entry into their own lives and to express their experiences in such a way that others may step into their shoes and empathize with them. The sharing of personal narratives further encourages understanding and empathy within the learning community as students inevitably find common ground when they see themselves in one another. The following personal narrative was written by a third grader who was invited to write about a difficult experience in her life during which someone showed her empathy.

One day my berother [brother] took a toy wen I was playing with it. Then we got into a fite and I got in trobl. Then I got an oreng [orange] and then I whent to go play, with my frend next dor. Wall [while] I was playing I felt a sead [seed]. Well I thot it was a sead so I spit it out. Just in case I checet [checked] if my wigally tooth was still ther it was . . . int! I started to voning [?] to my dad. Then we all me my broter [brother] and dad looked for my tooth and never found it.

"Sally [pseudonym], I know you canet [can't] find your wigelly tooth that you spit out. Do you want me to HELP you? You must be verey sad."

One can imagine how easily this writer's classmates empathized with her story since losing baby teeth is such an important experience in their young lives.

Fiction

In addition to personal narrative, fictional stories can also be effective vehicles for student writers to explore emotional experiences that resonate with their peers. Sometimes it's less risky for a student to explore their thoughts and feelings through the vehicle of a fictional character. In the sample story that follows, sensory details and interior reflection were two empathy-inspired craft elements the teacher had asked students to incorporate into their narratives. This sixth-grade writer wrote about what it was like to turn into a squid in science class—a fictional account, obviously—but also an expression of what it's like to be a new person in school, stared at for being different, and perhaps even bullied.

I stepped into the room, the smell of the class was unusual. I was being stared at by thirty other kids, they looked weirded out by me. The teacher scowled and told me to take my seat, she didn't even introduce me. I hung my head down and took my seat. I could taste the sweat dripping down my face from the pressure.

Then the teacher asked a question. "Is anybody in here scared of squids?" Everybody raised their hands, I felt a bit embarrassed and even felt my cheeks turn red and hot. I thought squids are cool. Then, they were staring at me again, so I raised my hand up. Then, my hand and arm felt week [weak]. Then, it turned purple and fell to the floor, and it turned into a tentacle. Before I know it, I feel my head turn pointy and my legs turn into tentacles. I hear kids screaming and they throw their pencils at me. "STOP!!!!" I scream, but they don't listen.

Then I wake up and say "Phew!"

As you can see, empathy is being evoked in this fictional story where the reader is inspired to "step into the tentacles" of the narrator—thus fulfilling the

> *Fiction can inspire reader empathy just as effectively as a well-told personal narrative. Both genres can speak to our human condition, which is our common ground.*

heart of the invitation to "write about a time when you felt wonder, oh-my-gosh amazement, or even shock," modeling a chapter in *Saving Wonder*. It's also worth noting that this writer evoked common ground with his audience as a pathway into gaining their empathy with his main character. What sixth grader hasn't felt embarrassed in a new situation to the point of feeling like a monster—or, in this case, a squid? Fiction can inspire reader empathy just as effectively as a well-told personal narrative. Both genres can speak to our human condition, which *is* our common ground.

Poetry

Many of poetry's craft elements—such as sensory details, evocative images, and metaphors—are perfectly designed for immediate emotional engagement with the reader or listener, all working together in a poem to elicit a reader's empathic connection. Here's an example of a poem in which a fifth-grade poet used eco-empathy to imagine the life of a now-extinct species.

Dead Letter to the Eastern Cougar
Nina, Grade 5

sometimes I feel like your
death is our race's fault and
now your soul is

gone with the river I wish you
could see the moths that flitter
around

in my own backyard
sometimes I can hear
the birds whistling in your mourn

and maybe again

you will soon see the daisies
grouped in your mountain

Home

Nina's teacher, Karen, used an old form of poetry called *dead letter poems* to inspire her students to write tributes to now-extinct animals, an assignment inspired by the class reading of *Saving Wonder*. In a wonderful example of empathy-infused writing, the student poet has used vivid imagery packed with emotion to draw the reader into the poet's world, a world once shared by the Eastern cougar.

Craft Elements That Lend Themselves to Empathy-Infused Writing

Just as a student's proficiency in reading deepens with the CoreEmpathy approach, so does their proficiency in writing—particularly as they play with those craft elements that lend themselves to evoking reader empathy, a purpose that goes deeper than writing for clarity or even to entertain. Writers use these elements to *engage* the reader, to give them an experience through the life of their stories. In this section, we'll take a look at some of these elements. Many were originally discussed in Chapter 4, but this time we'll view them through a writer's lens.

Sensory Details and Active Verbs

In a *New York Times* essay entitled "Your Brain on Fiction," Annie Murphy Paul (2012) writes, "Brain scans are revealing what is happening in our heads when we read a detailed description, an evocative metaphor, or an emotional exchange between characters" (para. 2). She goes on to cite specific studies that show how specific parts of the brain are activated by reading a line of text just as they would by living the experience itself. Sensory details and active verbs are among the significant craft elements that light up these parts of a reader's brain—which is why writers want to use them (Paul, 2012).

For instance, when a sixth-grade girl writes about the smell of "fajitas and dirty socks," our olfactory centers light up as we feel her disappointment in a princess idol gone bad. When we read another student writer's account of his vacation—"My toes sunk into the soft hot sand. The fresh saltwater tickled my nose"—our sensory cortex helps us imagine the experience of being at the beach. And when a young girl writes about the day she was adopted and how the soft seats "spun around where you could see the whole court," our motor cortex is activated, and we empathize with that sensation of spinning. We might even get a sense that the experience made her feel "dizzy," and, empathetically, we might feel a little dizzy ourselves with how overwhelming this experience must have been for a young child. "The brain, it seems, does not make much of a distinction between reading about an experience and encountering it in real life," concludes Paul (2012, para. 6). A writer's purpose is to blur this distinction as much as possible.

Craft Elements Related to Characterization

Other craft elements that are particularly adept at blurring this distinction and inspiring empathy are ones that develop characterization, beginning with *point of view*. With the empathy-infused approach, student writers practice perspective-taking on the page, learning ways to make their characters or narrators feel real to their readers. Other writing craft elements related to characterization, such as *dialogue, descriptions of facial expressions and body language*, and *interior reflection*, or what we call *the inside view*, are all ways a writer evokes a character's thoughts and emotions, inviting the reader into the character or narrator's inner life.

Plot, Conflict, and Emotional Arc

A student's understanding of plot and conflict will deepen as they "read like a writer" and explore the emotional arc of the main character of a shared story—that is, the arc that drives a plot forward as the character's feelings and beliefs change. (See the Reading Like a Writer section in the Phase One learning flow below.) Once examined, the student writer will be ready to model the text by creating emotional arcs for their own characters.

Emotional Tone and Voice

Language itself, as well as setting, can be explored for emotional tone, as student writers play with how certain words, colors, and descriptions can convey emotions. And, as we mentioned in the introduction to this chapter, all of these empathy-evoking elements contribute to the development of a writer's voice—that unique presence behind the words.

> *The application of empathy not only engages the reader— it engages the writer, too.*

In the section that follows, we'll show you how to integrate these craft elements into empathy-infused writing instruction. As your students explore and practice these craft elements through an empathy lens and practice them in their writing, their understanding of them will deepen. Even better, the activity of writing itself will become more joyful. The application of empathy not only engages the reader—it engages the writer, too.

Preparing to Teach Empathy-Infused Writing

You've already chosen an empathy-infused book that you and your students love. In that choice, you've identified the story's writing elements that will lend themselves both to the exploration of empathy and the writing craft elements you wish to teach. Furthermore, you've already laid the most beautiful foundation for writing by teaching empathy-infused reading lessons that have deepened your students' understanding of the story while grounding them in empathy. It's time to take a deep breath and celebrate how far you and your students have come. And then . . . hold on, because it's time to ride that wave.

This is the elegance of the CoreEmpathy approach. Each phase of learning arises out of what has come before, and yet, like a wave, it curls back in on itself to give the previous learning even more power.

Each phase of learning arises out of what has come before, and yet, like a wave, it curls back in on itself to give the previous learning even more power.

In other words, the reading learning supports the writing learning and vice versa. They are interwoven, each learning modality stronger because of its connection with the other. Furthermore, the CoreEmpathy approach gives teachers not only a reason but also a greater purpose to interweave reading and writing without sacrificing anything—and, in fact, gaining a great deal.

Finding the Core of What You Want to Teach

Although we've covered the criteria for choosing an empathy-rich book in Chapter 3, we think they bear repeating in relation to teaching empathy-infused writing. Remember, you're looking for the following: What craft elements does this author do particularly well? Of those, which ones does the author use to engage reader empathy? And what is unique about how the text is written? In other words, what *shimmers*?

For example, in *Leonardo, the Terrible Monster*, Mo Willems (2005) does a great job of showing how his protagonist's feelings change after the other character, Sam, reveals what he's feeling and why—a shimmering moment of empathy. You might make the choice, as we did, to focus your student writers' attention on this moment between the two characters, exploring how the author revealed each character's feelings and then inviting student writers to explore a similar moment in their own lives using a similar strategy.

One follows the same strategy for chapter books, searching for those chapters or scenes that will provide good models for empathy-infused writing. For instance, *The One and Only Ivan* is particularly strong on characters that model empathy, so you might want to draw your students' attention to the most impactful empathy moments, inviting students to model how the author conveys this deeper understanding. The novel *Saving Wonder*, on the other hand, offers opportunities to examine how dialogue can reveal the underlying feelings and beliefs of characters in conflict with each other—the perfect setup for dialogue writing and for exploring the empathy skill of perspective-taking.

Once you have identified the craft elements that shimmer and the core of what you want to teach, you're ready to design and implement the flow of your instruction.

The Learning Flow for Empathy-Infused Writing

All the empathy-infused reading and analysis that has come before has created a wonderful foundation for the writing to come. For kindergarten teacher Heather, this seamless flow between reading and writing is one of CoreEmpathy's greatest strengths:

> I loved how the reading of the book flowed into their writing. I think what I enjoyed most is that it wasn't just a reading or just a writing lesson, but rather they went hand in hand. I think this helped the kiddos grasp what they were learning.

Here's what the basic flow of your empathy-infused writing instruction will look like. As you will discover in the explanatory text that follows, you can easily practice the CoreEmpathy approach in single, stand-alone experiences with your students simply by utilizing the first three steps in Phase One. Once you discover how easy empathy-infused literacy instruction is, you can then practice going deeper with empathy, utilizing the steps described in Phase Two.

Learning Flow of Empathy-Infused Writing

Phase One: Connect

1. Align empathy with a writer's purpose.
2. Invite reading like a writer.
3. Release the writer within.

Phase Two: Deepen

1. Engage feedback through the CoreEmpathy writing community.
2. Invite students to revise for empathy.
3. Invite sharing and appreciation.

We want to emphasize that it's completely up to you as far as how much time you will spend in writing instruction and even which of the above phases you emphasize according to your knowledge of your students and their grade level.

For instance, primary-grade students may not be developmentally ready for much, if any, time spent in revision, so you may decide to move from "unleashing" your students into writing and then into "sharing and celebration." Some teachers have designed the learning flow to occur over several days, while others might move from reading into writing on the same day. Regardless, be sure to give your student writers ample time to write.

Phase One: Connect

As you probably have already figured out by now, we believe one of the best ways to learn something is to explore a model of it, so, in this section, we invite you to take a look at some examples of how we and other CoreEmpathy teachers have designed empathy-infused writing instruction using the flow we've outlined above. For more models, there will be integrated reading *and* writing lessons in Chapter 6 for you to explore and implement as you desire.

Like all good models, the following examples are here only as a framework to inspire your own creative thinking. Successful ideas will naturally emerge from the empathy-rich books *you* love and from what you already know about your learning community.

Aligning Empathy with a Writer's Purpose

Just like the beginning of every reading lesson, we begin every writing lesson by grounding ourselves in empathy. The difference in a writing lesson, however, is that that focus now shifts from what empathy is or where it shows up in the text to *aligning empathy with a writer's purpose.* If empathy is still a relatively new concept for your students, you are welcome to begin by asking your class what they remember about empathy from the reading and discussion of the story.

> Feel free to continue using the Empathy Visual and/or hand motions in your discussion.

Once you are satisfied that they are ready to move on, the alignment with a writer's purpose may sound something like this: "We write with empathy so that our readers can step into our character's shoes, and thereby imagine what our character sees, thinks and feels." Or, when applicable: "If we are writing a personal narrative, then we write with empathy so that our readers can step into *our* shoes, and thereby imagine what we see, think, and feel." With this greater purpose in mind, you might add something like:

You're giving them a key to something powerful here. You have a purpose for teaching empathy, and they have a purpose to learn it.

As writers, our words have the power to inspire our readers to laugh and to cry, to feel anxious, surprised, and sometimes even afraid. Our words also have the power to transport our readers into other worlds and other lives, sometimes very different from our own. This is the power of our words when we write with empathy.

Above all, you want them to know that you're giving them a key to something powerful here. You have a purpose for teaching empathy, and they have a purpose to learn it.

Reading Like a Writer

Now that you've reestablished the empathy focus and aligned it with a writer's purpose, it's time to ask your students to shift how they're viewing the text—from seeing the text as a reader to seeing it as a writer. This phase of writer engagement we've named in deference to the award-winning writer Francine Prose (2007), who wrote a book on this subject called *Reading Like a Writer: A Guide for People Who Love Books and for Those Who Want to Write Them.*

As Prose comments in her book, reading like a writer is a method of learning the writer's craft that's as old as time, wherein writers study and explore a text as a model for their own writing. First one reads for enjoyment, Prose suggests—a step that we (teachers) may forget all too soon in the rush to make something productive of our students' learning. After this first read, however, she advocates for a closer read, examining the work for *how* the author did what they did, what craft elements they used, and why they made certain choices (Prose, 2007). Prose writes about her own writing education according to this method as follows:

> I read closely, word by word, sentence by sentence, pondering each deceptively minor decision the writer had made. And though it's impossible to recall every source of inspiration and instruction, I can remember the novels and stories that seemed to me revelations: wells of beauty and pleasure that were also textbooks, private lessons in the art of fiction. (p. 3)

As you probably have already realized, Prose's idea of "reading closely" to examine an author's craft aligns beautifully with the concept of close reading we discussed in Chapter 4. In fact, the phases are so similar that some teachers may bridge the two by using a story chart created in empathy-infused reading instruction as an aid for viewing the text once again, this time through a writer's lens. However, it's important to note that, while the main goal of close reading is to deepen a reader's understanding of the story, the goal of reading like a writer is to deepen the *writer's* understanding of how the author uses craft to inspire reader empathy.

In this important phase, students begin to see themselves applying these craft elements, techniques, and strategies, as they shift their focus from seeing themselves as readers to seeing themselves as writers. In other words, you'll be guiding your student writers to read again, this time focused on the craft strategy you want them to notice and then practice.

CONNECTING QUESTIONS

There's no better way to guide this process of reading like a writer than through asking connecting questions that connect empathy with a writer's craft. In that you already have a specific craft element in mind you are wanting to teach, invite your students to notice that element in the story—or a section of text within the story—as they read like writers. Once the element is noted, invite them to *think* like writers by asking craft-focused, empathy-infused questions, such as:

- If you take a minute to step into the character's shoes, what is the character feeling here? What words or phrases make you think that? Or, what about the writing makes you think that?

- How does this word/sentence/dialogue/description/action/scene inspire reader empathy for the character or narrator? How does it help you, the reader, step into the character's shoes, feel what they feel, see from their perspective?

"What" questions help focus students on the specifics of the element you want them to explore, such as characterization, dialogue, setting, and the like. "How" questions invite them to move beyond simply recognizing a literary element to examining the author's craft, a first step in discovering how that element may be modeled in their own writing.

Your "how" question will always be reflective of the craft element your students will soon be practicing. For example, Laura's first-grade students, as they prepared for readers theater, watched for the places in *My Friend Is Sad* where author Willems (2007) indicated a character's big feelings or excitement with exclamation marks. A guided question during this reading-like-a-writer phase might be: "How does the author show the reader that Gerald is having *big feelings*?"

This is a perfect example, incidentally, of how reading and writing instruction are interconnected—one seamlessly flowing into the other. The readers theater experience gave Laura's students practice in reading fluency and inflection,

while also helping them notice the writerly function of punctuation—specifically exclamation marks—in helping readers empathize with a character's feeling
state. Indeed, the exuberance with which Laura's students expressed themselves in readers theater carried over into their writing experience, and Laura
was able to ride that wave of energy effortlessly from empathy-infused reading
to empathy-infused writing instruction—all in the same day. Let us say it again:
sometimes empathy-infused reading and writing instruction occur simultaneously. That's powerful instruction.

In addition to focusing on how an author uses a specific craft element in
their work, you also can ask broader questions that focus on an author's purpose. These questions often center on plot choices or character motivation and
can be simply phrased: "Why do you think the author made this choice?" For
primary students, you'll want to make sure that you anchor the question with
a concrete focus, such as: "Why do you think our author, Mo Willems, used so
many exclamation marks?" Or, in relation to *The Stray Dog* story: "Why do you
think the author showed us what the family was feeling every day of the week?"
Or, for *Leonardo, the Terrible Monster*: "How does the author show us that the boy
is feeling sad?"

When I (Mary) do author visits in schools, students often ask me why most
of Curley's family is dead at the beginning of my novel. I like to turn the question back to them, inviting them to put their author caps on. "Why do *you* think
I did that?" Answers are often insightful: "Because you wanted to make life
harder for Curley, so he could overcome more" or "Because you wanted us to
feel sorry for him." And then there was this answer: "Curley's parents dying
sets up the whole book," one student said emphatically. "It sets up his relationship with Papaw, and it sets up the whole arrangement they make with the coal
company. If his parents hadn't died, the story couldn't have happened."

"Wow," I said. "Spoken like a true author!" Indeed, she was reading and
thinking like a writer.

I share this example to illustrate how one simple question—"Why do you
think the author made that choice?"—can unleash a wave of insights that will
lead to greater learning about writing. Better yet, connecting questions help students discover the learning for themselves, making it more meaningful. That's
literacy instruction with a greater purpose.

TRACKING THE ELEMENTS

As your student writers make observations about how an author achieved a
certain effect, there are options to anchor those ideas. You can write their observations on a whiteboard, use a chart or document camera to help students better see these craft elements at play, or, as we've mentioned before, use a chart

already created during empathy-infused reading that you can now review during this writing phase, inviting students to see that element through a writer's lens.

For instance, during close reading of *Leonardo, the Terrible Monster*, second graders charted how each character's feelings changed as the story progressed and where empathy was revealed (Figure 5.6). During empathy-infused writing, they read the text again as writers, reviewing the discoveries they had already made, but this time focusing on *how* the author showed his characters' feelings. Once students read like writers and noticed how Mo Willems revealed this change in his characters' emotions through dialogue, they were ready to apply their learning, writing about a time when, like Sam, they had a difficult or challenging day, and where, like Leonardo, someone stepped in and showed them empathy.

"I am an Empathy Detective!"	
Feelings	
Sam	Leonardo
1. sad, crying	happy, excited
2. angry, hurt	proud, mean
3. upset, sad	sad, sorry
4. sad	sad
5. happy	happy
Leonardo changes	
Beginning of story	End of story
Sad	Happy

FIGURE 5.6. Story chart: How feelings change.

As you can see in the writing example in Figures 5.7 and 5.8, the student is showing all aspects of her learning—about dialogue, about how a character's emotions change, and about how empathy happens. They all come together to produce this engaging piece of writing through which the writer's voice is clearly heard. Another example of the empathy effect.

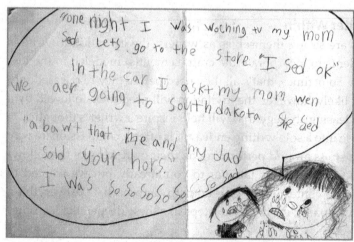

FIGURE 5.7. Bubble drawing and story: "One night I was watching TV …"

FIGURE 5.8. Second bubble drawing and story: "The next day …"

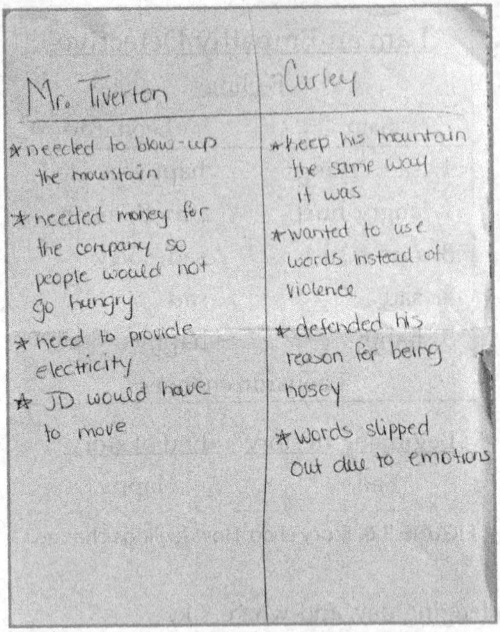

Mr. Tiverton	Curley
* needed to blow-up the mountain	* keep his mountain the same way it was
* needed money for the company so people would not go hungry	* wanted to use words instead of violence
* need to provide electricity	* defended his reason for being nosey
* JD would have to move	* words slipped out due to emotions

FIGURE 5.9. T-chart: Mr. Tiverton and Curley (*Saving Wonder*).

Tiffany's fifth-grade class in South Charleston, West Virginia, used Chapter P in *Saving Wonder* as a mentor text, focusing on the scene in which the coal boss, Mr. Tiverton, and Curley have a conversation about Tiverton's plan to mine Curley's mountain through a devastating mining process called *mountaintop removal*. After rereading this scene using readers theater, the class reviewed the text as writers and created a T-chart (Figure 5.9) showing how the author revealed the two characters' viewpoints or perspectives through dialogue—an empathy-infused craft element that also offers practice in perspective-taking, a core empathy skill. This reading-like-a-writer T-chart experience took students deeper into what motivated Curley to use certain words in his defense—"wanted to use words instead of violence" and "words slipped out due to emotion"—thus revealing an even closer read of the text than otherwise anticipated. It also helped make the perspective-taking part of dialogue writing more evident, so that students could use the learning more consciously in their own writing. You'll see in the next section how Tiffany also used this chart as a releasing strategy into student writing.

Releasing the Writer Within

Now that students are seeing themselves as writers, the invitation to write is issued, asking students to incorporate the craft element(s) modeled in the text in their own stories. Sometimes, that's all they need before they're released into their writing. Most likely, however, the invitation will need to be followed by a brainstorming or releasing strategy that will help inspire a writer's thoughts.

A gradual release into a solo writing endeavor is often a compassionate way to relieve a writer's stress around performing on their own. Most of the following release strategies are probably familiar to you already, but we wanted to discuss them within the context of the CoreEmpathy approach. Like everything else, when you add empathy, even interim steps like these deepen the learning.

THE INVITATION TO WRITE

First, it's important that young writers understand the goal they're moving toward. For instance, after guiding her first-grade class through an interactive read-aloud of *My Friend Is Sad*, followed by a readers theater experience focused on big feelings, Laura's invitation to write might have sounded something like this:

> Today, as writers, we're going to focus on using exclamation points at the end of our sentences to express the feeling of excitement. On the top half of your page, you will draw a picture of something you once saw that made you feel excited. And then, below the picture, you will write about what you saw and the big feeling it gave you—making sure you use an exclamation point to express that feeling of excitement. Here, let me show you what I mean.

Laura then modeled that invitation.

MODELING THE PROCESS

Once your students have examined a part of the book's text as a model for their own writing, they still might not have a mental image of the writing process itself. This is something only you as their teacher can demonstrate in real time. Especially in primary grades, student writers often need to see how someone else thinks through the writing process as they put words and pictures on paper.

After presenting the invitation to write, Laura then modeled it by relating an experience from her own life that students would not be tempted to copy. Drawing and writing about a time when her husband was away on a business trip, Laura wrote: "When I opened the door, I saw flowers! Red and white and purple flowers! I love flowers!" Notice that she did not say, "I was excited!" but rather let the vividness of her description and the exclamation points *show* how she was feeling. Good modeling!

It's interesting to note that even though vivid description was not a writing element Laura and her students discussed, it showed up in a lot of her students' writing, demonstrating a theory that Francine Prose (2007) makes about modeling other writers: "The truth is that this sort of education more often involves a kind of osmosis" (p. 3).

The examples of student writing in Figures 5.10 and 5.11 show how well this osmosis worked as a direct result of Laura's modeling. More important, by the time Laura released them, her students were eager to write with an enthusiasm that extended into more writing the next day. We love how this story offers an intriguing plot line in just three sentences. This is also an instance where the writer's voice really shines through—perhaps because she's been invited to show that "big feeling," to bring it out to the front of the story where readers can clearly see it.

FIGURE 5.10. Student drawing and story: "My friend's dog …"

My frains [friend's] dog! Dos [does] not like the cat I got the cat! It was Amasing [Amazing]!

Figure 5.11 is another example of voice that bursts through the writer's words. Writers often use contrast like this to deepen an emotional effect. Where a reader might expect an anxious shout, an author's choice to have a character speak in a restrained whisper may create a more suspenseful edge. It's the "whisper" in this story that makes the feeling of wonder more dramatic, without having to name it—an excellent strategy for engaging reader empathy. We feel this writer's awe.

FIGURE 5.11. Student drawing and story: "Baby deer ..."

(whisper) Baby deer. I love baby deer. Mom come here quietly. There is baby deer!

Although this first grader probably wasn't aware of using this strategy, Laura could have brought it to the young writer's awareness by saying something like, "I wonder if your choice to 'whisper' your excitement makes that feeling even bigger? What do you think?" Such a question might just plant the strategy into the writer's awareness to show up at another time.

DRAWING FIRST

In early elementary grades, pictures are an integral part of storytelling, but drawing first before engaging in writing can be helpful at any age. As demonstrated in Laura's lesson above, drawing the experience first can help student writers organize their thoughts in much the same way as other brainstorming strategies such as clustering or mind-mapping do, and, as such, can be a good bridge into a student's writing experience. These preliminary pictures often contain more information about the story or experience than the student will initially write about and can provide a wonderful jumping-off point for you, the teacher, to ask the student for more details that, depending upon the student's ability and enthusiasm, may be added to their writing as a first step into revision.

VISUALIZING QUESTIONS

Another releasing technique that works in a similar way to drawing the story first is to ask questions that help students not only visualize the setting and context of their stories, but the emotional core as well. Sometimes, visualizing questions are an effective way to inspire a student's own thinking after you've offered them a model of the invitation to write. The following is an example of how one writing phase can flow seamlessly into the next, ending with visualizing questions as a final release into student writing.

Shannon, a kindergarten teacher in Issaquah, Washington, and her class had recently read the book *Happy*. After engaging an empathy-infused reading lesson, Shannon pointed to the word *happy* on the cover and asked students to think of a time when they felt that way. Then she issued the invitation: "Today, we're going to draw a picture of a time we felt happy or something similar and then write about it. Here's what it will look like." She then modeled her thinking by relating a time when she felt happy—drawing a picture of that experience as she talked—and then by writing a simple statement about that feeling and time (Figure 5.12). Once again, notice that Shannon chose an experience that her young writers wouldn't be tempted to copy.

Once her model was established, Shannon invited her kindergartners to reflect silently: "What is a time when you felt happy or a feeling similar to happy?" After pausing a few moments to allow time for their memories to click in, she primed the pump of that inspiration even more with questions like:

FIGURE 5.12. Teacher model drawing and story: Maui.

- Where were you?

- What did it look like around you?

- Who was there with you?

- What was happening that made you feel so happy?

Again, she made sure to pause after every question. These visualizing questions helped her students find the connection between an emotion and a personal experience—a connection that forms the core of all personal narratives. While the memories were still fresh, she then invited her students to draw and write their stories as she had, helping them record them using phonetic spelling.

As you will notice in the teacher's example above, Shannon modeled *setting* (where it was—Maui) as well as *plot* (what happened—she got married) and the *emotional tone* or feeling of that experience (happy). As you enjoy the student writing that follows (Figures 5.13 and 5.14), notice how the elements of setting, character, and action are present in these student samples without the teacher specifically asking for them as part of the assignment. Through modeling and visualizing, the source of the writing came from within each writer's mind and heart.

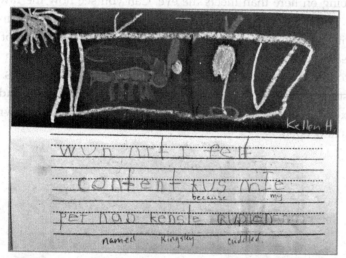

FIGURE 5.13. Student drawing and story: "One night, I felt content…"

One night I felt content because my pet named Kingsley cuddled.

FIGURE 5.14. Student drawing and story: "One day, I felt surprised…"

One day I felt surprised becas I made a new frend

Because her students wanted to do more writing, Shannon followed this same design for another lesson the following day, asking writers to find a different feeling inspired by a different experience. Notice the honesty of the story in Figure 5.15. This may seem like a simple writing lesson, but, as you see, a lot more is going on here than meets the eye. Can you see how the raw honesty expressed in this brief story would inspire reader empathy? Certainly, many of this writer's classmates were able to empathize with his feeling of jealousy. Shannon said her students enjoyed this writing experience so much that they chose to continue to write about their feelings for the next few days. It's as if, once her students had this experience of expressing their feelings and the subsequent experience of their classmates' empathy after sharing their writing, the floodgates flew open.

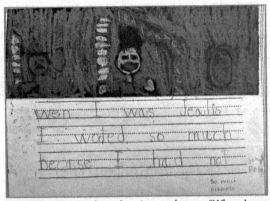

FIGURE 5.15. Student drawing and story: "When I was jealous…"

Wen I was Jealis I wanted so much because I had not so much presents.

And that's how it works. When *all* feelings are welcome inside of our classrooms, empathy grows.

STEMS

Releasing techniques do not need to be hard or convoluted to work. In fact, the simpler the strategy the better, allowing a writer's own creativity the space to shine. For instance, the use of stems—a few words or a phrase that relates to the topic or theme of the lesson that helps the writer begin their thought process—is a tried-and-true technique for releasing student writers of any age into empathy-infused writing, particularly when the stem is designed to connect the writer with their feelings.

Stems may be used alone or as repeating phrases, such as the ones suggested in the easy-use lesson (Phase One) in Chapter 6 with the empathy-rich story *The Day You Begin*. The stems "On the day I begin . . . ," "There will be times when . . . ," or "There was a time when . . ." prime the writer's creative pump, giving the brain something to come back to in order to spark a new idea. On the other hand, sometimes a single stem is all that is necessary to get the writing started.

T-CHARTS AND WRITING WITH PARTNERS

All the above releasing strategies work well for all grade levels, including intermediate. Some strategies may be better suited, however, for teaching a specific craft element, such as characterization, and how it evokes empathy. The following is an example of how one intermediate teacher adapted the use of T-charts and partner writing as releasing strategies that illuminated both an element of craft and a CoreEmpathy skill.

Tiffany wanted her fifth-grade student writers to focus on dialogue, using the empathy skill of perspective-taking to guide their writing. She adapted what she knew about T-charts and turned it into a releasing/brainstorming strategy that helped her students step into the perspective of, first, a story's characters, and, second, the characters in their own stories.

After reviewing the T-chart her students created in response to a dialogue scene in *Saving Wonder*, Tiffany invited her students to work as partners in creating their own T-charts of two differing perspectives, each student taking one side of an argument. She gave each student pair their own scenario between two wacky characters, such as "a cheeseburger that doesn't want to be eaten" and "a hungry kid," or "a monster under the bed" and "the child it's trying to scare." She then asked each pair of writers to step into the shoes of the characters they represented and develop a T-chart of the two perspectives, taking the form of a dialogue.

She gave students only a few minutes for this task, to keep the brainstorming hopping, and then asked for volunteers to perform their dialogue/skits in front of the class. As duos performed their skits, the laughter that followed helped create a lively environment for the solo writing to come. Figures 5.16a and b are an example of a T-chart of a dialogue between a child and the monster under their bed that got a lot of laughs. A teacher might not need to do this intermediary step of the partner-created T-charts for students to feel confident in writing their own dialogue scenes. However, in Tiffany's classroom, this step made all the difference in the energy with which her students approached their writing.

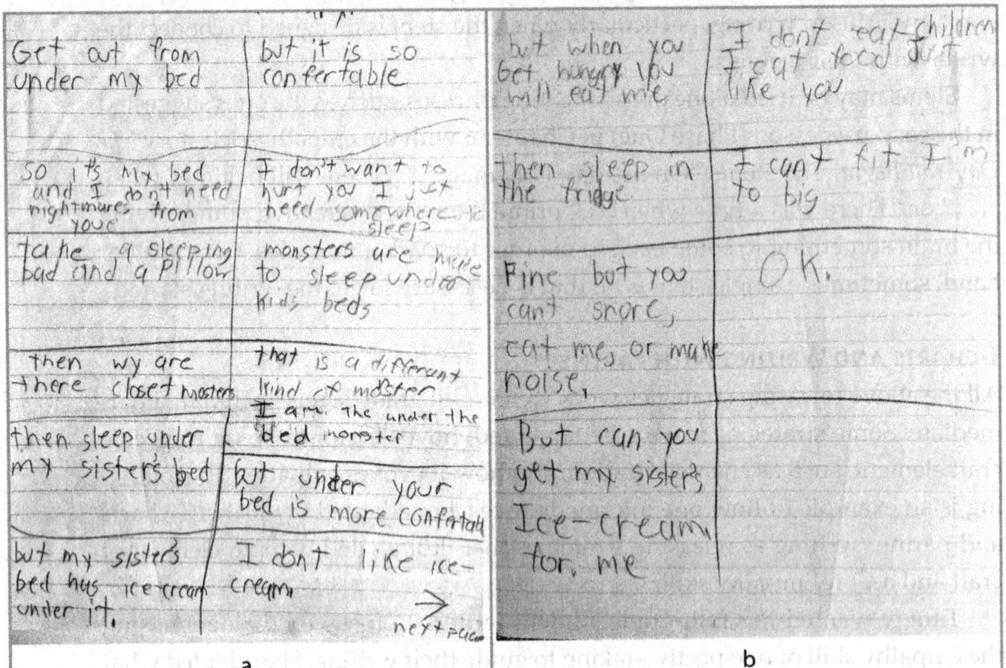

Get out from under my bed	but it is so confertable	but when you get hungry you will eat me	I dont eat children I eat food Just like you
So it's my bed and I don't need nightmares from youe	I don't want to hurt you I Just need somewhere to sleep?	then sleep in the fridge	I cant fit I'm to big
Tahe a sleeping bed and a Pillow	monsters are here to sleep under kids beds	Fine but you cant snore, eat me, or make noise,	OK.
then wy are there closet mosters	that is a differant kind of monster I am. The under the Bed monster		
then sleep under my sisters bed	but under your bed is more COnfortable	But can you get my sisters Ice-cream for me	
but my sisters bed has ice-cream under it.	I dont like ice-cream → next page		
a		b	

FIGURE 5.16. Students' T-chart: Dialogue.

Once Tiffany's students had limbered up their dialogue-writing muscles in these partnerships, they were ready to be released into writing an imagined dialogue on their own—this time between themselves and another person about something that mattered to them and about which they and the other person disagreed. Again, Tiffany encouraged them to create T-charts of the conversation first, as a way to brainstorm their thoughts prior to writing their dialogues.

The following writing sample was inspired by its writer's desire for a cell phone. In the process of creating this fictional dialogue—first by brainstorming via a T-chart—"Cameron" (a pseudonym) used empathy to step into his mother's perspective as well as his own.

"Why can't I have a phone?" I asked.

"You are too young for a phone," mom says. That's usually the response when I ask for a phone.

My face got red after that and then I say, "But I am very responsible. I have good grades and I don't lose stuff."

Now she looks like she doesn't know what to say, but right then she says, "I don't [know] when you are going to understand that you are not old enough. The rule has always been 6th grade." Now I don't know what to say, then she says, "You already have a lot of electronics. You can wait until 6th grade."

At that moment I say, "I bet you couldn't wait until next year for something you wanted." I can't believe I just said that out loud.

Then she says, "I know it can be hard to wait until 6th grade, but if your brothers can do it than you can do it too."

"But what if it is an emergency and I need to call you or if I would get lost or need to call you?" I ask.

"Some people don't even get a phone until high school, for that matter some kids don't even get electronics ever."

Then I stood up and said, "So you wouldn't care if I was in an emergency."

"I'm not saying that, plus other people you know, if it is an emergency, will be there and you can use their phone," mom says.

"Well, everybody else in my class has a phone," I say.

"It doesn't matter what they have, that doesn't mean they have all the electronics you do."

"What if I got one this summer instead of next Christmas?" I hopefully ask with my fingers crossed behind my back.

"If you keep good grades and you show responsibility then yes, that would be possible," mom replies smiling at me.

That was it. I finally convinced her that I should get a phone this summer!

Tiffany believes that inviting student writers to find the subject matter they are passionate about was one of the keys to the success of this writing experience—particularly with previously reluctant writers. Most people have heard that advice often given to writers: "Write about what you know." As writing teachers, we can extend this idea further by inviting our students to "write about what you care about" or "what inspires you." When students are invited to write from their emotional core, they are more likely to generate empathy-infused writing. Learning can't always be designed this way, but, when it can, aligning the learning with your students' curiosity, passions, and interests increases their chances for writing success and, just as important, enjoyment.

....

All of the strategies mentioned here—and so many others you undoubtedly have in your tool chest—will provide your students with a compassionate release into writing. They don't take much time, and they provide the safety and confidence students need to write on their own. Most important, when connected with empathy-inspired craft elements, these releasing strategies inspire writers to find the connection between a life experience and the emotions it evokes—an important CoreEmpathy skill.

For the little bit of extra time that one or more empathy-focused releasing strategies take to create a foundation for student writing, you are deepening your students' academic *and* emotional learning, and the payoff is great.

Phase Two: Deepen

After releasing the writer into their writing, an empathy-infused writing lesson can easily end there, perhaps followed by sharing. However, the following deepening phases of an empathy-infused writing flow can make all the difference between merely adequate writing and writing excellence. Certainly, primary teachers need to be aware of simplifying this flow for their young writers so as not to overwhelm them, but the intention behind the deepening process can still be realized. And what is that intention? A writing experience that inspires writers to deepen their skills while giving them that feeling that keeps them coming back for more. And what is that feeling that writing with empathy offers? The joy of being seen and heard.

Creating the CoreEmpathy Writing Community

Once your students have embraced the invitation to write and unleashed their creative powers in the process—hopefully to their amazement as well as yours—what's next? Now that students have their empathy-infused writing in hand, it's time to discharge that empathy into the classroom through sharing and feedback.

Now that students have written their first drafts, it's time to invite them to come together into a writing community where small groups of two, three, or four students gather to listen, share, and receive supportive feedback. "What's working" or "what shimmers" is always the first response from readers, followed by "What I'm curious about." These wonder questions are always guided by wanting to know more about the character or narrator's perspective and emotional or sensory experience.

Much like the "making the empathy learning real" phase in empathy-infused reading (Chapter 4), during which students are encouraged to practice empathy in the real world, a CoreEmpathy writing community is one of the best places for your students to consciously practice their empathy skills with one another. After all, the classroom *is* their world. The empathy skills activated in this feedback process are:

- active listening—not just for the words, but also for the feeling behind the words,
- finding and expressing common ground, and
- giving and receiving appreciation.

The first step in creating your classroom's writing community will be for the students themselves to empathize with what it's like to be both the giver and the receiver of feedback. This grounding in empathy will guide them in the creation of the writing community's intentions for how writing colleagues interact with each other.

Many writers who have developed their craft and become professionals will tell you that they've had the opposite experience from the one we're about to describe. Horror stories abound about a writer's spirit being crushed in a writing group in which one person—sometimes even the leader—has delivered critiques in a demeaning way.

Of course, we would hope this could never happen in the nurturing environment of an elementary school classroom. That said, most children feel vulnerable when they've dared to express their feelings in writing, particularly if those feelings are related to a difficult or challenging experience. They are concerned that something they share will make them seem "different" from their peers and kick them out of belonging.

Friends, this is a big deal. However, don't worry: setting up the CoreEmpathy writing community will be one of the easiest classroom management experiences you will ever have. Why? Because empathy is already in the room.

Creating Empathy-Infused Guidelines for Your Writing Community

Just as you set up your classroom guidelines at the beginning of the school year, you'll want to invite your students to work together on their own list of empathy-infused guidelines for their writing community. This should happen at the beginning of the school year, or at least as preparation for the time you decide your students are ready to give and receive feedback. Primary-grade writing communities will look more like a circle of writers sharing and celebrating their work, rather than offering any wonder questions regarding what more a reader or listener may want to know. The same empathy-infused guidelines will work just as well regardless of how deep the feedback goes.

Once you introduce the concept of this community, start the group's conversation by talking about empathy first. Then, invite students to engage their empathy as you discuss the kind of environment you want to create together. Here are some questions you might want to ask:

From the Point of View of the Writer

- When we share our writing with each other in partners or small groups, what's it like to be the one sharing?
- How does it feel when you read what you've written?
- What are some thoughts that might go through your mind?
- What kinds of things would you like to see or hear from your colleagues that will help you feel supported as a writer?
- What kinds of things would you want to know about your writing that will help make your writing better?
- What are some ways that you can support a writer who is sharing their work?

From the Point of View of the Writing Colleague/Listener/One Giving Feedback

- What is it like to be the one listening to someone sharing their work?
- What kinds of feelings might you feel?
- What kinds of thoughts might you think?
- What is fun or interesting about listening? And about giving feedback?
- What, if anything, is challenging about listening? And about giving feedback?
- What can a writer do when they're reading their writing aloud that would help support you as a colleague as you listen? And to give feedback?

Naturally, you will word these questions appropriately for your students' grade level. Tracking their answers on a chart or whiteboard also would be helpful.

From this chart or brainstorming session, they can create their own empathy-guided intentions to be posted in your classroom. Because everyone usually wants the same thing in a feedback situation, your classroom's empathy-guided intentions may include something of the following list (don't worry, a much shorter version appears at the end!).

> Please note that this is a comprehensive list and your class list of intentions will be *much shorter*.

Please note that this is a comprehensive list and your class list of intentions will be *much shorter*. However, we've made it comprehensive so that you may refer to it now and then for supportive things to say to your class as you release them into the writing community experience. These guidelines will also give you a good idea about what a CoreEmpathy writing community looks like, sounds like, and *feels* like in practice.

As the Writer Sharing

- Before we start, we take a deep breath and believe in what we've written.
- We read slowly and with inflection.
- We read so that everyone in our group can hear us.
- We pause now and then to breathe and let our words sink in.
- When we read, we remember what we were feeling when we wrote it.
- We read with that feeling.
- After we share, we listen carefully and with curiosity to our colleagues' feedback.
- We listen even when it feels hard, remembering that feedback is only someone else's opinion.
- We thank each person for their feedback.

As a Writing Colleague

- When someone is sharing their writing, we listen with our full attention. This means we sit facing them. Our bodies are comfortable but still. Our eyes are on them only, and not on anyone or anything else in the classroom.
- We listen not just to the words, but also to the feeling behind the words.
- We listen for what we appreciate about the writing, for what *shimmers*.
- We listen for vivid words or phrases that make the writing come alive.
- We listen for *common ground*—for what we have in common with the narrator or characters in the story.

- We listen for what our teacher invites us to listen for!
- When we give feedback, we share what we appreciated *first*, what got our attention, what made the story come alive for us, what made us *feel* something and what that feeling was.
- When it occurs to us, we tell the writer what we have in common with the narrator or character in the story.
- After we say what we liked, we *never* offer advice.
- We share what we wonder about, what more we'd like to know, and perhaps what confused us.
- We respect each person for being the author of their own writing.

And now for the shorter version of what your class workshop guidelines might look like:

In Our Writing Workshop . . .

- we share with empathy,
- we listen with empathy,
- we offer feedback with empathy,
- we *always* show appreciation for each other.

How's that? Simple, right? We trust you, the teacher, to know how to facilitate the guidelines for your classroom's writing community and to shepherd your own, unique, empathy-infused writing culture. Remember, just as it is with everything related to empathy, so much of what happens is in the *practice*.

As student writers practice their empathy skills in their writing community, they will be more inclined to dive back into their writing to revise. Once revision happens—as discussed in the next section—you may want to invite the writing groups to reconvene to share their revised stories with each other. Writers may want to talk about what changes they decided to make and why, but this final feedback is focused on *appreciation only*. We want to reinforce that feeling of satisfaction that comes when we dare to revise.

Empathy-Infused Revision

As you undoubtedly know by now, revision is usually not something writing students are excited about. In fact, we're pretty sure most teachers have heard the collective groan at some point in their teaching career when they've asked students to dive back into their writing to revise or edit their work.

Let's take a moment to empathize with your students. In fact, when you hear that collective groan, you might ask, "Tell me what you're *really* feeling. Name those feelings! I want to hear them." Here are some comments we've heard in response:

"It's frustrating!"

"I feel mad because I thought I was *done*."

"When my teacher says to revise, I feel hurt. I think she doesn't like what I wrote."

It's important to remind yourself and your students that all feelings are valid and welcome in the CoreEmpathy classroom. "I hear you" and "I know just how you feel" are wonderful things for you to say in response to your students daring to express their true feelings. You might even share how challenging revision has been for you, telling them about a time you felt frustrated by a teacher asking you to revise. Once this common ground is established with your students, they will be more ready to hear what you've learned about revision.

You might want to say things like "Revision is where the art is" or "It's where you get to go back into your story and really make it sing." In response to students who have expressed a worry that you're not happy with them, you might say, "I hear you, and maybe I believe in you and your story so much, I know you can make it better." Really, it's not so much *what* you say; it's the *attitude* you hold about revision that says more than your words.

It's important for you and your students to distinguish the difference between editing and revising early on. *Editing* is the process by which a writer looks for ways to make the writing more understandable or accurate, usually by paying attention to grammar, punctuation, word phrasing, word choice, and the like. *Revision* is a deeper process whereby the writer looks for ways to tell the story more effectively, usually by focusing on the craft elements themselves and looking for ways to deepen the emotional tone of the story. Revision is the process by which the writer as sculptor shapes the story or poem into the form that they have envisioned.

It's important to develop the practice of revision early on—at least as soon as your students are developmentally ready for it. Even kindergartners and first graders can be encouraged to look at the pictures they've drawn for a detail about their story that wasn't expressed in words and *tell* it to you or a classmate. With the help of their colleagues in their writing community, student writers will become grounded in the effect their writing is having on their reader-audience and will be motivated to make changes that will enhance or change the effect they really want.

As always, this revision phase of the writing flow will be guided by empathy. Your role as writing instructor is crucial, as you guide young writers in focusing the process—most likely suggesting only one or two craft elements they might change or add to their first drafts to make the writing more engaging to their readers. One of your main goals will be to help your students establish a revision practice, along with delivering the message that "revision is writing, too."

Revision is writing too.

Teacher-Guided Revision

Once students have written and you decide you want to deepen their writing practice with a revision experience, you can choose between two methods: (1) initiate peer feedback through a form of writing community in partnerships or groups, as discussed above, or (2) use a teacher-guided revision process informed by—what else?—empathy. For simplicity's sake, we've provided an outline of that process:

1. Remind them of their writer's purpose: "We revise to deepen reader empathy." For younger students, we might say: "We revise so our readers will feel even *more* of what we or our characters are feeling."

2. Then draw your students' attention to the craft elements they practiced in their stories—the ones the class explored through reading like a writer and then applied in their writing.

3. Ask students to mark that element with a checkmark, underline, or circle, or with a colored marker.

4. Once students have indicated all the places where that element occurs in their writing, congratulate them and perhaps ask for examples.

5. After a few writers have shared, remind them of your previous instruction concerning that particular craft element and how it evokes reader empathy.

6. Then invite them to "revise for empathy," mindful of that element's purpose you've just discussed. This usually means adding another word, phrase, or sentence that reflects that element or making what's already written more engaging. You'll always use this opportunity to remind students of how this element helps readers empathize with the characters or narrator.

7. This same process is repeated if there are other craft elements writers practiced in their stories, this time using a different mark or color to differentiate this next element from the previous one.

The following example shows what this teacher-guided revision process might look like, based on a classroom scenario at an elementary school in Batesville, Indiana. Fifth-grade students wrote personal narratives, focusing on three empathy-infused craft elements: sensory details, inside view (i.e., written reflections of what the narrator is feeling or thinking), and vibrant verbs.

Students were first asked to review their personal narratives for sensory details, putting a checkmark by each one. Once this was accomplished and appreciated through group sharing, the instructor talked about how seeing is often our go-to sense, but that details expressing sound or smell, for instance, can really help our readers step into our narrator's shoes. Student writers were then invited to add one more sensory detail, using a sense they hadn't used yet.

This same process was followed by asking writers to examine their first drafts and underline any inside views—a craft element that inspires readers to empathize, to see what the narrator or character is thinking and feeling. After sharing, they were encouraged to revise for empathy by adding one more inside view or adding to a reflection already written. Students repeated this process one more time, circling all vibrant or descriptive verbs and then revising in a similar manner.

The student writing sample shown in Figure 5.17 is a result of this revision workshop, a narrative by a fifth-grade writer named "Allie" (a pseudonym). As can be seen, the paragraph to the right of Allie's first draft is her revision (Figure 5.18), in which she added sensory details about the snow cone she eats before she goes on that first roller-coaster ride. The arrow in the original draft shows where this revision is supposed to go. This revision for empathy really added to Allie's narrative. The snow cone offered a wonderful contrast to how hot the day was, as it also set up the nauseous feeling to come with details that engaged the reader's senses and helped them step into the narrator's shoes.

A side note: The above revision experience was facilitated during one of my (Mary's) author visits, in which I facilitated a writers workshop. I wanted to optimize my time with students, which is why I worked with three craft elements in a single setting. Normally, a teacher would probably not choose to do this, and for good reason. We absolutely do not want revision to feel like work. We want it to feel like *play*.

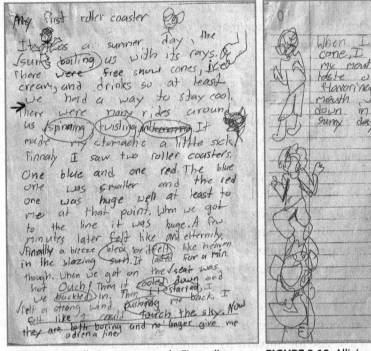

FIGURE 5.17. Allie's writing sample: First roller coaster.

FIGURE 5.18. Allie's writing revision sample.

Sharing and Celebration

Regardless of how quickly your class moves through an empathy-infused writing flow, or even if you skip feedback and revision due to time constraints or for developmental considerations, taking time for students to share and celebrate their written work is crucial for them to feel a sense of completion. After all, we write to communicate something to others. We want to know our writing has been received. It's one of the reasons we write.

In this phase, writers share their work by reading their writing aloud to the whole group, a small group, or a partner. Most of the guidelines for the Core-Empathy writing community apply in this process. Writing colleagues listen respectfully and eagerly, listening for what shimmers or tugs at their empathy, ready to speak their appreciation after the piece has been shared. For sure, this is *not* the time for criticism. Appreciation *rules*.

A Review of the Learning Flow for Empathy-Infused Writing

Teaching empathy-infused writing starts with applying empathy-infused reading instruction to an empathy-rich story, allowing student writers to appreciate not just how the author uses the story's craft elements to achieve a particular effect, but how writing with empathy inspires readers to care. You can practice the CoreEmpathy approach to writing by trying out one of our sample lessons in Chapter 6, or by designing your own lessons. You can also check out our website (www.CoreEmpathy.com) for more sample lessons. Meanwhile, the following is a quick review of the steps to the learning flow for empathy-infused writing instruction.

Phase One: Connect

1. Align a writer's purpose with empathy, reinforcing the idea that we write with empathy to help our readers see, think, and feel with our characters.
2. Invite students to read the story again, this time exploring it through a writer's lens. Use connecting questions to focus their attention on how the story's craft elements inspire reader empathy.
3. Release students into their writing, inviting them to use what they've learned about craft in their own stories. Use one or more empathy-infused releasing strategies.

Phase Two: Deepen

1. Students share their writing and offer empathy-inspired feedback within a CoreEmpathy writing community—whether it's the whole classroom, a small group, or as partners.
2. After receiving feedback from either you or their writing community, students revise their writing in order to deepen reader engagement. The revision process may be guided by you or initiated on their own in response to peer feedback.
3. Students share their final drafts with the whole class or within their writing communities. Listeners focus their feedback on what they appreciate about each other's work, as you encourage a spirit of celebration.
4. Enjoy your classroom's transformation!

Reengaging Greater Purpose: The Transformative Power of Empathy-Infused Writing

Perhaps the most meaningful result we've witnessed in student writing inspired by the CoreEmpathy approach is the transformation student writers experience when they can see themselves in their own empathy-infused stories. This doesn't happen in every piece of writing, of course. Much depends on how open the student writer chooses to be. When feelings are talked about openly in an empathy-rich classroom, however, and students feel safe in doing so, they generally feel safe on the page as well and their writing will reflect that.

A poignant demonstration of this happened in a classroom that had only been experiencing the CoreEmpathy approach for a little over a week. A first-grade student who was a self-selected mute—someone who had never spoken in the classroom so far that year—chose to write about herself, much to the teacher's surprise. She felt safe enough in the empathy-infused classroom to express, through pictures and the written word, something that had been bottled up inside.

And then there was that school where a bully group calling themselves the "Redneck Mafia" was formed, seeking to terrorize students they considered different from themselves. Several years later, at a school within that same district, sixth-grade students experienced empathy-guided writing workshops for the first time. Their teacher, Michelle, had been working diligently with them for the previous month in close reading the novel *Saving Wonder*, as well as inviting them to write their personal responses to the characters' inner lives. Her students were well prepared for the CoreEmpathy writing lesson that followed.

The *Saving Wonder* text that students were invited to read like a writer was a scene in Chapter D in which the characters Curley and Jules meet up at their favorite tree and see a magnificent elk for the first time. The scene is filled with sensory details intended to evoke a feeling of quiet wonder and awe. Students were invited to notice these details along with other elements that inspired readers to step into the shoes of the characters. The invitation to write, issued by Michelle, was "to write about a time when you felt wonder, surprise, or even shock" using vivid sensory details and internal reflection—or what Michelle called "thought-shots"—to engage a reader's empathy.

These sixth graders' personal narratives covered a wide range of experiences—from a young boy's account of the day his parents told him and his siblings they were getting a divorce, to the student who wrote an account of what it's like living with an addicted mother and having to be the grown-up. Other student writers in Michelle's class told coming-of-age stories, like one boy's account of what it felt like to go hunting with his father and kill his first deer: "I could smell the smoke from the gun. And everything goes quiet." Or the young girl's discovery of how her favorite princess idol was a mere mortal: "I came to realize she was a fony [phoney]. She didn't even smell like royalty, simply fahetas [fajitas] and dirty socks."

The result of this empathy-infused writing lesson, Michelle said, was some of the best writing she'd seen from her students all year, even from those who had previously demonstrated lower-level ability. One such student, "Maya," wrote from the point of view of her little-girl self about the day she was adopted and what it was like in the courtroom:

> I really was wondering why they recorded us on a big camera. The seats we sat in were soft, they spun around where you could see the whole court. When we went to the Judge's desk, I banged the gavel or mallet. I thought that I was going to put a scare [scar] on her desk.... It was a thrill to look out the windows. You could see the bridge from there. I felt as if I were going to fall out. All of the people were clapping and screaming for us. Out of nowhere, a lady yelled "Wait a second!" I tasted my sweat wondering who it was.

Notice how some of the sensory details convey conflicting emotions. For instance, the height of the windows is both thrilling and scary. One can only imagine how this writing helped this student process this experience, perhaps inspiring compassion for the little girl she was at the time—a demonstration of the transformative power of writing as a writer looks back on their past *with empathy.*

As you adopt the CoreEmpathy approach to both reading and writing instruction, not only will your students be learning and practicing literacy goals in a deeper way, they'll be experiencing the joy, satisfaction, and self-understanding that only empathy-infused literacy learning can bring. As your students read for greater understanding of themselves, others, and the world around them, and as they write for deeper reader engagement and then share that writing with each other, empathy in the classroom will naturally blossom and grow.

If this isn't literacy instruction with a greater purpose, we don't know what is.

6

CoreEmpathy Literacy Lessons

Empathy. That's something I've been thinking a lot about lately. The ability to walk in someone else's shoes, the recognition that someone else's experience has value, too.

—*Michelle Obama, former First Lady of the United States*

There's nothing like seeing an actual lesson to help a teacher visualize what a certain strategy or approach might look like in their classroom. This chapter contains a wide range of lessons that have already been discussed in the reading and writing chapters (Chapters 4 and 5). Naturally, you will explore these offerings and find creative ways to adapt these lessons to address the needs of your unique learning community.

The first easy-use lessons include Phase One steps for two of our anchor books. These lessons require minimal preparation and class time for maximal effect. They are basically empathy-infused, interactive read-alouds with empathy-infused writing ideas. All that you've learned about the approach in the previous pages will help make this format a great way to practice your CoreEmpathy instruction skills.

The rest of the chapter offers reading and writing lessons on four of our anchor books in a more extended format. These lessons will help you teach Phase One: Connect and Phase Two: Deepen for both reading and writing instruction, complete with guidance in learning targets and lesson flow, teacher talk, connecting questions, charts, and student practice in "making the empathy learning real." You'll find additional lessons on our website, too: www.Core Empathy.com.

◎ Easy-Use Lessons (Phase One Only)

The Day You Begin by Jacqueline Woodson

Empathy Focus

This picture book tells a lyrical story for empathy practice as readers step into the shoes of each character and see themselves. It also introduces the idea of self-empathy—suggesting that there is a "brave self" that is always standing with you, reminding you of your value. We also love this book for the idea that empathy flourishes when people tell their stories, and that empathy is a key to everyone feeling they belong, wherever they are, because where empathy lives, so does community.

Read-Aloud Using Connecting Questions

Begin with Empathy First, then introduce the book by title and author. Tell your students that this book offers a chance to practice empathy in order to understand the story more deeply. As you read, invite your students to imagine what it is like to be the characters, exploring what they see, think, and feel.

In the beginning of the story, ask:

- Have you had this experience? What did it feel like for you? How can it help you understand what the girl in the story feels like? (That's empathy in action.) What do you imagine the girl (or boy) is feeling in this part of the story?

- Is the girl (or boy) feeling "on the inside" or "on the outside"?

- What might you have in common with this boy (or girl)?

In the middle of the story, ask:

- Did the teacher use empathy with Rigoberto? What makes you think that? What difference did that make for him? What makes you think that?

- Have you ever felt like this in the lunchroom? (Tap your heart, if you have.)

- Did the girl's friend, Nadja, use empathy or not? Did she understand how her friend was feeling? What makes you think that? How would empathy make a difference here?

- How could empathy make a difference in this situation? Or, using your empathy, if you were one of these children (*point to a picture of the group of children, presumably on the "inside" of things*), what are some things you could do or say to help the girl (or boy) feel a part of the group?
- Even when the boy seems to feel sad, is he really alone? What makes you think that?

Toward the end and after reading the story, ask:

- On "the day she begins," what does Angelina begin to do that changes the way she feels? Do you think empathy made a difference in the way she feels about herself? What makes you think that?
- Can you have empathy for yourself? What would that look like? Or feel like?
- What does Angelina discover when she tells her story?
- What part does sharing our stories play in allowing empathy to grow?
- In what ways are you alike and in what ways are you different from a friend, neighbor, or sibling?

Empathy-Infused Quick-Write Ideas

After reading, have your students write and draw inspired by the story. Model the writing idea first, or use pages from the book that model the focal craft, and then choose from the following writing invitations:

- Taking inspiration from one of the situations in today's story, write about a time when you felt "on the outside" and what, if anything, happened that changed the way you felt.

And/or:

- Write about a time when you felt like you were "on the inside," and what, if anything, happened that changed the way you felt.
- Write about a time when you discovered that you had something in common with another person you thought was different from you.
- Using empathy, write a letter to your brave self.
- Use the story that Angelina shares about how she spent her summer as a model for your (*student*) writing:

"My name is _____ and I spent my summer
(school break, weekend, holiday) _____."

(*Invite writers to find something unique or special about that time, even if it initially felt boring or stupid.*) Share what this time meant to you and why.

- Use inspired phrases from the story as stems or repeating phrases where every new thought or statement begins with it. Examples from the story:
  - On the day I begin . . .
  - There will be times when . . .
  - There was a time when . . .

- Draw "feelings outside of" or "feelings inside of" (*this is a way to release students into their writing*). (*Sharing writing with partners, in groups or with the whole class will infuse empathy into the classroom.*)

Sit-In: How Four Friends Stood Up by Sitting Down by Andrea Davis Pinkney

Empathy Focus

This book draws the reader in to a depiction of true events with dynamic illustrations conveying the energy of the nonviolent aspect of the Civil Rights Movement inspired by Martin Luther King Jr. The story begins with the historic sit-in at the Woolworth's lunch counter in Greensboro, North Carolina, in 1960. Keenly aware of her young audience, author Andrea Davis Pinkney uses empathy to draw her readers into the story, helping them imagine what it must have been like for those four black college students to be refused service simply because of the color of their skin while putting their lives on the line through peaceful means. We also love this book for its language, particularly Pinkney's use of food and recipes as an extended metaphor for the story's themes of integration, racial equality, and justice for all.

Read-Aloud Using Connecting Questions

Begin with Empathy First, then introduce the book by title and author. Tell your students that this book offers a chance to practice empathy in order to understand the story more deeply. As you read, invite your students to imagine what it is like to be the characters, exploring what they see, think, and feel.

In the beginning of the story, ask:

- Looking at this picture of four young college students at a lunch counter, what do you imagine they're waiting for? What do the words say they were feeling? What do *you* imagine they were feeling?

- The author uses something everyone in the world understands—food and recipes—to talk about big ideas. Why do you think she does this? Let's watch for every time she uses a cooking term, food, or recipe to talk about a big idea.

- What must it feel like to be treated like "the hole in a doughnut"?

- Putting yourself in their shoes, what do you imagine the four friends were thinking as they sat there?

In the middle of the story, ask:

- What kept those four friends strong in their conviction to "ignore the law" of "whites only" and "refuse to leave?" What inspired them?

- The author uses bold words throughout her story, such as "Be loving enough to absorb evil." Why do you imagine she does this? What changes in you when you see/read them?

- What could you imagine their evening was like when they got home after the first day?

- (*After reading about what the sit-in students often did at the counter—read schoolbooks, finished homework—ask a question about common ground.*) What things do you have in common with these students back in the 1960s?

- As the students get treated poorly, they continue to sit in what the author describes as "practicing peace." What can you imagine was happening inside of them? What did "practicing peace" mean to them?

Toward the end and after reading the story, ask:

- How would you feel if you were sitting there with them? (*Encourage the expression of all feelings, including strong or hopeful or bored.*)

- Stepping into the shoes of the people who treated these students so poorly, why would they do this? What were they feeling, do you imagine?

- What part did empathy play in helping people to join the students in their work for integration and equality?

Empathy-Infused Quick-Write Ideas

After reading, have your students write and draw inspired by the story. Model the writing idea first, or use pages from the book that model the focal craft, and then choose from the following writing invitations:

- Modeling the "recipe for integration" on the last page of the story: If you were to create your own recipe for peace in the world right now, what ingredients would be included? What directions—numbers 1 to 10—would you give to make your recipe come true? (*This could be done in partnerships, imagining what it was like for the four friends at the lunch counter working together for justice.*)

- If you were to create your own recipe for peace or love or hope in your life right now, what ingredients would be included? Make a list of those ingredients, and then write the directions for how everything needs to be prepared and served.

- Choose one of the four college students who sat at the lunch counter on February 1, 1960, and write a letter to a friend about that day as if you were that student. Write from the first-person point of view.

⊚ Literacy Lessons (Phases One and Two)

Happy by Mies van Hout

Reading Lesson

Reading Level—PreK–K

Empathy Focus

Although an early step in empathy is beginning to recognize how others might be feeling, children must first recognize those feelings in themselves and develop a vocabulary of feeling words to express them. This book helps students recognize and name a wide range of feelings by seeing them in the expressions of the fish and the corresponding words. Each everyday emotion is well depicted in crayon through the fish's body language and facial expressions, so that students can also begin to practice "reading" their own feelings and those of others.

Phase One: Connect

CoreEmpathy Target

I can recognize feelings that I feel every day. Others have felt that feeling, too. And when I feel something difficult, I know it will go away and I will feel something else soon.

Literacy Learning Targets

Within the Literacy Learning Targets sections, grade-specific standards—identified by their strand and number (or number and letter, where applicable)—are noted in parentheses alongside each target (Common Core State Standards Initiative, 2021).

- I can ask and answer questions about key details in the text. (RI.1)
- I can identify the topic and retell key details of the text. (RI.2)
- I can describe the connection between two details in the text. (RI.3)
- I can ask and answer questions about unknown words in the text. (RI.4)
- I can use illustrations and details in the text to describe its key ideas. (RI.7)
- I can clarify and determine the meaning of unfamiliar words. (L.4)
- I can explore how words are related and how words are similar and different. (L.5)

- I can convey ideas using empathy and literacy vocabulary. (L.4, L.5)
- I can engage in collaborative discussion. (SL.1)

ENGAGING THE STORY (2 MIN.)

TEACHER: This year, we are reading books that will help us know our feelings. Feelings are very important to all of us. We all have them because we all can feel! Let's find words for feelings and what they are through this book titled *Happy*.

TEACHER: Hey, did you recognize a feeling already? Sure! The name of the book is a feeling, isn't it? Happy is a feeling I'm feeling right now because I have all of you in front of me. I also notice that this fish is feeling happy, too. Do you agree? How do you know? (*Have students describe what they see on the cover.*)

TEACHER: Do you think feelings are inside of us or outside of us? (*Accept all answers.*)

TEACHER: If you said "inside of us," you are right! We feel *inside*. And, if you said "outside of us," you are right, too! Although we feel inside, we often show it outside on our faces. Just like the fish on the cover.

ENGAGING EMPATHY THROUGH STORY (15 MIN.)

TEACHER: I'd like to read you the book *Happy* now. As I read, look at the word and the fish to see how it is showing us what that feeling looks like. (*Read the book out loud with exaggerated inflection. Let your voice and your body express the emotion. Be sure to pause on each page to let the word and the definition, by means of the fish picture, settle in. Stop when you get to "Surprised."*)

TEACHER: Oh yes, *surprise*. Raise your hand if you have ever felt surprise? Wow, look around you! Has anyone else in our class ever felt surprise? (*Be sure to raise your hand, too.*) Yes, we all have felt surprise before. Do you suppose other kindergartners who aren't in our class have also felt surprise? (*Let class respond.*) How do you know? Do you suppose every child at our school has ever felt surprise? How do you know that?

TEACHER: Yes, that's true. All kindergartners and even every child at this school have felt surprise. That's because we all feel. Show me your face when you feel surprise—maybe even a face like the fish in our story.

TEACHER (*go through more feelings, asking the same questions, only this time stop at a difficult feeling like furious*): Do all feelings feel good? No, they don't, but that's okay, because feelings go away after a while. We feel them only for a short time. We can always do something to make ourselves feel better, like doing something we enjoy or talking about our feelings with someone. I like playing the guitar (*replace "guitar" with what you like to do*) to help me feel better. Or, I might ask for a hug from a member of my family. (*Finish the rest of the story. Stop and ask the same questions, focusing on the idea that others feel the same feelings we do and that feelings come and go.*)

MAKING THE EMPATHY LEARNING REAL (1 MIN.)

TEACHER: Today, let's pay attention to our feelings. Think about what words you would use to describe how you're feeling. Did that feeling go away? What did you feel next? Were there others who felt that same feeling with you?

TEACHER (*throughout the day, when you notice that the majority of your students are feeling a certain way—tired, confused, happy, surprised—stop and ask them what they are feeling, as follows*): What word would you use to name your feeling? Are there any other words for that same feeling? How many of us are feeling this way? How many are feeling something a little different?

TEACHER: Many of us share the same feelings. Sometimes we don't. But one thing is for sure: we *all* feel!

Phase Two: Deepen

CoreEmpathy Target

I can recognize words that describe feelings and what they mean.

LITERACY LEARNING TARGETS

Same as reading lesson (Phase One), plus:

- I can identify the front cover, back cover, and title page of the book. (RI.K.5)
- I can name the author and illustrator and identify their roles in the text. (RI.K.6)

ENGAGING READING (2 MIN.)

TEACHER (*hold up the book, showing the cover*): Yesterday, while we read this book, we learned that feelings are felt by everyone. Which feelings do you feel inside of you? (*Put your hand over your heart.*) Which feelings do all people feel? (*Let students respond openly with feelings found or not found in the book.*)

TEACHER: We also learned that, although some feelings feel good and some don't, both are fine because we all feel! Feeling is part of being *us*. What are some feelings that feel good? What feelings don't feel so good? Are both okay? Yes, because feelings come and go, and we can always do things that make us feel better.

Revisit the Story (15 min.)

Teacher (*turn everyone's attention back to the book*): Readers often read books more than once. They do this to understand a book more deeply and also to find details they didn't notice the first time.

Teacher: Let's look at our book *Happy* by Mies van Hout. Here, she is the author and the illustrator. The title and author/illustrator names are on the front cover to tell a reader what the book is called and who wrote it. The illustrator is the person who drew or painted the pictures. In our book, the illustrator drew the pictures with crayon. Have you ever drawn with a crayon like the illustrator? What kinds of things did you draw? When you look at a drawing in crayon, how do you know it was drawn with crayon?

Teacher: Today, we are going to read our book again and deepen our understanding by looking at the fish pictures and noticing which details in the illustrations help us know what each fish is feeling. We'll also pay attention to the feeling words and see how they match the pictures.

Teacher: Let's try one. Let's look at the nervous fish. What kind of details do you see in the drawing to show that the fish is nervous? (*Model if necessary. For instance, mention the squiggly lines as an example.*) When you are feeling nervous, do you shake? Let's try putting a little shaking into our body. (*Continue to go through the book like this. Ask for the telling details in each illustration, and then invite students to express that emotion in their faces and bodies. Model the details when necessary.*) Which details are we and the fish expressing that are the same?

Teacher: There's an interesting thing about feelings: some of them are similar. Some fish in our book's pictures look almost the same as each other. This is showing us that some feelings are alike. (*Put the fish pictures and the words from Figure 6.1 on the chalkboard ledge or board, one pairing or set of three at a time. Explain each one. For example, "I can feel angry when I'm furious." Ask the students to join you by describing how the pictures of the fish are similar. Explain that is because the words are similar in meaning. Have students make a face/body movement that is the feeling in the left column, then say, "You are also looking [say the feeling word from the right column] because the words have a similar meaning."*)

Extensions and Variations

Discuss how some feeling words are opposites of each other. Or show a word and have the students show you the feeling by making the face, expressing it in their bodies, or describing what it is with words.

Similar Feelings in the Book	
furious	angry
happy	glad, delighted
proud	brave
content	loving, sure
surprised	astonished

FIGURE 6.1. Story chart: Similar feelings.

TEACHER: Today, we learned that not only do all people have feelings, but sometimes they also feel similar things. We also learned that there are different words for feelings that are very much alike. We can sometimes tell what a feeling is by looking at the details of a picture, or, in our everyday life, by looking at the details of a person's face or their body expressions. We express our feelings in our faces and our bodies!

MAKING THE EMPATHY LEARNING REAL (2 MIN.)

TEACHER: Today, think about what you are feeling. Does someone around you have a similar feeling? Does their face look like yours? Think of another word you might use to describe that feeling. It is good to have words for our feelings! Feeling words can help us say what we're feeling, so that others can understand us better and we can understand them. Using our feeling words will help make our classroom a safe and fun place to be!

Writing Lessons

Phase One: Connect

CoreEmpathy Target

I can recognize words that describe feelings and the situation when I have felt them.

LITERACY LEARNING TARGETS

- I can ask and answer questions about key details in the text. (RI.1)

- I can identify the topic and retell key details of the text. (RI.2)

- I can describe the connection between two details in the text. (RI.3)

- I can ask and answer questions about unknown words in the text. (RI.4)

- I can identify the front cover, back cover, and title page of the book. (RI.5)

- I can name the author and illustrator and identify their roles in the text. (RI.6)

- I can use illustrations and details in the text to describe its key ideas. (RI.7)

- I can use a combination of drawing, dictating, and writing to narrate a single event or several loosely linked events. (W.3)

- I can recall information from experiences or gather information from provided sources to answer a question. (W.8)

- I can clarify and determine the meaning of unfamiliar words. (L.4)
- I can explore how words are related and how words are similar and different. (L.5)
- I can convey ideas using empathy and literacy vocabulary. (L.4, L.5)
- I can engage in collaborative discussion. (SL.1)

READING LIKE A WRITER (20 MIN.)

Choose two words and matching fish pictures from the previous day's synonym chart. Display them on a bulletin board. Read each one, facilitating the face and body activity.

TEACHER: We've talked about how everyone feels these feelings. Now, I want you to think about a time when you felt these feelings. Let's take one at a time. As I look at the feeling word *happy*, I'm remembering a time when I felt that way. (*Tell a quick story while you sketch it onto a black piece of paper. Be sure to make it non-relatable to the children in your class so they won't "adopt" your story as theirs.*) That's a time when I felt "happy." If I wrote it, it would look like this. (*Model phonetic spelling by writing your story briefly under the sketch.*)

TEACHER: That's a time when I felt this feeling. What is a time when you felt this way? Think of that now. What was happening when you felt it? Who was there? What was around you? Think of that now. Remember in your mind what was happening to you. Remember this is your story . . . when you were feeling that way. Turn and tell that story to your neighbor.

Repeat this sequence with two more words from the chart and their matching fish pictures, inviting students to share their stories with their neighbors.

TEACHER: Now you are going to draw and write your feeling story on this paper. You have choices with this! Choose either one of the stories you told. Which one do you want to write and draw? (*Students draw and write personal narratives using their feeling stories.*)

ENGAGING APPRECIATION, SHARING, AND CELEBRATING (5 MIN.)

TEACHER (*invite writers and illustrators to come up and share their pictures and stories to the class; after sharing, say the following*): These are beautiful ways to make our classroom a feeling place. This is a classroom I want to be a part of! And you know what? You all have had a feeling that I have had, also! (*Display the students' pictures and stories under the fish–emotion match.*)

Phase Two: Deepen

Choose two *different* words and matching fish pictures from the synonym activity. Display them on a bulletin board. Read each one. Do the face and body activity and then proceed with the writing from the first lesson. After sharing, display the writing under the different feeling captions.

Fireflies! by Julie Brinckloe

Reading Lesson

Reading Level—Developmental Reading Assessment (DRA) 24; Grade 2.5; Guided Reading K; Lexile 630

Empathy Focus

In *Fireflies!*, the main character looks at a jar of fireflies losing their light and feels sad. Recognizing they are also losing their life, he makes a decision to release them into their natural environment. This compassionate act stems from his experience of eco-empathy—the ability to take the perspective of another living being in the natural world.

Phase One: Connect

CoreEmpathy Target

I can empathize through noticing, appreciating, and perspective-taking. I can act with compassion.

Literacy Learning Targets

- I can ask and answer questions about key details of a story. (RL.1)
- I can gather information to find the central theme. (RL.2)
- I can describe how characters respond to and meet challenges. (RL.3)
- I can describe in detail the differing points of view among main characters. (RL.6)
- I can collect information from illustrations and text to demonstrate understanding. (RL.7)
- I can convey ideas using empathy and literacy vocabulary. (L.4, L.5)
- I can engage in collaborative discussion. (SL.1)

Engaging Empathy First (5 min.)

Teach the Empathy First lesson.

Engaging the Story and Charting It (25 min.)

Teacher: Today's story is *Fireflies!* by Julie Brinckloe. It has a lot to show us about empathy and how we can empathize with something in the natural world. We call that *eco-empathy*. Eco-empathy is the ability to imagine what an animal or other living thing may be feeling. *Eco-* is short for the word *ecology*, which is the study of the earth and the environment. (*Write "eco-empathy" and its definition on the top of the story chart under the title and author.*)

TEACHER: Let's read the word and definition together. (*Chorally read the top of the chart.*) Let's look for how empathy or eco-empathy happens in this story. (*Hold up the book and show the cover. Choose among the following questions to discuss predictions.*)

- What might we know about today's story from its cover?
- What might we be able to tell about the story from the artwork on the cover?
- Can we tell who the characters might be? *Where* do you think they are?
- What do you think the title might be telling us about the story? What genre do you think this story is? In other words, will it be fiction or nonfiction? What tells you that?

TEACHER: As we might have predicted from the cover, today's story is about a boy close to your age who catches fireflies. Give a thumbs-up if you have ever caught fireflies. What was it like? What can you tell us about fireflies? (*Choose students to share.*)

TEACHER: As we read, let's keep our eyes and ears out for the things that the boy feels and does to show us where empathy is happening. Also, we are looking for clues (*textual evidence*) to tell us which genre it is. Let's read with those two things in our minds. (*Read the story. Stop at "'Don't let your dinner get cold,' said Momma."*)

> **Teacher Tip**
>
> The beginning of a story is the best time to collect information that orients a reader to the story: genre, character names, traits, and setting information. Record these on the story chart. *Fireflies!* is realistic fiction because it is a made-up story grounded in real-life circumstances (setting) and characters without a fantastical element. Find "moments" of this in the pages for textual evidence of genre, but also talk about what is not there—talking animals, magic, and so on.

TEACHER: Which genre are you thinking the story is? Why do you think that? What pages, words, and pictures help you to know that? (*Explain realistic fiction.*)

TEACHER: Now that we know we are reading realistic fiction, we can turn our attention to the characters and setting of our story. We are at the beginning, the best place to pay attention to the information the author is giving us about characters and setting. Who are the characters in our story? What traits do they have? What information do we have about the setting? (*Talk about what information has been gathered so far in order to summarize it. Add to the story chart, which might look like Figure 6.2.)*

TEACHER: As we read this next part, let's read for more clues about who our main character is and what he is about to do. (*Invite students to read the next part with their eyes as you display it on the document camera, and continue reading aloud from "I forked the meat" to "I poked holes in the top of the jar with Momma's scissors."*)

Story Chart *Fireflies!* by Julie Brinckloe Eco-Empathy: (definition)	
Genre	Student Reponses
Main character Traits Setting Problem	

FIGURE 6.2. Story chart: *Fireflies!*

TEACHER: What is our main character about to do? How do you know? How is he feeling? What other character traits can we add to our chart? Did you notice new information about the setting? (*Continue to write answers on your story chart under the headings Main Character and Setting.*)

TEACHER: Now that we have gathered information about the characters and setting, let's switch our attention to what the main character is doing and how he feels as he is doing it. Read along with your eyes as I read the next section, thinking about what the boy is doing and how he is feeling. (*Continue to read from "The screen door banged" to "waving our hands for more."*)

TEACHER: What is our main character doing and how is he feeling? (*Record on story chart.*)

TEACHER: The next section of a story is often when the author presents us with the problem. Read with your eyes as I read it aloud. Be thinking about and be ready to discuss what the problem he faces could be. (*Read from "Then someone called" to "and fell to the bottom, and lay there."*)

TEACHER: After the boy's excitement and playfulness of catching the fireflies, what is happening? What is the problem he is facing? (*Accept all answers. Add to story chart under the heading of Problem. This finishes today's chart. Put the book down or turn off the document camera for a moment.*)

ENGAGING THE STORY'S EMPATHY AND CENTRAL MESSAGE (5 MIN.)

TEACHER: We've talked about what empathy is, but our story's ending shows us *how* to do it. Let's learn the steps of empathizing by listening closely to the story's ending. The main character shows us how to empathize. (*Point to the Empathy First visual—"I empathize when . . ."—and refer to the first step: "I notice by watching and listening."*)

TEACHER: The first step of empathizing is noticing by watching and listening (*point to your eyes and ears*). Do the motion with me as we read the first step out loud, "I notice by watching and listening."

TEACHER: The boy in our story is doing that on these pages. (*Show the pages that begin "The light in the jar ..."*) Looking at the illustration, show me with your hand motions the step of empathizing he is in. (*Students point to eyes and ears.*) Yes, he is noticing by watching and listening. Turn to a partner and whisper what he might be noticing. (*After students finish sharing, read the page out loud.*) He is noticing that the fireflies' lights are dimming, isn't he? I wonder: What are *you* feeling as you read this? (*Pause to let that question settle in.*)

TEACHER: You are feeling empathy, too, aren't you? That's the second step of empathizing: "I feel ... what the other might be feeling." (*Do the motion as you reread the second step on the Empathy First poster. Invite students to join you.*) Read the second step with me as we do the motion together.

TEACHER (*as you show the following page that begins "I shut my eyes," ask the following questions*): What do you think the boy is feeling? Is that the same or different from what you were just feeling? (*Give a moment for responses.*) First, the boy noticed something about the fireflies, and then he felt something in response to what he noticed. (*Read the page out loud.*)

TEACHER: The last step of empathizing is to act. (*Beginning with both hands over your heart, reach your hands out, palms up, toward your students as you read, "I act ... with kindness and compassion."*) Let's do this motion as we all read this last step together.

TEACHER: The boy in the story shows us this last step of empathizing. Here's what he does. (*Show the next page that begins "I flung off the covers ..."*) Look at the illustration and tell me what he decides to do? Yes, he lets them go! Here's what the author writes. (*Read the page out loud.*) Do you think that was a difficult decision to make? Share with your neighbor what you are thinking.

TEACHER: Sometimes a decision is not easy, but it feels right anyway, doesn't it? Those are the steps of empathy! Our character showed us how to do them. I'm going to flip back through the pages so you can show me with the motions and tell me the step that he is doing. (*Quickly show the pages again as the students respond with each step and the corresponding motion.*)

TEACHER: Now let's enjoy the rest of the story. (*Read to the end with excitement.*)

TEACHER: Now we have read a story that helps us understand empathy for another living being. This is called *eco-empathy* because the main character was empathetic to something in the natural world. Where is that word and definition for us to refer to? (*Indicate story chart.*)

TEACHER: How did our story help us to understand what empathy is? Did you find yourself feeling empathy for the boy? How could you tell you were feeling empathy?

Making the Empathy Learning Real (1 min.)

TEACHER: Today, think about the natural world around you—the plants and animals. What do you notice? Imagine what it might be like to be that part of nature. What might that tree, or bird, or insect be feeling in the moment as you watch? What are they seeing? What would it be like to be that living being for a day?

Phase Two: Deepen

CoreEmpathy Target

I can listen for descriptions of how someone else feels.

Literacy Learning Targets

- I can gather information to find the central theme. (RL.2)
- I can describe how words and phrases supply meaning to a story. (RL.4)
- I can collect information from illustrations and text to demonstrate understanding. (RL.7)
- I can read a story with fluency to understand it. (RF.4)
- I can convey ideas using empathy and literacy vocabulary. (L.4, L.5)
- I can clarify and determine the meaning of unfamiliar words. (L.4)
- I can understand word relationships and nuances in word meanings. (L.5)
- I can use words acquired through reading, being read to, and conversations. (L.6)
- I can engage in collaborative discussion. (SL.1)

Engaging Background Knowledge (5 min.)

TEACHER: Yesterday we read the book *Fireflies!* and discovered how a character can show us what empathy is. We also learned that we can empathize with a character. What does that mean we did? Let's look at what we discovered as we read. (*Revisit the story chart, reading both columns: the story elements and the students' responses. This can be done through students reading, partner reading, or choral reading. Revisit Empathy First, connecting it to the story's events.*)

Revisit the Story: Engaging Language (20 min.)

TEACHER: Writers use language to help us as readers see pictures in our mind, feel something in response, and imagine what life in the story might be like. Julie Brinckloe does this in *Fireflies!* Let's go through parts of our story, paying attention to what we see, feel, and imagine. Let's also pay attention to which words or phrases help us to see, feel, and imagine.

TEACHER: Yesterday, we looked at the illustrations as we read. Today, we are going to just listen to the words as we concentrate on what is inside our minds and hearts. Then, we're going to zoom in on the words and phrases that the author uses that create those reactions in us. (*Read one or two pages out loud at a time—see below for good examples of sensory language. You may want to make a copy of the book's pages you decide to use to glue onto the language chart. After each example, pause to ask: "What words help you see, feel, or imagine?" Record responses.*)

The following pages contain beautiful language evoking images and sensory responses demonstrating Julie Brinckloe's craft as an author:

- The jars were dusty, and I polished one clean on my shirt. Then I ran back up, two steps at a time.
- The screen door banged behind me as I ran from the house. If someone said, "Don't slam it," I wasn't listening.
- The sky was darker now. My ears rang with crickets, and my eyes stung from staring too long. I blinked hard as I watched them – *Fireflies!* Blinking on, blinking off, dipping low, soaring high above my head, making white patterns in the dark.
- I thrust my hand into the jar and spread it open. The jar glowed like moonlight and I held it in my hands. I felt a tremble of joy.
- The fireflies beat their wings against the glass and fell to the bottom, and lay there.
- The light in the jar turned yellow, like a flashlight left on too long. I tried to swallow, but something in my throat would not go down. And the light grew dimmer, green, like moonlight underwater.
- Then the jar began to glow, green, then gold, then white as the moon. And the fireflies poured out into the night.
- Fireflies blinking on, blinking off, dipping low, soaring high above my head, making circles around the moon, like stars dancing.

TEACHER: Those are beautiful words that Julie Brinckloe used! Sometimes we call these *descriptive* words, or lively or interesting words. They are not ordinary, everyday words. They are the words that help readers get pictures in their minds and react with their senses to stories.

Deepening language: Focus on the word parts and grammar more closely. For example, moonlight *is a compound word in which each part helps to determine the meaning of the whole. Also, many of the words are verbs that have an ordinary word pairing, such as* soaring *(going),* poured *(flew),* thrust *(put), and* beat *(hit). Compare and contrast the impact of both on the reader.*

Revisit the Story: Engaging Fluent Reading (15 min.).

Teacher: I have copies of the book *Fireflies!* for you to read with a partner. You may choose to read it taking turns, with one partner reading a page, then the other reading the next. (*Model this by sitting with a student and having the book in between both of you.*) As you read the story, enjoy the words and images as they flow naturally. Another choice is to retell the story, page by page, using as many words from our language chart as you can. (*Model this for a few pages. Partner students and have them make a choice where to read together.*)

Making the Empathy Learning Real (3 min.).

Teacher: What a beautiful story of a boy showing *eco-empathy*—that is, empathy with the natural world! He noticed what the fireflies were doing, and knew that it was not good for them, and he felt deeply for their situation. That helped him to act with kindness and compassion. The author's use of lively, interesting words in the story helped to make the boy's experience real for us. They helped us feel empathy for him! Today, let's listen for both lively and descriptive words in our books and experiences. Also, pay attention to the natural world you encounter. Think about how you would describe it using descriptive, lively words like our author did.

Writing Lessons

Phase One: Connect

CoreEmpathy Target
I can recognize and appreciate what someone else feels.

Literacy Learning Targets

- I can describe how words and phrases supply meaning to a story. (RL.4)
- I can describe in detail the differing points of view among main characters. (RL6)
- I can collect information from illustrations and text to demonstrate understanding. (RL.7)
- I can convey ideas using empathy and literacy vocabulary. (L.4, L.5)
- I can clarify and determine the meaning of unfamiliar words. (L.4)
- I can understand word relationships and nuances in word meanings. (L.5)

- I can use words acquired through reading, being read to, and conversations. (L.6)
- I can engage in collaborative discussion. (SL.1)
- I can write using information from experiences. (W.8)

ENGAGING FEELINGS (10 MIN.)

TEACHER: Learning about empathy is learning about feelings. Imagining how someone feels helps us to be empathetic toward them. I have a list of feelings. Let's get to know them and then use them to imagine how a person is feeling. (*Show feeling words and synonyms on the board, as in Figure 6.3.*)

TEACHER: Let's read the poster together. Listen for the word that you know. You can use it as a guide to learn new feeling words. (*Read the poster aloud with your students. Explain that the words in the right-hand column are "synonyms"—words that have similar meanings and can be used interchangeably.*)

TEACHER: The synonyms are not ordinary, everyday words. Using them can help a reader see, feel, and imagine, because they are lively and descriptive. Now let's imagine those feelings in someone else. This is also an important part of being empathetic. We can find this on our Empathy First poster. Which step is it? Yes, after we notice, hear, or see someone or something in nature, we begin to recognize and understand what they are feeling.

TEACHER: I'm going to show you a face. See if you can recognize the feeling I'm expressing. You are welcome to use the poster for help! (*Choose two or three emotions from the feeling chart. Show one on your face for your students to discern. If they use one of the most common emotion words, such as happy or sad, affirm the emotion and then ask which other emotion words they might use to express the same feeling.*)

TEACHER: Now you try it with each other. The person you are sitting next to is your partner. (*You are also welcome to assign them.*) Take turns, one of you showing a face that expresses a feeling on our chart and the other trying to recognize it. Be an *emotions detective* by looking for clues on your partner's face and in their body language.

Emotion/Feeling	Synonym
Happy is like	cheerful, playful, silly
Mad is like	angry, irritated
Sad is like	gloomy, blue
Scared is like	afraid, frightened
Excited is like	thrilled, full of anticipation
Guilty is like	ashamed, embarrassed
Confused is like	perplexed, puzzled
Sure is like	confident, to know for certain
I feel worried when . . .	I didn't do my homework.
I feel wonder when . . .	I look at a sunset or sunrise.

FIGURE 6.3. Poster: Emotions/feelings and their synonyms.

Reading Like a Writer (10 min.)

Teacher: Now you have just learned an important step in being empathetic! Imagining how someone else feels helps us to see the world the way they do. Let's do the same thing with the boy in our story.

Go through the following pages with a pace that moves fairly quickly. As you show the pages, ask questions like "How is the boy feeling here?," "Have his feelings changed?," "Why?" You may choose to read some of the words that provide clues to the boy's feelings beyond the illustrations. Continue to praise your students for their ability to recognize how someone feels, as well as for their use of the new emotion vocabulary. Continue to refer to this as an important step in empathizing. Show the pages that begin:

> "Then we dashed about ..."
> "I climbed the stairs ..."
> "In the dark I watched ..."
> "The light in the jar ..."
> "I shut my eyes tight ..."
> "I held the jar, dark and empty ..."

Releasing the Writer (20 min.)

Teacher: Well done on recognizing the main character's feelings. We read some of the words that helped give us clues to the boy's emotions. These were the lively, descriptive words that the author used to help us imagine the story fully. Yesterday, we made a list of these words. Let's take a look at them and read them aloud, reminding ourselves of words that help us see, feel, and imagine. (*Read language chart chorally.*)

Teacher: I'm going to show you a list of sentences. One sentence does not create pictures in our minds and the other does. Choose which one you think has the lively, descriptive words similar to the ones on our language chart. (*The sentences below demonstrate the use of language to create pictures in the mind of a reader and those that do not. Add more that apply to your room. Refer back to the reason why we use words; namely, "words create pictures in the minds of our readers," "readers 'feel' in response to our writing," and "words give the reader an opportunity to 'imagine.'"*

Have your students compare and contrast simple sentences with sentences that help them to have a mind picture. Write the sentences, circling the sentence that contains the lively words. Underline which words make it effective and briefly discuss why and what part of speech it is. Model your thinking on how to choose a lively word. Ask them to join you in transforming the sentences.

I got up from my chair. I shot out of my chair because I was surprised.

The ant went by me. The ant scrambled over a rock by my feet.

The leaves moved. The leaves wriggled as the wind blew.

Invite students to convert these next sentences individually, using lively, descriptive words:

The bird flew.

The sun was out.

The cat was happy.

The clouds moved.

Engaging Appreciation, Sharing, and Celebrating (2 min.)

TEACHER: Who would like to read their lively sentence for "The sun was out"? Listeners, we are going to listen for the word or phrase that helps us to feel, imagine, and picture what is happening. Please raise your hand when the writer is done reading and tell the writer which word or phrase helped you feel, imagine, and picture. (*Continue to have writers share, moving through all the sentences.*)

TEACHER: Well done, descriptive writers! You've just written like Julie Brinckloe, using words that help readers feel and imagine.

Making the Empathy Learning Real (3 min.)

TEACHER: As you go through your day, think about what you are experiencing, and how you feel while experiencing it. How would you describe it to someone? What words would you use?

Phase Two: Deepen

CoreEmpathy Target

I can imagine and appreciate what life might be like for plants and animals in the natural world.

Literacy Learning Targets

- I can convey ideas using empathy and literacy vocabulary. (L.4, L.5)

- I can use accurately grade-appropriate conversational, general academic, and domain-specific words and phrases. (L.6)

- I can engage in collaborative discussion. (SL.1)

- I can engage in collaborative discussions about the main ideas in a story while asking and answering questions with a speaker. (SL.2, SL.3)

- I can write opinion pieces in which they introduce the topic or book they are writing about, state an opinion, supply reasons that support the opinion, use linking words (e.g., *because, and, also*) to connect opinion and reasons, and provide a concluding statement or section. (W.1)

• I can write using information from experiences. (W.8)

READING LIKE A WRITER (5 MIN.)

TEACHER: This week we've been reading a book about a character who shows us eco-empathy. Empathy is … (*invite students to do the hand motions from Empathy First: seeing, walking, feeling*). Yes, so eco-empathy is … (*do all three hand motions and phrases from the Empathy First poster*) for the natural world. When I say "natural world," I mean all the plants and animals that live on earth with us. Let's put these two ideas together—what we know about empathy and what it means as we think of the natural world. Let's finish the phrase, "I feel eco-empathy when …" (*have students respond*).

Review the pages from Fireflies! *that expressed the "lively" language used by the author.*

RELEASING THE WRITER (20 MIN.)

TEACHER: Today, we are going to look at two pictures of the natural world and write about the one that inspires the most eco-empathy in us. We also have learned that authors use colorful, descriptive words. Talk to each other about what colorful, descriptive words do in a story for the reader.

TEACHER (*show two pictures in nature from posters or the internet of your choosing*): Let's talk about what kinds of plants and animals might live in each one of these natural settings. (*Examining each picture one at a time, invite students to join you in a discussion, imagining and describing what plants and animals live in that setting—seen in the picture and not seen. You might also discuss what they eat, why they live there, and how their life fits that habitat.*)

TEACHER: As you look at each picture, think about how you feel. Which setting are you most curious about? Which one makes you feel like you want to be there? In which setting is it easier for you to imagine what life might be like for the plants and animals that are making their homes there? Can you picture how they might be living? How do they find food? Is it difficult? How are they happiest? How do they like to live? (*Accept all answers, as this is the preparation for their opinion writing.*)

TEACHER: Choose the natural setting that makes you feel the most eco-empathy. It is the one that you answered our questions for most easily. In your opinion, that is the natural setting that evokes the most eco-empathy. You may want to begin by drawing a quick sketch of the setting that you've chosen with the plants or animals that you imagine are there.

TEACHER: After your quick sketch, write sentences telling your readers which setting evoked eco-empathy for you and why. You will begin by telling them what eco-empathy is, because you are now experts on this. It will be the opening for your writing. Also, be sure to tell your readers why that setting makes you feel eco-empathy. Finally, describe that setting using lively and descriptive words.

Invite students to open their writer's notebooks and write. Remind them that their writing does not need to be edited today, but to focus on forming an opinion using lively words. You may want them to use the paragraph frame that is offered in the Releasing the Writer preparation section above if you'd like to give your students the additional scaffold.

ENGAGING APPRECIATION, SHARING, AND CELEBRATING (5 MIN.)

Invite students to share while others "listen for" why the setting made the writer feel eco-empathy. When the writer finishes, the other students can tell the writer what they heard.

MAKING THE EMPATHY LEARNING REAL (1 MIN.)

TEACHER: Beautiful work today, writers! You've connected your empathy learning with the natural world using lively, descriptive words. Any time you notice the natural world today—perhaps on the playground, on your ride home from school, or in a park or your yard—think of the plants and animals that may live there. What do they need? How might you help them get what they need? Like the boy in our story *Fireflies!*, we can notice through eco-empathy what a plant or animal or insect might need, and, if it's possible, help them. Their lives are important to all of us.

Through Grandpa's Eyes by Patricia MacLachlan

Reading Lesson

Reading Level—DRA 28; Grade 3.7; Guided Reading L; Lexile 560

Empathy Focus

A young boy, John, learns a different way of "seeing" the world through being with his blind grandfather. For John to "see" as his grandfather sees, he needs to *empathize*, to step into his grandfather's shoes, to experience the world through the rest of his senses other than sight—just as his grandfather does. The story demonstrates not only what we might need to do to empathize or understand one another, but also how we might *invite* someone into *our* world to help them understand or empathize with us, as Grandpa in the story does with his grandson, John.

Phase One: Connect

CoreEmpathy Target

I can empathize through perspective-taking, listening, appreciating, and finding common ground.

Literacy Learning Targets

- I can gather information to find the central theme. (RL.2)
- I can describe how characters respond to and meet challenges. (RL.3)
- I can describe in detail the differing points of view among main characters. (RL.6)
- I can collect information from illustrations and text to demonstrate understanding. (RL.7)
- I can convey ideas using empathy and literacy vocabulary. (L.4, L.5)
- I can engage in collaborative discussion. (SL.1)

Engaging Empathy First (5 min.)

Teach students the definition of empathy by using the Empathy First lesson.

Engaging the Story (20 min.)

TEACHER: Today's story is *Through Grandpa's Eyes* by Patricia MacLachlan. (*Show the book cover.*) It has a lot to show us about empathy, and how we can empathize with another person—particularly someone we care about in our family. Let's look for how empathy happens in this story.

Choose among these questions to help students make predictions from the cover:

- What might we be able to tell about the story from the artwork on the cover?
- Can we tell who the characters might be or where the story might take place?
- What do you think the title is telling us about the story?
- How might the title relate to our Empathy First poster?
- What questions do you have about the story when you look at the cover?

Read the story through to the page that says "even though they are not sharp at seeing." Ask students to keep their eyes and ears out for some of the things that the boy, John, discovers as he learns to empathize with his grandfather—what he learns "through Grandpa's eyes." After reading, confirm and alter predictions that were previously made.

In this beginning section, record the story elements you want your students to notice, such as characters and setting, on your story chart. At this stopping point, return to your purpose to read "How John is empathizing with his Grandpa" and record what readers are learning about empathy from the poster as the character, John, learns about his grandfather's world "through Grandpa's eyes." Use turn and talks or whole-class discussion interchangeably throughout the lesson.

CHARTING THE STORY'S CORE (20 MIN.)

Now that you've established the basic elements of the story, remind students that "we're still looking for the ways John learns to empathize in our story." Continue reading aloud until the page that says, "I make my plate of food a clock, too, and eat through Grandpa's eyes." Ask, "How is John learning to empathize with his grandfather?" and "How does this help you understand our Empathy First poster?" Record answers.

TEACHER: In our book, each page has helped us to understand what empathy is. You've noticed that empathy is imagining what life might be like for another, and that John is doing that with his grandfather. (*Refer to the Empathy First visual and hand motions.*) Here is another thing we can notice: Grandpa is helping John imagine his world by using his five senses. That's *how* John is imagining what Grandpa's life might be like.

Ask students to name their five senses and point to the body part that helps them experience that sense. Invite students to tap their eyes, ears, nose, and mouth and to rub their fingertips (for "touching") along with you as each sense is named by either you or the students.

Tell students that today's reading is showing what happens inside Grandpa and Nana's house, and that, tomorrow, they'll be following John and Grandpa outside the house. Meanwhile, flip back through the pages of the first half of the story and ask students to notice where John uses his five senses to empathize. Record answers. After reading and completing the chart (see Figure 6.4), ask: "What sense do you see the most? Least? Why do you think that is?"

Story Chart
Through Grandpa's Eyes by Patricia MacLachlan
Characters and setting:
What the story is helping us learn about empathy:
How John learns to empathize:
The senses John uses to understand Grandpa's world:

FIGURE 6.4. Story chart: *Through Grandpa's Eyes.*

MAKING THE EMPATHY LEARNING REAL (3 MIN.)

TEACHER: After school, pay attention to your five senses as you go about your life at home today. What are some of the things you see, hear, smell, taste, and touch? Is there anything you see at home or any sound you hear that makes your home unique or special to you? Is there something in your home that feels soft or maybe rough to the touch? What does it smell like when someone is cooking in the kitchen? How does this help you imagine what life might be like for someone else?

Phase Two: Deepen

CoreEmpathy Target

I can empathize through perspective-taking, listening, appreciating, and finding common ground.

Literacy Learning Targets

- I can gather information to find the central theme. (RL.2)
- I can describe how characters respond to and meet challenges. (RL.3)
- I can describe in detail the differing points of view among main characters. (RL.6)

- I can collect information from illustrations and text to demonstrate understanding. (RL.7)
- I can read a story with fluency to understand it. (RF.4)
- I can convey ideas using empathy and literacy vocabulary. (L.4, L.5)
- I can engage in collaborative discussion. (SL.1)

> **Teacher Tip**
>
> The Phase Two reading lesson may be done in two parts at different times of the day, or all at once, depending upon student engagement.

ENGAGING READING (20 MIN.)

Before you begin reading with your class, ask them what they remember about the story from their reading yesterday. They may refer to yesterday's story chart. Accept all responses. Then, review the five senses. As in lesson one, ask students to tap their eyes, ears, nose, and mouth and rub their fingertips (for "touching") along with you as each sense is named by either you or your students.

TEACHER: Now that all our senses have been awakened this morning, just like John's senses were awakened in the story, let's bring what we know about our senses into our reading time.

Read the last half of the book aloud without stopping, so that student readers begin to feel a sense of flow and continuity. Begin where you left off yesterday at "Grandpa and I walk outside. . . ." Ask students to read along silently and to tap the sense that John is using to understand or empathize with his grandfather as you read. You can join in with them for the first few occurrences, but then allow students to point to their senses on their own as you read to the end of the book.

TEACHER: How does John's grandfather help John empathize with him? (*Encourage students to name the ways Grandpa helps John understand what it's like to be blind through each sense—hearing, smell, taste, and touch—and add these to the list on the story chart, adding a page if necessary.*)

TEACHER: After reading our story and putting yourself in Grandpa's shoes, just like John did, what would you say about what it's like to be blind? (*Allow students to respond.*) Great! By imagining what it's like to be Grandpa in today's story, we are feeling empathy, aren't we? (*Tap heart.*)

Making the Empathy Learning Real (2 min.)

Teacher: As we go through the rest of the school day—at lunch and on the playground—let's pay attention to our five senses: what we are seeing, hearing, smelling, tasting, and touching. Then, let's share what we are experiencing with a friend. If something we eat tastes sour or sweet, we can share that. If a sound hurts our ears or if a song makes us feel happy, we can talk about what that's like, too. Just like John's grandfather in today's story, we can use our five senses—as well as what we are feeling inside—to help others understand or empathize with us.

Phase Two: Deepen (*continued*)

Revisit the Story: Engaging Fluent Reading (20 min.)

Pass out copies of the book *Through Grandpa's Eyes* for students to read on their own, aloud with a partner, or in a small group with you. Invite students, as they read, to enjoy the words and images as they flow naturally, to focus their attention on reading fluently—making the words sound like they are talking. Encourage them to pause where it would add meaning to the story and to adjust their voices according to each punctuation mark at the end of a sentence.

Teacher Tip

You may want to have the students read for a time frame, so that, if finishing times differ, fluent reading can still be practiced. Explain to the students that, if they get to the end of the story and there is still time left to read, to begin again, getting yet even more proficient at fluent reading. The development of fluent reading is actualized from rereading a text three to four times (National Reading Panel, 2000).

Teacher (*allow everyone the opportunity to reread the story without interruption*): What did you notice? What moments of empathy stood out for you? How did your attention to your five senses help you to notice or understand new details in the story?

Teacher: What a beautiful story of a boy showing empathy in his family! He noticed what life was like for his grandfather in many different ways, and he felt deeply for his situation. That helped him act with kindness and compassion. The author's use of description in the story helped make John's experience real for us. It helped us feel empathy for *him*!

Making the Empathy Learning Real (1 min.)

Teacher: Today, at home, think about how you can practice empathy in your family. Can you put yourself in someone else's shoes? What would it be like to be your brother, or sister, or parent—or even your pet? When someone in your family expresses frustration, or sadness, or excitement, how can you show them you understand or empathize with how they feel? Or, if you are the one having these feelings, how can you help *them* understand or empathize with *you*?

Writing Lessons

Phase One: Connect

CoreEmpathy Target

As a writer, I can use point of view and sensory details to help readers empathize with my characters.

Literacy Learning Targets

- I can use narrative techniques, such as dialogue, description, and pacing, to develop experiences and events or show the responses of characters to situations. (W.5B)

- I can use concrete words and phrases and sensory details to convey experiences and events precisely. (W.5D)

Engaging Empathy First

Teach or reteach Empathy First as you deem necessary.

Engaging a Writer's Purpose

Teacher: Good writers inspire readers to empathize with their characters—to imagine what a character's life is like by seeking to understand what that character sees, thinks, and feels. Our story's author, Patricia MacLachlan, did a really good job of helping us imagine what it was like to be both John and Grandpa in our story, *Through Grandpa's Eyes*.

Teacher: As you imagine what it was like to be John in our story, what are some of the things he was seeing? What were some of the things he was hearing? What was John thinking and feeling as he watched Grandpa do things? What was it like to be Grandpa? (*You may want to write student responses down on a chart or whiteboard.*)

RELEASING THE WRITER: EMPATHY WALK

TEACHER: Today, we are going to practice empathizing with both John *and* Grandpa by going on an empathy walk. You will have the chance to be both John (leading) and Grandpa (being led).

Choose the best place for the walk in your school. We're suggesting using a hallway in the experience below. Pair up your students and explain the boundaries of their empathy walk.

TEACHER (*to the students "being Grandpa," say the following*): What one thing can you do right now to get a sense of what it's like to be Grandpa in today's story? (*"Close my eyes."*) That's right! As your partner leads you down the hall, keep your eyes closed, as best you can. If you peek once in a while, that's okay, but the more time you spend with your eyes closed, the more you will know what it's like to be Grandpa in today's story—the more *empathy* you will feel for him. It's like you're walking in his shoes. Like Grandpa, you can use your senses other than sight to help you know where you are. Pay special attention to sounds.

TEACHER (*to the students who are "being John" and leading their partners, say the following*): Remember how kind John was to his Grandpa, and how gently he led him outside? I invite you to use the same kindness and gentleness as you lead your partner down the hall. Don't worry about whether they are keeping their eyes closed. That's not your job. Your job is to imagine being John leading Grandpa—your partner—safely down the hall. Is everyone ready?

After the partners make their first trip down the hall, invite them to switch roles as one leads the other back. Remind them of their new roles by repeating the above directions.

TEACHER: Now that we've experienced an empathy walk and walked in the shoes of John and Grandpa, did you discover anything more about them that might not have been in the book? What was it like not being able to see? What was it like being the one leading? What more do we know about empathy?

Invite students to write about the experience as they complete the following writing stems. Present writing stems on a document camera or whiteboard. Invite students to expand their writing by suggesting that they are welcome to write beyond the stems—whatever occurs to them.

When I was being led, I felt _____. I heard _____. I kept thinking _____.

When I led my partner, I felt _____. I tried to _____.
I kept thinking _____.

Engaging Appreciation, Sharing, and Celebrating (5 min.)

Invite students to share their writing in their partnership or with the class as a whole. Invite listeners to look for common ground—what thoughts or feelings they held in common with the writer.

Phase Two: Deepen

Reading Like a Writer

Ask students to take out any notes they've made from their "five senses at home" homework from the previous reading lesson so that they can reference it for the next writing experience. If they don't have any of those written notes available, the writing experience can be adapted.

> Teacher: Patricia MacLachlan is really good at waking up our senses with her words. In your reader's imagination, see if you can listen and hear the sounds the characters are hearing. See if you can notice how the author inspires us to hear these sounds. (*In the second half of the book, read two pages aloud, beginning with "When we come to the riverbank" and ending with "'Honkers,' he insists. And we both laugh."*)

> Teacher: What are some of the sounds John and Grandpa heard on these two pages? (*After students have answered, you might want to invite readers to look back at the word-sound "Conk-a-ree" that the blackbird makes, saying the following.*)

> Teacher: Look at this interesting word! What an interesting sound! Would anyone like to try making that sound out loud? The author has made up a word for this sound. Does anyone know what it's called when a writer makes up a word that sounds like the sound itself? Onomatopoeia. That's right! (*Display the word. Say more about it or offer examples, if this is the first time most of your students have heard the word.*)

Releasing the Writer

Invite students to take out their five senses notes, if they have them. Reassure the ones who don't have notes that they can "start fresh" with the questions you will ask.

> Teacher: What are some sounds at your house that are familiar to you? Write these down. If you want to try your hand at onomatopoeia, try creating a word phonetically that sounds like the sound itself. Have fun with this! (*Invite students to use a web or cluster to brainstorm sounds. After allowing a few minutes for brainstorming, ask the following question.*) Can you remember a time when a sudden or weird noise or sound at your house either surprised or startled you, or made you really curious? Write a story about that experience. Include in your story:

- a description of your house using your "five senses" notes or what you remember

- what happened and when, telling your reader about this sudden or weird sound

- what you were thinking or feeling when you heard it

- onomatopoeia, a made-up word that sounds like the sound itself

ENGAGING APPRECIATION, SHARING, AND CELEBRATING

After students have completed their stories, invite sharing in whatever way feels right in the moment—with partners, small groups, or the whole class. Invite writers to read their writing with feeling and loud enough for everyone to hear. Invite listeners to listen with empathy (*tap heart*).

TEACHER: What would "listening with empathy" look like? (*Possible answers: "with full attention," "body facing speaker."*) Put yourself in the speaker's shoes and listen like you would want someone to listen to you. Listen and imagine what that character's life is like. Imagine that character's point of view as you listen.

TEACHER (*after each writer shares, ask listeners the following*): Name one thing you heard that really helped you imagine what the writer's life is like in their home.

MAKING THE EMPATHY LEARNING REAL

Invite students to reflect on ways their homes are the same, even though they also may have significant differences. You may want to chart their responses under the title "What Our Homes Have in Common." This will help establish common ground in your learning community—an important foundation of empathy.

The One and Only Ivan by Katherine Applegate

Reading Lesson

Reading Level—DRA 40; Grade 3–5; Guided Reading S; Lexile 570L

Empathy Focus

Katherine Applegate has written a novel, narrated by Ivan the gorilla, that evokes reader empathy on every page. Immediately, the reader is drawn into Ivan's point of view when we see his environment, his friends, and all that happens both through his eyes and his large, caring, silverback heart. Our empathy for Ivan and his friends has us rooting for them on every page. Many of Applegate's characters are also beautiful models of empathy, showing readers what it means to walk in another's shoes—or paws—and inspiring us to take action to help make life better for other living beings. Eco-empathy is alive on these pages, as well as giving plentiful opportunities for classroom discussions about how we as human beings treat animals and how we might treat them better.

Phases One and Two Reading Lessons: Connect and Deepen

As this is a longer-term read for your class and you'll be stopping at certain sections of the book to enter into discourse, connecting and deepening are happening throughout the experience.

CoreEmpathy Target

I imagine what the characters' lives might be like in order to understand the story more deeply.

Literacy Learning Targets

- I can refer accurately to the text when explaining what the text says explicitly and when drawing inferences from the text. (RL.1)
- I can determine the theme of the story and summarize it. (RL.2)
- I can describe the characters, settings, or events of a story, drawing on specific details in the text. (RL.3)
- I can describe the point of view from which a story is narrated. (RL.6)
- I can make connections between the text and visuals where the different versions reflect description and direction. (RL.7)
- I can compare and contrast themes and patterns of events in stories. (RL.9)

- I can write an opinion using supporting information from a text. (W.1)

- I can conduct a short research project to build knowledge on a topic. (W.7)

- I can draw evidence from literary text to support analysis and reflection. (W.9)

- I can convey ideas using empathy and literacy vocabulary. (L.4, L.5)

- I can engage in collaborative discussion. (SL.1)

ENGAGING EMPATHY FIRST (5 MIN.)

Teach the Empathy First lesson. Adapt it as necessary before reengaging the story on subsequent days.

Note to Teacher

To follow is a guide divided into manageable parts to help your learning community closely read *The One and Only Ivan*. As the person who knows your students and your classroom practices, choose the instructional reading model that suits it best, whether it be as a read-aloud, a small-group read, individuals reading, as an audiobook, or a combination of these. As you read and discover, keep track of your community's thinking by charting it electronically or on paper. If appropriate, invite your students to record their own thinking through journaling reader responses. Finally, divide the reading as you see best fitting the learning needs, engagement, and stamina of your students.

ENGAGING THE STORY

Katherine Applegate was inspired to write *The One and Only Ivan* from a real gorilla who lived in a mall in Tacoma, Washington. One approach might be to introduce the story by investigating him, in addition to the main idea, and inferring and predicting (e.g., "Meet 'Ivan': The Gorilla Who Lived in a Shopping Mall"; Block, 2013).

TEACHER: Now that we have an idea of what empathy is, let's explore how it can work within our reading of *The One and Only Ivan* by Katherine Applegate. Reading through an empathy lens can help us understand a story more deeply. It's like empathy is the glass or lens to see the story through. (*Show the cover of* The One and Only Ivan *by Katherine Applegate and explain that it is about a gorilla who lives in a mall. Ivan makes friends with animals and people who live or work there.*)

TEACHER: What do you notice in the illustration? What do you think the title and illustration may be telling us about the story?

ENGAGING EMPATHY-INFUSED READING: CHARTING THE STORY'S CORE

The following is an empathy-inspired learning series for the practice of close reading *The One and Only Ivan*. Based on the needs of your students and classroom, divide the series as it works best for you. Timing is completely in your control. Keep track of what your students say through charting it on large paper or in a document to project, perhaps with the title heading each section. See pages 65 and 66 (Figures 4.5 and 4.6) for one teacher's use of story charts for *The One and Only Ivan*. Regardless of how you choose to record your students' responses, make it work for you!

Part I of the Story: The Setup—Ivan Reveals Himself and Others

Possible chart title: "Here's What We've Learned"

TEACHER (*set the purpose or intention of the reading*): Authors describe their characters and where they live at the beginning of a story. We can closely read using an empathy lens to collect details about these important elements of story in order to understand its setup. We can imagine their lives, their world, their struggles, their feelings by seeing it from the character's point of view. Let's continue to think about that as we read the beginning of the book. Keep in your mind the following question: "As I imagine Ivan's world, what do I learn about it?"

TEACHER (*read through to page 10*): What do you imagine it is like to be Ivan? How might he feel about himself and his life? What did Ivan say to inspire those ideas? (*Record responses.*)

TEACHER (*continue to read through to page 26*): What new information did you learn about Ivan's life? How does he feel about it? Do you feel empathy for him? If so, how?

TEACHER: Yes, we can feel empathy about a character because we begin to care about them. Also, a character can feel empathy for another. In these next short chapters, we see that happening. Ivan empathizes with others. Let's read to find out in which way Ivan is practicing empathy and with whom.

TEACHER (*read through to page 36*): Whom does Ivan empathize with? How do we know he is empathizing? Use words from our Empathy First definition to help explain your response. (*Continue to record your students' responses in your chosen manner.*)

TEACHER (*read through to page 59 for the entrance of the remaining characters, asking questions about them using empathy; also, invite empathetic reader response by asking the following questions)*: Do you care about the characters? Who? Why? What part of the reading helped you to feel that way?

Students will now have many ideas about how Katherine Applegate set up Ivan's world. Using the tools you've created (charting, journaling, etc.), summarize what has been learned and discussed by having your students write or draw. It could begin "When I think of the details of Ivan's life, here's what I imagine. . . ."

Part II of the Story: The Rising Action—The Story Turns toward a Promise

TEACHER: We have a shift or turn coming in our story. This is important to make note of and talk about to see how the characters' relationships with one another start to change also. Authors move their story forward this way. Empathy can help us notice those changes clearly, as we continue to imagine the lives of the characters we are getting to know. Let's keep reading pages 60 to 82, reading with an empathy lens by asking, "What shift or turn is happening?" "How does that turn change other things?" I can't wait to hear what you think.

TEACHER (*read through to page 82*): What big happening occurred at the Big Top Mall? As Stella was telling the story of Jambo at the zoo, do you think empathy was at work when the boy was not killed? Why? How do you imagine each character (*or suggest certain characters*) is feeling now?

TEACHER (*read through to page 113, where Ivan makes Stella a promise*): What do you think about Ivan's promise? As a reader, are you feeling empathy for any of the characters? Who? Why? How might Stella be feeling?

Part III of the Story: The Turning Point—Grief, Change, and a Plan

Read through to page 120 about the loss and grief that the characters feel. Sometimes, strong feelings in characters bring strong feelings to readers. Be ready for this . . . hear it, write about it, and help your students move on by explaining that all feelings shift, too.

TEACHER: What do you imagine the characters are feeling during this important time? Do you empathize with them?

TEACHER (*read through to page 147*): What new things have you learned about Ivan? Do you imagine him differently now? If so, how?

TEACHER (*read through to page 173, a powerful part of the story where Ivan himself changes; tell your students that the change in Ivan is what propels the story to change, too*): What do you imagine is happening inside of Ivan? What is he feeling? Describe (through charting and journals) the change in the story (often referred to as the *turning point*) by using empathy and imagining being Ivan. What can you imagine coming from this change?

Part IV of the Story: Conclusion—The Plan in Action

TEACHER (*read through to page 199*): What are the details of the plan that Ivan imagined? What do you think about it?

TEACHER (*read through to page 222*): How does empathy help Julia understand Ivan's plan? How does Ivan, or Ruby, or Mack feel about the plan? Use stepping into each character's shoes to list ideas.

TEACHER (*read through to page 248, where Julia draws for Ivan; also, reread the chapter on "Finally," beginning on page 215, to discuss common ground*): What common ground do Julia and Ivan have? How does the common ground—another aspect of empathy—that Julia and Ivan share help her to solve his puzzle?

TEACHER (*read to the end of the story; engage your students in an open discussion to invite their thinking of the conclusion; include questions such as the following*):

- Have you empathized with a character? Which ones?
- Can you find the importance of "12"?
- How did home change for Ivan?
- Is Mac a bad guy? Can you empathize with him and see things from his perspective?

DEEPENING UNDERSTANDING THROUGH EMPATHY

TEACHER: What did reading with empathy do for you as a reader? (*Invite your students to reread out loud parts of the story that were important to them. Suggest they look for a meaningful part, a part where a change occurs, or a part where they used empathy, for instance.*)

TEACHER (*afterwards, make a web on a chart with "Home" in the center; as offshoots, draw lines out from the central idea, and then write the names of the main characters at the end of each line and circle; invite students to do the same in their reader-response journals*): As you use your empathy lenses to step into the lives of the characters, imagine what home means to each of them. Write down your ideas as offshoots from each name, indicating the place in the text that inspired that idea.

OPTIONAL WRITING OR DISCOURSE PROMPT

To compare and contrast a central message or theme of the story, invite your students to write whether they think it really was "home" or not, using the web as inspiration for their writing. Their webs could alternatively be used as inspiration for discourse in partners, small groups, or the class as a whole.

Making the Empathy Learning Real

> TEACHER: What is home to you? Think about what makes home to you and share that with your class as they share their ideas. How can these ideas help us to understand each other? (*Record their ideas through a new chart, add to the one already built, or record in journals.*)

Extending the Story (optional)

Invite students to research and read articles about the real Ivan who once lived in a mall in Tacoma. You may have already read one during the earlier Engaging the Story element of this lesson; if so, extend that exploration by including various articles. Remind students that it is Ivan's real-life story that inspired Katherine Applegate to write *The One and Only Ivan*. To explore the differences between fiction and nonfiction, invite them to compare and contrast aspects of each.

Phases One and Two Writing Lessons: Connect and Deepen

CoreEmpathy Target

I can use point of view, comparisons (similes and metaphors), and other writing craft elements to help readers empathize with my characters.

Literacy Learning Targets

- I can describe a character in depth, drawing specific details in the text. (RL.3)
- I can apply what I've learned about a character in a story to reflect on my writing. (W.9)
- I can use narrative techniques, such as dialogue, description, and pacing, to develop experiences and events or show the responses of characters to situations. (W.3B)
- I can orient the reader by establishing a situation and introducing a character. (W.3A)
- I can use concrete words and phrases and sensory details to convey experiences and events precisely. (W.3D)

Prewriting Bridge between Reading and Writing Lesson

This writing lesson is intended to be experienced after your students have read the entire novel and completed the reading lessons. The day before you begin this writing lesson, ask students to choose a pet or favorite animal, bird, reptile, or insect they are familiar with at home or in their yard. While at home, they should practice empathizing with that animal, noticing its behavior and imagining what that animal's life might be like, taking notes of their observations and imaginings. Ask them to bring their notes to class for the following day's writing lesson.

Engaging Empathy First

You may want to use the CoreEmpathy visual and hand motions to reengage empathy if you feel your students could use the review before adding the following writing focus.

Aligning with a Writer's Purpose

TEACHER: Good writers inspire readers to empathize with their characters—to imagine what a character's life is like by seeking to understand what that character sees, thinks, and feels. Empathy is the key to creating characters that readers care about, just like Katherine Applegate inspired us to care about Ivan and his friends.

TEACHER: Who was a character you really cared about? What was it like to be that character?

Reading Like a Writer

TEACHER: Today, we're going to go back to the very beginning of the novel and reread the first five pages, where the author Katherine Applegate introduces us to Ivan. This time, however, we're going to read like a writer, searching for how the author inspired us to empathize with Ivan—that is, how she helped us see the story-world through Ivan's eyes or his point of view. (*Share anything about point of view you believe is important, such as that the story is told from the "first-person" or "I" point of view.*)

TEACHER: We'll also be looking for other craft elements that the author used to help create a character we could empathize with. The process by which a writer creates a character is called *characterization*. That's what you'll be doing today: reading like a writer and then creating a fictional character from what you've observed about the pet or animal you care about or find fascinating. (*Invite students to take out their prewriting notes from the previous day's observations at home. If you need to review what "fictional" means, do so now.*)

> **Teacher Tip**
>
> This gives students an idea of what they're working toward, as they "read like writers." They'll start to imagine how they might use the tools you'll be discussing in their own writing. Also, you may want to write some of these writing craft terms or student responses on a chart or whiteboard.

As a group and with their writing notebooks handy, ask students to reread pages 1 to 5, pausing at the end of each page to ask the following questions and invite brainstorming.

TEACHER (*after reading page 1, chapter "Home"*):

- How does the author capture your interest or curiosity about Ivan on the very first page?
- Whose point of view are we hearing in these first pages—that is, who is telling the story?
- Which of these three sentences on this page is a statement of opinion, as opposed to a statement of fact? (*"It's not as easy as it looks."*) Knowing what you know about the story now, why would Ivan say this?

TEACHER: Another term for a character's opinions or thoughts is *inside view*. As a writer, Applegate is helping her readers empathize with Ivan by showing them his inside view—what he's thinking about his life, his past, other characters, and everything that happens. What thoughts or opinions might the pet or animal you observed hold about their life? In your writer's notebook, take a minute to make notes about that. (*Note: If you've taught a brainstorming technique such as clustering or web-making, feel free to invite students to use that—clustering ideas around "inside view."*)

TEACHER (*after reading page 2, chapter "Names"*): On this page, the author is showing more of Ivan's inside view.

- Which sentences reflect Ivan's thoughts about something?
- Who or what does he hold strong opinions about?
- What *simile* does the author use to express how Ivan feels about humans and their words? Why would the author choose "banana peel" as a comparison to get Ivan's point of view across to us? (*It's what Ivan knows and cares about.*) The comparisons we choose to use as writers help our characters seem more real to our readers. They are part of characterization.
- In your notebooks, jot down a few objects that your animal is familiar with—objects you might use in a character sketch to create a comparison. Also, jot down possible names others might call your character, as well as the name your character calls him- or herself.

TEACHER (*after reading page 3, chapter "Patient"*): When we create a character, we want to show our readers the qualities of their personality.

- In this chapter, how does the author reveal an important quality about Ivan's character?
- Knowing what we know about Ivan now, did this quality change as the story progressed?

- What qualities does your animal have that you may want to include in your writing? Jot these down.

TEACHER (*after reading pages 4–5, chapter "How I Look"*):

- What are some more things the author is revealing about Ivan through his point of view?
- What sensory details does the author use to help us "sense" more about Ivan's physical being?
- From these pages, how do you think Ivan feels about himself? How does he feel about humans? Chimps?
- What does your animal look like? What sensory details might you use to describe him or her? How does your animal feel about him- or herself? Jot down your ideas.

RELEASING THE WRITER

Now that your students have done their brainstorming, it's time to release them into their writing. Invite them to refer to their notes and create a character sketch of their fictional character by modeling Applegate's structure, as well as the craft elements they've just noticed in her writing.

> **Teacher Tip**
>
> If you think your students' writing will be more successful if they write immediately following the brainstorming for each model chapter, please feel free to facilitate the lesson that way.

A character sketch helps the reader imagine who that character is and what that character's life is like. It differs from a story in that it's only about the character and not necessarily a complete story with a beginning, middle, and end. In this writing exercise, the most important thing student writers will be modeling is the use of the first-person or "I" point of view, writing as if their character were the one doing the speaking.

Suggest that students write similar "chapters" as the first five chapters in the book, making them at least several sentences long. Encourage them to use the same titles, although their "Patience" chapter should be titled with the one character quality they want to emphasize about their fictional animal.

ENGAGING APPRECIATION, SHARING, AND CELEBRATING

After students have completed their character sketches, invite sharing in whatever way feels right in the moment—with partners, small groups, or the whole class. Invite writers to read their writing with feeling and loud enough for everyone to hear.

TEACHER (*invite listeners to listen with empathy—tap hearts*): What would "listening with empathy" look like? (*Possible answers: "with full attention," "body facing speaker."*) Put yourself in the speaker's shoes and listen like you would want someone to listen to you. Listen and imagine what that character's life is like. Imagine that character's point of view as you listen.

TEACHER (*after each writer shares, ask the class, or group, or partner the following question*): Name one thing you heard that really helped you understand or empathize with the writer's character.

MAKING THE EMPATHY LEARNING REAL

TEACHER: Take your character sketch home and observe your pet or animal again. What more comes to mind? What have you missed? What are they trying to tell you about their life? Revise your sketch, adding anything that would help your readers empathize with your character.

7

The CoreEmpathy Classroom

Good teaching is an act of hospitality toward the young, and hospitality is always an act that benefits the host even more than the guest.

—Parker J. Palmer, American author, educator, and activist

This book could easily end right here. However, we know you have the rest of your classroom to run. Through an empathy lens, we have ideas to make that smoother and more joyful for you.

After exploring the plentiful examples of lessons, strategies, and practices contained in the previous chapters, you have a vision of what the CoreEmpathy approach to literacy learning can look like—and, perhaps more important, feel like—in your classroom. Most of all, we hope you are feeling some stirrings, a desire to "get out there and teach," inspired by a deeper connection with what got you into this teaching business in the first place. Your purpose—now even greater. And that, our teaching friends, is more than enough.

However, we're willing to bet that, once you see how an empathy lens transforms literacy learning, you'll start thinking of even more ways you can integrate empathy into other areas of your day. We've written this chapter to help get you started. It's full of ideas to create a CoreEmpathy classroom—a place where empathy assists classroom procedures, routines, and practices. It also contains ideas on how to extend learning beyond literacy because empathy is already a practice in your classroom. Teaching literacy is a large part of your work, but there's more to your job. You want a classroom that runs smoothly and is an exciting place to learn. Empathy can help with that, too.

Again, because we're dealing with a lens here, we're suggesting that an empathy-infused classroom is a matter of *how you see* these practices combined with *what you do* to make them work. It's a matter of focus. In this chapter, you will read how to influence your classroom culture through these practical ideas:

- setting up your classroom guidelines and rules with empathy
- creating a welcoming classroom with empathy
- facilitating classroom meetings through an empathy lens
- inviting appreciation and empathy and building the bridge between
- applying empathy to challenging behavior
- integrating the expressive arts, empathy, and literacy learning
- expanding eco-empathy into the classroom
- applying empathy to other subjects and curricular goals
- exploring still *more* strategies for cultivating an empathy-rich classroom

Suffice it to say, once it's introduced into the environment, empathy will seep into every aspect of your classroom. You won't be able to keep it from expanding, so you might as well guide it. Let's start with how you can let it guide the classroom routines you create that make the school day flow smoothly. By our way of thinking—that is, empathy-infused thinking—it all begins in September, with your students entering your classroom.

Guiding Classroom Routines through an Empathy Lens

Greeting Your Students in the Morning

There's no substitute for a teacher's warm greeting for each student every morning as they walk in the door. This simple act sets the tone for the day, eases nerves, and gives everyone a moment to transition from their home life to school life. And this welcome is never more important than on the first day of school. It turns out that a warm greeting at the door is a simple act with a powerful impact on the first day and every day.

A 2018 study involving hundreds of classrooms revealed just how powerful this classroom practice can be. The study, reported in an article by Youki Terada (2018) on the Edutopia website, showed that a simple morning greeting contributed to students' sense of connection and belonging, which in turn increased the time and effort they wanted to put into their learning. In fact, learning engagement went up by 20 percent and disruptive behavior decreased by 9 percent. More learning, less disruptions—every teacher's dream, right? Not surprisingly, the teachers themselves felt better about their day, too, when they initiated this welcoming practice, setting a positive tone for everyone (Terada, 2018).

Clearly, these first moments of the day carry an impact that only beginnings hold. We know a teacher who puts an empathy twist to this warm morning greeting. Sarah, a first-grade teacher in Bellingham, Washington, greets her students every morning at the door as she sits on one of their chairs. She models empathy by putting herself in the seat of her students, literally, so that she can greet each one at eye level as they cross the threshold.

Besides setting a positive tone for the day, Sarah also uses this welcoming time to gain valuable information about each student, she says. Utilizing the empathy skill of observing facial expressions and body language, she picks up clues about each child's emotional state. "Their eyes and faces tell me how their morning has been and how they are feeling," she explains. Some give her a high five, others a sideways hug, but they all get a smile and a warm greeting from her each morning.

Like Sarah, Laura has also committed herself to "being fully present" as she greets her first graders every morning. She gives this practice top priority, she says, even when mornings are busy with meetings, because she sees how the positivity that her welcome generates sets the tone for the entire day. "If a meeting runs late in the morning, I no longer feel badly about politely excusing myself to be that warm greeter every day. I have made it a priority. No exceptions."

Establishing Classroom Norms to Start the Year

On the first day of school, we know you establish your classroom guidelines after greeting your students. This is the time when your students begin to understand how your classroom will be a healthy community of learners. Let empathy assist you. It will help your students understand their role in that healthy community.

Laura sets classroom guidelines at the beginning of the school year and then uses empathy practice as the way these guidelines are realized in the learning environment. She asks her students two important questions at the beginning of the year in order to begin to set the community guidelines with the empathy intention: "What kind of environment will help you learn?" and "What do you want to feel in your classroom that will help you learn?"

Each year brings different answers, Laura tells us, but they can be synthesized into three primary responses. Her students want safety, energy, and happiness. Once that is recognized, the classroom norms can be established as ways safety, energy, and happiness can be achieved. She favors having her students generate the norms while she writes their ideas. She helps to form them into four or five clear statements that are posted on the walls as a permanent reminder of how the learning community functions in a healthy way.

In earlier chapters, we've discussed how cultivating empathy can support academic learning and growth. Classroom routines and practices can also be supported. Empathy is the how. Through empathy practice, you and your students can create a "safe, energetic, and happy" learning environment. Now let's look at how the school year progresses in a classroom where everyone feels welcomed and everyone knows they belong.

Morning Circle Meetings to Start the Day

After receiving the warm greeting from a teacher, your students are ready to start their day. A *morning circle meeting* is a classroom practice that we suggest after you greet them to transition into learning. You've already modeled a welcoming way to enter in your classroom at the door; now your students can welcome each other as they move into the circle.

Laura's students enter the circle by looking at someone while tapping their hearts—a gesture, according to Laura, that was initiated by the students themselves, and, incidentally, the CoreEmpathy hand motion for empathy. This simple gesture seems to say, "The heart in me greets the heart in you." Thus, the school day begins with a warm welcome from everyone to everyone, and empathy is integrated seamlessly into the classroom routine.

Creating a Welcoming Classroom

Of course, empathy won't stop there. This empathy-infused welcome inevitably permeates the learning culture throughout the day. If your classroom is like most, people come and go throughout the day—students and adults—and it can feel disruptive. The practice of empathy can ease these transitions, and, in fact, offer a sense of belonging right away.

Beth, a kindergarten teacher in a small community northeast of Everett, Washington, shows the impact of that first moment when a newcomer walks in the door and how it sets the stage for a welcoming classroom. My (Christie) first moment in her classroom was so powerful, it took my breath away in much the same way an expansive mountain view does. Only I was looking down rather than up, because what I was viewing was just over three feet tall. I was looking into the big brown eyes of a five-year-old boy.

It was December when I arrived in Beth's classroom to mentor a teacher candidate in the final weeks of her internship. A helpful school employee pointed the direction to her classroom after giving me a neon sticker that read "Visitor" in black ink. Scurrying to the classroom door as fast as I could while still using my "walking feet," I opened it looking for an inconspicuous seat in which to observe. Two steps in, my brown-eyed greeter appeared with an outstretched hand, ready to shake mine just like we were greeting each other before a business meeting. "Hello, my name is Xavier. What is your name?" said an innocent young voice. Surprised, I stumbled to answer, "Mrs. Kesler." He smiled and took my hand, then shook it. With our hands awkwardly pumping up and down, he replied, "Mrs. Kesler, we are learning math right now. Please come in and join us."

In a moment, I felt welcome. I knew I belonged.

In a moment, I was not inconspicuous or invisible; I was a part of the learning and the classroom. In a moment, I didn't want to look for a place in the room to watch the action; I wanted to be a part of it. In a moment, I felt welcome. I knew I belonged.

Of course, this experience didn't happen by accident. Beth assigns a student every week to be the classroom greeter. In September, her entire classroom is trained in the art of greeting: using eye contact with a smile, the outstretched hand, the introduction, the question, and the explanation of what is happening in the room. They learn to say the visitor's name to get to know them, and even how to shake hands. Are you seeing the career skill being built here, simultaneous with the goal of creating welcome? I sure did.

But the skill building for success now and in the future goes even deeper with the inclusion of empathy. Beth introduces this classroom routine at the beginning of the school year by inviting her students to step into the shoes of a newcomer. In essence, she introduces the idea in this manner: "We are doing this to help visitors feel welcome. Have you ever entered a place where you were uncertain what was happening and who was there? That's how our visitors might be feeling, too. By greeting them warmly, we can help them feel welcome."

And, boy, did that welcome practice work for me. Even the language her student used made a difference in how I felt, an ever-important hug to my heart: "Please come in and join us." Not "watch us," not "take a seat," but "join us." What a message. And her students practice this welcome over and over, because that's how they get better at it. That's empathy in action. That's imagining what someone else might be feeling and then acting on that understanding with kindness. I wanted to stay all day. And that's how Beth's students feel *every* day.

It's the same for all of us, isn't it? This longing for welcome? Whether we're a newcomer or not, whether we're walking through a door we know or a door that's unfamiliar, we inevitably feel that moment of trepidation, when we hold our breath before entering. What will happen in this place today? More important, will I belong? A welcoming classroom helps ease this important transition for everyone.

It's important to remember that whenever a student enters the classroom—whether they enter just like any other day, or they've come in late, after an absence due to illness, or are returning to join their classmates from another activity—that student is momentarily in the role of newcomer. Essentially, a student's inner voice may be asking, "Will I fit in now?" Extending an empathy-guided welcome helps students reestablish their sense of belonging, a crucial factor in their feeling safe and their readiness to learn.

Remember the story we shared in earlier chapters about the student who returned to the classroom in the middle of a reading lesson and a group of students offered him a seat at their table, explained the activity, and gave him a role—all without teacher intervention? The students assuaged his trepidation by extending an empathy-guided greeting the moment he walked in. You can imagine that he, then, felt safe and welcomed, and that, in turn, created the space for him to be ready to learn. This is a perfect example of what happens in a welcoming classroom. That's the impact empathy can have.

Inviting Appreciation into Your Classroom Practices

Empathy and appreciation may be two different practices, but they are cousins to each other in that they connect people in positive, life-giving ways. Between these two cousins is a bridge. When this bridge is built in your classroom, a regular practice of students expressing appreciation for their learning, their teacher, and each other can create a beautiful foundation for the deeper dive into understanding that empathy inspires. Conversely, once we've stepped into another's shoes, it's easier to look for things we appreciate about them. When students feel the safety and interconnection that an empathy-rich classroom provides, they are much more inspired to express appreciation, which, in turn, heightens the possibility for more empathy. In a CoreEmpathy classroom, appreciation and empathy form a win–win bridge that runs both ways.

In this section, we'll explore how this appreciation and empathy bridge can become a part of your classroom routines, and what part this plays in establishing a healthy classroom culture. But first, let's explore how inviting appreciation into your classroom practice can provide a more accessible approach into empathy. Sometimes, strong feelings can hinder a person's

In a CoreEmpathy classroom, appreciation and empathy form a win–win bridge that runs both ways.

empathic abilities, for instance. When this happens and empathy practice is difficult to achieve, appreciation may still be reachable.

Appreciation as a Bridge into Empathy during Conflict Resolution

Rather than the level of engagement or change in perspective that empathy requires, appreciation asks only for a simple recognition of someone or something's positive qualities. In this very moment, there are undoubtedly people and things in your life that you can call to mind and appreciate with little forethought. We can, too. For example, we appreciate you being curious about empathy and how it can transform your classroom. Because appreciation is so accessible, it can become a powerful way to establish connection among classmates before entering into the deeper level of engagement that empathy requires.

Appreciation can be a more approachable first step than putting themselves in the other's shoes.

When conflict arises between classmates, you may be inclined to invite students to apply empathy to the situation in order for one to see the perspective of another. However, asking a student to imagine what someone else sees, thinks, and feels during conflict may be too challenging for them, particularly when the context is unfamiliar or when they're engaged in such strong feelings themselves that there just doesn't seem to be the space or room for anything else. Appreciation can be a more approachable first step than putting themselves in the other's shoes.

How can you establish appreciation as part of your classroom culture? First, define *appreciation* for your students as simply acknowledging a positive quality in something or someone. Then, start giving examples of what you appreciate about the people and things involved in the immediate context. Invite your students to join in.

As you introduce the concept of appreciation, be sure to tell students that you can appreciate something at any time, even if you don't necessarily like it. It helps to offer an example from your own life of how this can happen. A quick story I (Christie) often use with my students is about a time when my sweetie, Craig, invited me to a concert. It was a band he'd been crazy about for years but had never had the chance to see perform. Once we arrived at the concert and the music started, I knew it wasn't for me. However, I could still find so much to appreciate. I could appreciate Craig's sheer joy in being there, the musicianship of the band members, and the messages in their songs, even though I didn't enjoy the music itself. The good qualities I noticed weren't dependent on me liking it. All I needed to do was notice them. Just like that, a bridge was built, and I could more easily move into empathy with my sweetheart, seeing the evening through his eyes.

Once you establish what appreciation is and how it can operate through simply watching and noticing, your students can offer their own ideas of appreciation. Then it can become a regular classroom practice and work in similar ways. Let's look at how it can play a role as part of your process for resolving conflict. When challenging behavior is present, appreciation can form a bridge that can help mend fences between students, paving the way for greater empathy.

When challenging behavior is present, appreciation can form a bridge that can help mend fences between students, paving the way for greater empathy.

You undoubtedly already have a process for helping your students resolve conflicts. Once you've come to the point within that process when it's time to find resolution, consider inviting each student to find something they appreciate about the other. It doesn't have to be a big thing. It can be as seemingly insignificant as "I appreciate that you're good at math," or "I appreciate how well you draw." Now, a bridge is built between them.

Jordan, a second-grade teacher in Bellevue, Washington, relays a particularly disturbing incident that such an application of appreciation helped resolve. One classmate made a hurtful comment against another, and, in it, referred to that classmate's race. Jordan put an end to it quickly and decisively, but she was unsure of how to help them repair the damage done by the slur. Without resolution, the accepting classroom culture she had worked so hard to establish would be tarnished.

This is when she decided to try appreciation as a way to bridge the gap. After explaining what appreciation was in everyday language, Jordan invited the student who wronged the other to think of and then express "appreciations" to the harmed student—in writing first, and then in conversation. It was the first step in unlocking the discomfort between the students, she says, and it paved the way toward healing. They were then able to resolve the conflict, restore the relationship, and become a healthy part of the classroom community once again.

This situation helps us to understand appreciation's important role in restoration. Pam, the principal of an elementary school northeast of Bellingham, Washington, favors the restorative justice approach to problem-solving on a school level. Her approach to creating a positive, healthy school culture values how appreciation could play an important part. *Restorative justice* is a discipline practice that holds the goal of "making it right" in highest priority. Pam prefers to call it "restorative practice," however, since she believes the approach takes a combination of finesse and procedure to achieve.

Conversation is necessary in this approach, Pam says, to facilitate healing between a transgressor and the one wronged, requiring the use of "I" statements, active listening, and proactive steps for future problem-solving. Pam agrees that adding appreciation to these conversations—where students voice a unique, positive quality they see in each other—could enhance the process, and in fact help create a bridge between a contrived apology and an authentic one that allows true healing to take place.

Empathy as a Bridge into Appreciation

Let's reverse the direction one can travel over the same connecting bridge. Rather than appreciation leading to empathy, let's explore empathy-enriched experiences being the bridge to appreciation. As we said before, it's a complementary relationship.

In Chapter 4, we described first-grade literacy learning with *My Friend Is Sad* by Mo Willems (2007), and how dramatically students read with fluency during empathy-infused reading. In Chapter 5, we described how Laura used empathy-infused writing to enhance her students' writing skills as well. The empathy work in her classroom was rich and deep by the end of her unit, and it brought unexpected crossings into appreciation. Her students didn't just walk over that bridge, they ran over it.

Laura wanted to end the series of empathy-infused literacy learning by creating an *appreciation chart*, first asking her students to think about what they appreciated about the characters in the story, their situations, and the illustrations. They easily filled the chart with their story ideas. Then she asked them to appreciate each other as well as herself and the learning that happened during the unit, and, wow, the floodgate was opened. Appreciation didn't just flow; it was unleashed like the power of a river.

As her students expressed idea after idea, they filled the chart with so many sticky notes that they covered over Laura's titles and subtitles (Figure 7.1). But it didn't stop there. Asking for still more notes, Laura's students ran

FIGURE 7.1. Story-inspired appreciations and class-inspired appreciations.

out of room and wound up sticking appreciation all over the walls surrounding the overflowing chart! The feeling of excitement and positivity in Laura's classroom was palpable.

Laura believes, as we do, that all the empathy-infused reading and writing that preceded this activity fueled these written expressions of appreciation. Empathy was the bridge into appreciation, and both worked together to create this beautiful experience of an empathy-rich classroom.

Story-Inspired Appreciations

"I appreciate that Piggie and Gerald got a hug from each other."

"I appreciated that we read with a partner."

"I appreciated how Piggie said, 'ye haw.'"

"I appreciated that empathy happens."

Class-Inspired Appreciations

"I appreciate wen Gabe lisens and is nice."

"Ms. Hewson teaches in a fun way."

"I like when something falls we pick it up."

"I appreciate that everybody has a friend."

After teaching empathy-infused reading and writing through story, we suggest doing as Laura did and setting aside time for students to appreciate the book, the author, the central message, the teacher, and one another.

In addition to making appreciation charts, other ways to apply empathy-inspired appreciation to the learning may include:

- appreciating the author by watching interviews with them on YouTube

- creating an author corner with other empathy-rich books the author has written

- making an appreciation bulletin board, where random appreciations can be posted

- appreciating the subject matter explored in a fictional book by studying nonfiction books on the same subject (e.g., after reading *Fireflies!*, your class might read nonfiction books or articles about this amazing insect)

Beyond accentuating the literacy learning, we believe there are no limits to the role appreciation can play in supporting an empathy-rich classroom. Making appreciation an everyday part of your classroom expressions through note-giving and thank-you card writing may be something that you are already doing, for instance, but we'd encourage thinking of ways to expand the practice of appreciation into unknown territories. For example, classmates could spend time in appreciation toward a birthday boy or girl at the end of their special day. Or consider setting aside a day during which the people who work behind the scenes at your school (think nurses, psychologists, attendance help, and speech support) stop by your classroom for a visit. Then have your students write about and speak their appreciation for each person in making your school the place it is.

Simple expressions of appreciation such as these, or more involved appreciations through chart creations and active conflict resolution, can create the bridge toward empathy. We invite you to try these or discover your own. Then visit www.CoreEmpathy.com and tell us all about it!

Extending Empathy-Rich Literacy Learning through the Expressive Arts

Besides taking time to appreciate the book's author, its theme, and each other's contributions, one of the best ways to allow empathy to linger is to integrate an expressive arts component into a reading or writing lesson or to include it as an extension. Of course, this is something teachers have been doing since the dawn of education. We're including a discussion of it here, however, for you to view it through that now-familiar empathy lens, thus making the arts a more conscious part of your CoreEmpathy practice and to give them a greater purpose in your classroom.

The expressive arts represent a wide range of artistic expression. In addition to the literary arts, they include:

- the visual arts, such as drawing, painting, collage, murals, and sculpture
- the dramatic arts, such as readers theater, plays, puppetry, and mono- logues
- the arts of movement and music
- the media arts, such as videography, podcasts, or computer-aided graphics

Just as the literary arts have been proven to increase empathy in the reader and writer, so have the expressive arts in general been shown to do the same. In a research report published in 2019 entitled "Investigating Causal Effects of

Arts Education Experiences," researchers found that increased art education experiences significantly reduced the number of students receiving disciplinary infractions while also improving State of Texas Assessments of Academic Readiness writing achievement. These arts-related experiences also increased students' compassion for others. For elementary students (constituting 86 percent of the total sample of 10,548 third to eighth graders from forty-two schools), these added art experiences significantly improved school engagement, college aspirations, and arts-facilitated empathy (Bowen & Kisida, 2019).

Clearly, the above report supports the idea that the expressive arts enrich academic learning in much the same way empathy does. Add the two together—the arts and empathy—and you get a combination that amplifies the effects of each element. The following are just a few strategies—some you may already use—for incorporating the expressive arts into your literacy instruction.

Ever since cave dwellers drew pictures on cave walls, drawing a picture in response to a story or as the way to tell a story has been a vehicle into writing. Writing is prompted after reading *Leonardo, the Terrible Monster*, for instance, by students drawing a picture of themselves first, before writing the dialogue. By drawing first, a student's ideas for writing become organized and then unleashed, as discussed in Chapter 5. Often, emotions are also identified and expressed in students' drawings, further inspiring the student writers' words and putting them in touch with their emotional vocabulary.

In early elementary classrooms that are exploring emotional vocabulary as an empathy skill, teachers can enlist movement and music to extend the literacy lesson. Consider inviting students to "move or dance like a certain character" in order to express how they think that character is feeling. Of course, there's nothing like music to evoke emotions as well. Try asking students if certain music reminds them of a character or feeling in the story.

Another, more global strategy for developing emotional vocabulary is keeping a running list of feeling words in your classroom. Add to the list when a feeling is experienced and identified. Consider having a feeling puppet handy for helping younger students recognize and identify their feelings. You or a student can use the puppet to explain and perhaps express a feeling that has come up in the classroom.

Sometimes, the expressive arts can facilitate a student's entry into reading and writing, as discussed in Chapters 4 and 5. For instance, in the sample reading lesson for *My Friend Is Sad*, the dramatic art of readers theater offers a beautiful reentry into the story that inevitably deepens student understanding. Empathy is

When children play—which is what all expressive arts invite them to do—they relax into the learning.

inspired and practiced through the very process of stepping into a character's shoes in order to portray that character dramatically. And guess what? Using this expressive art as a channel for the story is also *fun*. When children play—which is what all expressive arts invite them to do—they relax into the learning.

Karen, a fourth- and fifth-grade language arts teacher at a public school dedicated to the arts in Lexington, Kentucky, integrated the art of mask-making with creative writing to deepen her students' experience of the environmental theme in *Saving Wonder*. In a lesson she calls "The Council of All Beings," she invited each student to write a persuasive speech from the point of view of a plant, animal, or other element of nature that would be affected by the practice of mountaintop removal mining—a source of major conflict in the novel. She then invited them to create masks representing those nature elements and deliver their speeches in a council format *as if they were that element*—a beautiful expression of eco-empathy. Thus, she incorporated art, writing, speaking, and empathy into one integrated lesson—with powerful results. Here are excerpts from the speech fifth-grade student Madison gave at the Council of All Beings, evoking the voice of the mountain (see also Figures 7.2 and 7.3).

"I Am a Mountain"

I am the mountain of life. I sprung from the soil long before any of the mountains in Appalachia, yet the humans deny the evidence. . . . Foolish beings, I was given a name by Mother Earth long before they came around. In the language of the mountains, *Adskedoncte*. In the language of humans, which we all understand, unfortunately, it means *The Youth of The Mountains*. Yet they threaten to decapitate me. That name speaks power. I could crush the humans, defeat them until they second-guess reality. But that is not the way of the mountains. That is not the way of *Adskedoncte*.

…

The original Humans of this land, the natives, respected all life. They respected me and knew my true name. They drank from the river and cut down trees and plants, but only necessarily. Nothing was wasted. I have stood here for hundreds of years, I plan to live hundreds more.

…

I long to be majestic again, to stand tall over everything, the ruler of Appalachia, as everything is at peace. Mother Earth is dying. And we cannot stop it. Only humans can stop themselves, realize the sincerity of what they are doing. Killing things for their own use. When us mountains are gone, they will be at a loss, no power, no amenities. Everything that separates them and the children of Mother Earth destroyed. Selfish beings.

…

I bathe in the Soil, as the Plants and Trees nest there, the River tumbling down like a cub at play. Insects make their home in the soil and Mammals prowl about. The Sky, contrary to its moods, hangs overhead, and Fish swim in the River as they splash and go about their ways. Reptiles peer from the Soil, like frightened children in bed, and the Amphibians hang out by the River flirting with the Fish. Birds nest in the Trees and entertain us with their music. And I support them. I am the Center of Appalachia, the oldest mountain in Kentucky, and I will not go down without a fight. We are the Council of Twelve Beings and we will not go down without a fight.

FIGURE 7.2. Madison as the Mountain.

Karen's integrative lesson is also a fantastic example of eco-empathy in action, whereby readers and writers step into the perspective of an element in nature and imagine what that element's life is like. Clearly, Madison is a gifted writer in a school that nurtures her talent, but this lesson including both visual and dramatic art allowed her to more deeply express that gift, as she took the mountain's perspective to heart.

FIG. 7.3. Council of All Beings.

As you can see from Madison's writing sample, integrating the creative arts with literacy and empathy is a powerful combination. Integrate expressive arts with literacy and empathy wherever you can, and you will be cultivating a thriving, empathy-rich classroom.

Everyday Empathy in the Classroom

In this chapter so far, we've explored empathy's role in a welcoming classroom environment, as well as setting an intention for empathy in already-established classroom practices. We've also examined the role of empathy's not-so-distant cousin, appreciation, in not only expanding the joy of learning and relationships, but in creating a bridge for empathy to grow even in the midst of conflict. Additionally, we've given a shout-out to the expressive arts as another way to deepen literacy learning while simultaneously cultivating even more empathy in your learning community.

As you probably have already realized, when it comes to creating an empathy-rich classroom, the possibilities are endless. We can't close out this chapter, however, without adding just a few more ideas to the CoreEmpathy mix—extended practices that can inspire empathy to have an even greater influence on your classroom culture.

Eco-Empathy in the Classroom

Many classrooms incorporate plants, insects, or small animals into the environment as a way for students to learn how to care for other living things while providing motivation for learning more about them. These already established relationships offer wonderful opportunities for the practice of eco-empathy in the classroom—that is, empathizing with another living being in the natural world.

When the opportunity presents itself, it's easy to ask, "If we were to put ourselves in the perspective of our plant/colony of ants/guinea pig, what do you think they might be needing right now?" Or if, for instance, the classroom is noisy and your class gerbil, Petunia, is running around her cage, jumping against its walls, you might ask, "Why do you think Petunia is acting that way? Can we put ourselves in her place and imagine what she might be feeling? Is there something that we can do or not do that might help her feel calmer?"

Once eco-empathy is inspired and practiced in your classroom, it isn't a stretch to imagine your students practicing it at home with their pets, other neighborhood animals and plants, and, beyond this, with natural beings from other environments. This is *exactly* how empathy moves from your classroom into the outer world.

An Empathy Reading Corner

Create an *empathy reading corner*, where your class's empathy-rich library can be stored and enjoyed. Record your voice reading the story you've just explored for students to play back and enjoy the story again. Or, better yet, invite students to create a recording or video of them reading the story, or suggest they read to each other in the empathy reading corner.

Independent Reading and Letting Empathy Linger

Create a signal for when empathy is found while you are reading aloud, or when your students are reading on their own, such as tapping the heart or signing an "E." Have your students spontaneously signal and discuss, when appropriate, what they read and how it demonstrates empathy in the story. They can leave tracks of empathy sightings in the pages of books during silent reading in the form of a sticky note with an "E" and a heart surrounding it.

Journaling Empathy

For those classrooms that invite students to write in a daily journal, consider making Fridays "Empathy Journaling Day," when students journal about an experience they had that week in which they either observed or experienced empathy. Knowing that Empathy Journaling Day is coming, students will be more alert for empathy throughout the week.

An Empathy Sighting Chart

Consider creating a classroom chart that will record a running list of empathy sightings that students observe in the classroom, lunchroom, bus, hallways, or playground. Invite them to create this chart with you, asking them what they think would be important to record: Names? Dates? What happened? Maybe empathy sightings will become so prolific, you'll need to create a new chart every week. Worse things could happen! Perhaps it could also become a part of your classroom meeting time.

Exploring Other Subjects through an Empathy Lens

When empathy becomes part of the classroom culture, it inevitably shows up in other subjects besides reading and writing. The "people subjects" of social studies and history are two logical areas of study conducive to empathy-infused instruction. When your class is discussing a culture, social issue, or challenging time in history, some empathy-focused questions might be:

- What do you imagine it's like to live in that culture? Or to live at that time in history?
- Can you step into those people's shoes? What do you think that was like?
- How do you think they felt when that happened?
- Where is/was empathy showing up in this?
- If you were to take the perspective of _____, what do you see, think, feel?

These social-oriented subjects are obviously ripe for an infusion of empathy in the learning, but an empathy lens also can be applied wherever math or the sciences intersect with human behavior or conditions. Math in the form of statistics, for instance, can offer an idea of the scope of a social problem that affects people on an individual level, perhaps inspiring empathy for that group of people. When real-world statistics reflect a character's condition or source of conflict within an empathy-rich story, reader empathy for those characters can deepen.

Empathy-infused science instruction can work much the same way. When Tiffany was teaching *Saving Wonder* to her fifth-grade class, for instance, she was inspired to teach a science class on water runoff to explore what happens to streams affected by mountaintop removal coal mining. She devised a hands-on experiment that showed how this kind of mining releases toxins into the soil that then leach into streams. (See www.maryknightbooks.com/educators.)

Each plastic bottle contained colored candy representing the toxic minerals within mountain rock. Whereas one bottle had hard-packed soil over the candy layer, the other bottle had the candy intermixed with the soil, representing what happens when the rock is obliterated through the mountaintop removal coal mining process (Figure 7.4a). Figure 7.4b shows how the runoff was tainted with the candy representing the toxic minerals. Students even noticed a "smell" to it.

By conducting this class science experiment through an empathy lens, Tiffany's students received a visceral understanding of the effects of runoff on a

FIGURE 7.4. Soil experiment.

community's water supply and what that can do to people's health. By stepping into the shoes of those affected by coal mining, students engaged in more empathy practice while simultaneously learning science and deepening their understanding of the story. Connecting science with *how* that science affects people provides students with *why* we study these things.

Are you seeing how empathy can inform instruction and thrive in all aspects of your classroom culture? What's more, it deepens the learning by adding meaning to what is already being taught and, even more powerfully, *lived*.

. . . .

We hope these stories have provided you with inspiring ideas. Each of these teachers made very small adjustments to practices and procedures they were already doing for empathy to enter the process. As you establish or reexamine the practices that help your classroom run smoothly, here are some questions to consider as you apply the empathy lens:

- Which first moments are important in your classroom?
- What classroom practices might add safety, energy, or joy to the life of your classroom if you were to add empathy as an intention?
- When you examine an established classroom routine from the perspective of your students, does the resulting empathy inspire any adjustments?

- As you introduce the practice, would it be helpful for your students to act like a character in a book you've recently studied in which the character showed empathy?

- As you teach this practice, ask students to think about what someone else might feel, see, or think as a result of doing it. Once identified, you can also ask: "How could we act with kindness and compassion?"

Again, we aren't suggesting you add any new practices to your classroom unless you absolutely want to. We are simply inviting you to apply an empathy lens to those practices you already do so that empathy can become a conscious part of their establishment and, in so doing, a conscious part of your learning culture. You make empathy conscious by naming it, by making it visible and audible. As you plan the ways you want to run your classroom, let empathy guide you. It will steer you and your students to the place you want to be—in a healthy learning community thriving with greater purpose.

8

CoreEmpathy for You

Talk to yourself like you would to someone you love.

—*Brené Brown, American author and research professor*

One of our first steps in the creation of CoreEmpathy involved creating curricula to distribute to teachers for field-testing the approach. At the beginning of every lesson, we invited teachers to take the first few moments of every school day before students arrived to reflect upon a quote about empathy and how it related to their lives. Basically, we were asking them to give themselves a little empathy—to fill up on empathy, so they'd have it to give. Makes sense, right?

Do you think they did it? Do you think your fellow colleagues took the three minutes we were suggesting to focus on their own needs . . . to take care of themselves . . . to fill themselves up with something wonderful? Come on now, be honest: would *you*? We can hear you chuckling.

That's right. *None* of the teachers we asked to field-test our CoreEmpathy curriculum took the time for self-empathy. Not one.

First, let us say that we understand where you're coming from. We've been there. We're still there at times. Both of us have this insane inner driver that pushes and pushes to get the work done at any cost. We don't have time for niceties. If something is bugging us, we tend to ignore it and plow through whatever is in our path. Sound familiar? Yeah, we thought so.

So, Team Empathy, what are we going to do about this empathy deficit in us? Keep on plowing? We wouldn't suggest it.

During the time we've been working on this project, we've had plenty of occasions when we've found ourselves in a bit of a tangle. In every case, trying to plow through that tangle never worked. What did? You guessed it: empathy. And most often, this meant giving ourselves empathy first.

Which is why we're ending this journey with you—our teacher-reader friend—focused on taking care of you. Would it surprise you to know that, in a CoreEmpathy classroom, you come first? We know that sounds weird, but it's true. The climate in your classroom begins with the climate in you. And so, we'd like to offer you a few empathy-inspired ideas that will nurture this climate, that will feed your energy and inspiration to do the work that is yours to do.

> **You *are the "core" in CoreEmpathy. It's been you all along.***

In this chapter, you'll find ideas for:

- how to give yourself empathy
- empathy-inspired partnerships
- becoming a role model for empathy
- preventing empathy burnout
- inspiring a greater purpose with a greater vision

But first, before we go any further, we want to tell you a secret. Perhaps it's something you've already guessed. *You* are the "core" in CoreEmpathy. It's been you all along.

Taking Care of You

Would it help if we told you that giving yourself the gift of empathy is also the best gift you can give your students? It's like that adage we've all heard by now: in case of an emergency on a plane, put your oxygen mask on first before you help the person next to you. Well, that's true with empathy, too. When you take a moment to step into your own shoes and, from your observer-self, imagine and feel what it's like to be you in the throes of all the challenges your life is dishing out, you are uniting with that part of yourself you've shoved aside for way too long in order to do your work.

That's the conundrum, isn't it? If we don't give ourselves that "empathy oxygen" first, we won't be able to show up fully in our work. Why? Because we haven't stopped long enough to offer ourselves the kind of self-understanding and appreciation that we're giving out to everyone else.

All we're suggesting is that you establish a two- to three-minute self-empathy practice at the beginning of your school day to reflect on where you are and what you need to take care of yourself in order to accomplish the big work ahead. This might mean taking time to feel the feelings of what's most present in your life right now, followed by giving yourself some appreciation for doing the best you can.

It could also mean looking back over the previous day and recalling the shimmering moments in your classroom—those moments when empathy showed up big time, when an inspired moment of instruction ignited your students' imaginations, or when witnessing an unexpected kindness touched your heart.

Perhaps you use this quiet moment to envision the day, to imagine and then feel how engaged your students will be as they open a new book and discover the gifts that lie within, waiting to be unlocked by reading it through an empathy lens.

Here are a few more suggestions for inspiring you to start the day with self-care, ones we first offered to our CoreEmpathy teachers during field-testing. Now that you know how important self-empathy is, perhaps you'll even take us up on it!

- How you treat yourself, particularly in challenging situations, will be reflected in how you treat your students. If you are inclined to be gentle with yourself when you make a mistake, for instance, then it will be far easier to have that same caring attitude with your students. Before your students start coming through the door this morning, ask yourself: What words of encouragement do I most need to hear today? Imagine that you are your own BFF. Identify three qualities that you love about yourself. After a few quiet moments of reflection, tap on your heart gently and bring this loving attitude into your classroom.

- As soon as we make an empathetic connection with another living being in nature, we are experiencing our connection with all of life. Just for a moment, feel your connection with something beautiful in nature, either through your imagination or perhaps with something right in front of you—a plant in your room or a tree outside your classroom window. Feel how it inspires you. Now remember a day when nature restored you. Rest in that memory. Steep yourself in gratitude for the natural world and all that it gives us.

- An active, thriving classroom can sometimes be noisy, right? What looks like chaos to an untrained eye may well be the height of creativity. Sometimes, however, a learning community needs silence for its members to reflect on their learning, to feel their feelings, or generate new ideas. Silence inspires receptivity, if given the chance. This morning, take a few minutes to simply sit in silence, imagining your heart and mind opening to this new day and all of its possibilities.

- Remember that, in order to give empathy to your students, you need to find a way to fill yourself with it first. If something has happened this week that has been particularly difficult or challenging, find a friend or colleague you can confide in who will listen to you and reflect back to you what you are hearing and feeling with an empathetic heart. If no one is available in the moment, try journaling about your experience and then read your entry back to yourself silently, offering yourself an empathetic ear. You can be your own best friend.

This last self-empathy reflection offers the perfect segue into the next section, as it reminds us that we really don't need to "go it alone."

Modeling Empathy and Empathy Partners

In addition to calling for the integration of social–emotional learning with academics, the report from the Aspen Institute National Commission on Social, Emotional, and Academic Development (2018) noted that "teachers and school leaders must be given opportunities to build their own social and emotional skills so that they can, in turn, model and support these skills in their students" (p. 12). The superintendent of Atlanta Public Schools and a member of the Commission Meria Carstarpehn added:

> It's hard for someone to give what they don't have. You can't assume that, just because they're adults, they [educators] have the skills and the mindsets they need to model healthy behaviors and understand the core knowledge of social–emotional learning. It's a wonderful thing when adults and kids grow together. (p. 12)

When it comes to empathy, we couldn't agree more. Of course, this "growing together" is what will happen naturally as you and your students apply the CoreEmpathy approach to literacy learning. A classroom environment in which everyone learns is a beautiful thing. But your students are not your only empathy partners. In our experience, there is no better place to practice empathy skills than with a trusted colleague. We know, because we've been practicing empathy with each other throughout the course of this project.

We knew going into the creation of CoreEmpathy that, working with such a deeply emotional soul-topic, we were bound to get many lessons along the way that were going to rock our world. After years of working together, suffice it to say, our world got rocked. However, after turning to empathy first when we encountered a challenge, not only did our partnership deepen as we practiced empathy with each other, but so did the work.

Sometimes as teachers we become so immersed in a challenge, it's impossible to give ourselves the empathy or compassion we so desperately need. This is when it's good to turn to a trusted teaching partner or school friend who is already steeped in the culture and practice of empathy. In fact, we suggest that you set up an empathy support agreement with a teaching partner ahead of time, so that, when one of you asks for empathy, the other partner knows just what to do.

Sometimes just knowing that an empathetic other is there for us is all we need to move forward in our day.

This doesn't have to be a long-winded conversation, nor are you asking for therapy, and we're certainly not suggesting you whine. Communicating what you are feeling in the moment and complaining are two entirely different things. When you approach a teaching partner for empathy, all you need to say is, "Hey, do you have a minute? I could use a little empathy," and the other immediately knows what's needed.

The empathy skills of close listening, being *with* and not fixing, hearing and feeling the emotions behind the words, repeating back what was said, and, finally, an expression of appreciation for what the other is experiencing all can be offered in just a few minutes. After all, in a school setting, a few minutes may be all you have. You can always agree to meet later for a deeper connection. Sometimes just knowing that an empathetic other is there for us is all we need to move forward in our day. And, of course, the time will come probably sooner than later when you will be the one offering the empathetic ear.

Within the Aspen Institute National Commission on Social, Emotional, and Academic Development's (2018) report, cochair of the Commission and professor emeritus at Stanford University Linda Darling-Hammond points to research that shows that "teachers who have honed their own social–emotional competencies have more positive relationships with students and peers, and are better able to create academically supportive classroom environments that engage students more deeply in their learning" (p. 15).

Empathy is a never-ending practice. As you cultivate your empathy skills with yourself and your colleagues, you'll also be developing and modeling those skills with your students. Children learn what they see, and, as you undoubtedly already know, you are an important role model in your students' lives.

Not to worry. In the case of empathy, practice doesn't make perfect. Practice grows more empathy—and that's good news for all.

Preventing Empathy Burnout

It isn't a great leap to consider that empathy-guided partnerships such as the ones we're suggesting above will not only help you build empathy skills you can model for your students, but they can also help prevent empathy burnout. While empathy can deepen our teaching purpose, it also has the potential to lead to being emotionally overwhelmed. In other words, empathy burnout is a potential hazard of being in the practice wherein we lose sight of our ability to separate our feelings from another's. As we discussed in Chapter 1 in relation to students, some people are more susceptible than others to absorbing other people's emotions. Empathy burnout happens when we take on too much of other peoples' suffering as if it were our own.

It's doubly difficult for teachers when it's one of your students who is suffering. As teachers, we often get a close-hand look at the challenges our students face in their family lives. What do we do with that heartache? How do we continue to empathize with our students without burning out emotionally? And, as any teacher knows, you don't need to be teaching at a Title I school to witness troubled lives. Issues of neglect, abuse, addiction, parental absence, or emotional loss occur across socioeconomic boundaries.

Tiffany's second- and third-grade classroom in a rural West Virginia school consists of many students who live in challenging conditions, as described in this book's introduction. Many live under so much stress, she said, that they take anti-anxiety drugs or prescriptions for depression. Their medications usually wear off halfway through the day, making the last half of the school day challenging for both learning and teaching.

When Tiffany was asked, "How do you feel empathy for your students and still teach?" she was quick with her answer: "I'm tough on them. I expect a lot. Yes, I'll sit with them and listen as they tell me about some terrible thing that has happened in their family, and I'll give them a minute or two to cry. But then I say, 'It's time to get back to work.'"

Although initially surprising, Tiffany's answer makes a lot of sense. There's a natural tendency for both teachers and parents to "bubble-wrap" their kids—

> *"No matter what is happening in our lives, we have the power to create our own story."*

that is, try to save them from experiencing negative or difficult emotions. According to Daniel J. Siegel and Tina Payne Bryson (2018b), authors of *The Yes Brain: How to Cultivate Courage, Curiosity, and Resilience in Your Child*, "Bubble-wrapping kids can prevent the full development of empathy, which often emerges directly from having experienced negative emotions themselves" (2018a, para. 12).

Although Tiffany allows her students to take a few minutes to feel those difficult feelings, she doesn't let them dwell there. She invites them to take action. "The kids and I talk about how, no matter what is happening in our lives, we have the power to create our own story. I tell them it's what they learn in school that will help them do that."

Not only does this attitude shift the student's attention from the challenges of what is to the possibility of what can be, but Tiffany's philosophy is also the perfect antidote to her own empathy burnout. Even though she may empathize first, Tiffany doesn't have time to dwell in the sadness of her students' life circumstances. She has a job to do and so do they. In other words, she's a teacher in touch with her greater purpose, and she's connected that purpose with a greater vision of what's possible in her students' future lives.

In our CoreEmpathy definition of empathy, we include that empathy is not just about stepping into someone else's shoes; it's also about acting with kindness and compassion according to your new understanding of the other. Sometimes that action looks like getting on with the work—that is, focusing our energy on what we can do, rather than what we can't. Taking action—preferably an action connected with our greater purpose—is the best remedy for empathy burnout there is.

At the first signs of becoming emotionally overwhelmed, then, it's important to check in with yourself, acknowledge your feelings, offer yourself a good, strong helping of empathy, and then turn toward your greater purpose. Suddenly, the world will become a lot clearer and you'll begin to feel empowered again. *Let us say to ourselves, "This is the difference I can make, right here and now."*

We know, because it's worked for us. Whenever we've gotten overwhelmed by events in our personal lives or the world at large, we remember to turn toward our greater purpose—this work with CoreEmpathy, for instance—and we say to ourselves, "This is the difference I can make, right here and now."

For you as a teacher, that greater purpose includes teaching literacy—hopefully, now, empathy-infused literacy—to your students. In overwhelming times, you can simply look into your students' faces and say to yourself, "*This* is the difference I'm making."

Connecting Greater Purpose with Greater Vision

Greater purpose becomes even stronger when it's connected to a greater vision, like how Tiffany connected her purpose for teaching to a vision of what is possible in her students' future lives.

You see, empathy is like a natural gas. As soon as it enters your learning environment, it will expand and seep into every nook and cranny, every heart and mind, every relationship, every subject explored, every story told and retold, until it fills your entire classroom. This is how empathy becomes more than a value, a purpose, or even a practice. This is how it permeates an entire learning culture. Empathy can fuel our greater purpose, yes, but it can also provide us with a greater vision—one that we all can share.

Once again, a greater vision begins with seeing your greater purpose through the right lens. In this case, an empathy lens. It's that simple. From the culture of your empathy-rich classroom, you and your students will become emissaries, bringing a more compassionate, empathic way of being into the world: from classroom to playground, to whole school, to family, and, before you know it, empathy has entered into the greater community. Hey, it could even expand to permeate the whole world. We're talking nothing less than an empathy revolution here—and why not?

In summary, empathy is core to a healthy learning community, but it's also important to take care of yourself to prevent empathy burnout, to hone your own empathy skills, and to become a role model for your students. Remember:

- Take a few moments to offer yourself empathy *first* every day.
- Develop empathy-inspired partnerships.
- Believe in the resiliency and potential of your students.
- Let empathy inspire you to act, fueled by your greater purpose.
- Connect your greater purpose with a greater vision, and then . . . watch that vision happen!

With everyone in your classroom practicing empathy, skills will be cultivated, understanding will flourish, and learners will feel safe to speak up, try new things, and collaborate with one another. Beyond your classroom, anyone who relates to the likes of you and your kids will automatically feel more joy without even knowing why. But *you'll* know. It's the empathy.

Appendix A

Teacher Aids

Empathy First Visual

Empathy Is . . . Imagining What Another's Life Is Like

It is seeking to understand what they . . .

see

think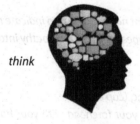

feel

I empathize when . . .

I *notice* by watching and listening.

I *imagine* what they see, think, feel.

I *act* with kindness and compassion.

Empathy First Lesson

As you say the following, point to the part of the definition on the visual and make the movement that corresponds to it. Invite students to read and make the movements with you or after you as an echo.

TEACHER: Let's take a look at our Empathy First visual and learn what empathy means: "Empathy is imagining what another's life is like."

HAND MOTIONS: *For "empathy," place hand over heart. Use this motion whenever you say the word. For "imagining," place fingers of one hand over forehead (mind) and "release" above. For "another's life is like," place one hand vertically in front of your eyes then rotate the other hand around it.*

Putting the hand motions and explanation together, it will look and sound as follows. The teacher puts her hand over her heart and says, "Empathy is," then she taps her forehead with her hand and moves it up and out while saying "imagining"; then, with her left hand vertically in front of her eyes, she rotates her right hand around it while saying "what another's life is like."

TEACHER: It is seeking to understand what they ...

   see (*point to eyes*),
   think (*point to head*),
   feel (*tap heart*).

Introducing the actions of empathy brings different hand motions to indicate how it is done. The next part of the lesson, below, describes how to put empathy into actionable steps.

TEACHER: I empathize when ...

   I notice ... by watching (*salute*) and listening (*cup ear*).
   I imagine (*same as imagining above—tap your forehead with your hand then move it up and out*) ... by what they see (*point to eyes*), think (*point to forehead*), feel (*tap heart*).
   I act ... with kindness and compassion (*with hand pausing on the heart, extend it outward*).

The lesson ends with an actual example of empathy, and can be altered to fit the learning by describing a time in your life when you thought empathy was present. You can change your empathy example to fit particular challenges that are happening in your classroom. Other times, you may wish to skip this step because the lesson is in review. Watch for a classroom example when students are practicing empathy right in front of you. Last, you can treat this step flexibly by asking for the example to originate from your students.

TEACHER: Let me give you an example of empathy. (*Feel free to give an example from your own life, making sure to model the above language within your story.*) A friend of mine talks to me about her visit to her grandmother's house, and I can imagine how happy she felt when she was there. In fact, I feel happy, too, just listening to her. That's empathy! I am able to see my friend's grandmother through her eyes. I'm imagining what my friend's experience was like.

Learning Flow of Empathy-Infused Reading

Phase One: Connect

1. Choose your book: narrative, loved, accessible to your readers, and empathy rich.
2. Peruse it and note the moments of empathy.
3. Design empathy connecting questions to ask at these moments.
4. Engage the Empathy First lesson.
5. Read the story, setting the purpose to look for empathy as you read, and ask connecting questions. Let the empathy-enriched discourse flow.

Phase Two: Deepen

1. Chart the story's core by capturing the book's key ideas and connections to empathy on a visual.
2. Discover the central message and theme while engaging common ground and the story's empathy by asking students a form of the question "How does the story (and its empathy) speak to your life?"
3. Revisit the story for reading goals and key literary elements.
4. Making the empathy learning real by applying empathy responses in your students' lives outside the classroom.
5. Enjoy your classroom's transformation!

Learning Flow of Empathy-Infused Writing

Phase One: Connect

1. Align a writer's purpose with empathy, reinforcing the idea that we write with empathy to help our readers see, think, and feel with our characters.
2. Invite students to read the story again, this time exploring it through a writer's lens. Use connecting questions to focus their attention on how the story's craft elements inspire reader empathy.
3. Release students into their writing, inviting them to use what they've learned about craft in their own stories. Use one or more empathy-infused releasing strategies.

Phase Two: Deepen

1. Students share their writing and offer empathy-inspired feedback within a CoreEmpathy writing community—whether it's the whole classroom, a small group, or as partners.
2. After receiving feedback from either you or their writing community, students revise their writing in order to deepen reader engagement. The revision process may be guided by you or initiated on their own in response to peer feedback.
3. Students share their final drafts with the whole class or within their writing communities. Listeners focus their feedback on what they appreciate about each other's work, as you encourage a spirit of celebration.
4. Enjoy your classroom's transformation!

Appendix B

Empathy-Rich Books and Resources

Empathy-Rich Books on Our Shelves

Double-asterisk notations (**) indicate texts that are used as anchors throughout this book and are featured in lessons presented in Chapter 6, as well as on www.CoreEmpathy.com. Full bibliographic details for these texts are provided in the Works Cited section. This list is dynamic and simply represents what was on our shelves prior to publication. We'd love for you to add your favorites and help us grow the list on our website.

Grades K–1

- *Chrysanthemum* by Kevin Henkes
- *Happy* by Mies van Hout**
- *How to Heal a Broken Wing* by Bob Graham
- *The Invisible Boy* by Trudy Ludwig
- *Jabari Jumps* by Gaia Cornwall
- *Leonardo, the Terrible Monster* by Mo Willems**
- *My Friend Is Sad* by Mo Willems**
- *My Many Colored Days* by Dr. Seuss
- *My Papi Has a Motorcycle* by Isabel Quintero
- *The Recess Queen* by Alexis O'Neill
- *The Stray Dog* by Marc Simont**
- *Sulwe* by Lupita Nyong'o
- *Tacky the Penguin* by Helen Lester
- *Yo! Yes?* by Chris Raschka

Grades 2–3

- *Alexander and the Terrible, Horrible, No Good, Very Bad Day* by Judith Viorst
- *A Bus Called Heaven* by Bob Graham

- *Charlotte's Web* by E. B. White
- *Circles of Hope* by Karen Lynn Williams
- *The Day the Crayons Quit* by Drew Daywalt
- *The Day You Begin* by Jacqueline Woodson**
- *Fireflies!* by Julie Brinckloe**
- *Fishing Sunday* by Tony Johnston
- *Last Stop on Market Street* by Matt de la Peña
- *Me . . . Jane* by Patrick McDonnell
- *My Brother Charlie* by Holly Robinson Peete and Ryan Elizabeth Peete
- *Ordinary Mary's Extraordinary Deed* by Emily Pearson
- *The Proudest Blue: A Story of Hijab and Family* by Ibtihaj Muhammad
- *Something Beautiful* by Sharon Dennis Wyeth
- *Through Grandpa's Eyes* by Patricia MacLachlan**
- *What Is Given from the Heart* by Patricia C. McKissack
- *When Aiden Became a Brother* by Kyle Lukoff

Grades 4–6

- *Because of Mr. Terupt* by Rob Buyea
- *Because of Winn-Dixie* by Kate DiCamillo
- *Bud, Not Buddy* by Christopher Paul Curtis
- *Flora & Ulysses* by Kate DiCamillo
- *The Great Wall of Lucy Wu* by Wendy Wan-Long Shang
- *I Am Every Good Thing* by Derrick Barnes
- *I Am Malala: How One Girl Stood Up for Education and Changed the World* by Malala Yousafzai with Patricia McCormick
- *Love That Dog* by Sharon Creech
- *The One and Only Ivan* by Katherine Applegate**
- *Out of My Mind* by Sharon M. Draper
- *Paper Wishes* by Lois Sepahban
- *Rules* by Cynthia Lord
- *Sadako and the Thousand Paper Cranes* by Eleanor Coerr
- *Sarah, Plain and Tall* by Patricia MacLachlan
- *Save Me a Seat* by Sarah Weeks and Gita Varadarajan

- *Saving Wonder* by Mary Knight**
- *Sit-In: How Four Friends Stood Up by Sitting Down* by Andrea Davis Pinkney**
- *The Undefeated* by Kwame Alexander and Kadir Nelson
- *Walk Two Moons* by Sharon Creech
- *When Zachary Beaver Came to Town* by Kimberly Willis Holt
- *The Wild Robot* by Peter Brown
- *Wishtree* by Katherine Applegate
- *Wonder* by R. J. Palacio

Resources for More Children's Books on Empathy or That Inspire Empathy

- #BooksMadeBetter—www.booksmadebetter.com, founded by Miranda McKearney (who created EmpathyLab)
- Common Sense Media—www.commonsensemedia.org/lists/books-that-teach-empathy
- Social Justice Books—www.socialjusticebooks.org/booklists

Adult Literature on Empathy on Our Shelves

Full bibliographic details are provided in the Works Cited section for all of the following books.

- *Assessing Empathy* by Elizabeth A. Segal, Karen E. Gerdes, Cynthia A. Lietz, M. Alex Wagaman, and Jennifer M. Geiger
- *The Empathy Effect: 7 Neuroscience-Based Keys for Transforming the Way We Live, Love, Work, and Connect Across Differences* by Helen Reiss
- *Empathy: Why It Matters, and How to Get It* by Roman Krznaric
- *Reclaiming Conversation: The Power of Talk in a Digital Age* by Sherry Turkle
- *Roots of Empathy: Changing the World Child by Child* by Mary Gordon
- *The War for Kindness: Building Empathy in a Fractured World* by Jamil Zaki

Other Media Resources on Empathy for Educators

- Ashoka—www.Ashoka.org, "everyone a changemaker"; www.StartEmpathy.org, "empathy and young changemaking"

- Brené Brown, "Empathy"—www.brenebrown.com/videos/RSA-Short-Empathy, an RSA Short animation/

- CoreEmpathy—www.CoreEmpathy.com, "literacy learning with a greater purpose"

- Greater Good—www.greatergood.berkeley.edu, reports on research into the roots of compassion, happiness, and altruism

- Roots of Empathy—www.rootsofempathy.org, an international school-based program

- Upworthy—www.upworthy.com, a website dedicated to positive story-telling

Works Cited

Applegate, K. (2012). *The one and only Ivan* (P. Castelao, Illus.). HarperCollins.

Arizpe, E., Styles, M., & Bromley, H. (2003). *Children reading pictures: Interpreting visual texts.* Psychology Press.

Asher, J. (2009). *Learning another language through actions* (7th ed.). Sky Oak Productions.

Aspen Institute National Commission on Social, Emotional, and Academic Development. (2018, January 23). *How learning happens: Supporting students' social, emotional, and academic development—an interim report.* Aspen Institute National Commission on Social, Emotional, & Academic Development. https://www.aspeninstitute.org/publications/learning-happens-supporting-students-social-emotional-academic-development

Baron-Cohen, S. (2012). *The science of evil: On empathy and the origins of cruelty.* Basic Books.

Barrentine, S. J. (1996). Engaging with reading through interactive read-alouds. *The Reading Teacher, 50*(1), 36–43.

Beers, K., & Probst, R. E. (2013). *Notice and note: Strategies for close reading.* Heinemann.

Block, M. (Host). (2013, June 13). *Meet "Ivan": The gorilla who lived in a shopping mall* [Radio broadcast]. NPR. https://www.npr.org/2013/06/13/191053327/headline-here?t=1610469591769

Bowen, D. P., & Kisida, B. P. (2019, February). *Investigating causal effects of arts education experiences: Experimental evidence by Houston's Arts Access Initiative.* Rice University and Houston Education Research Consortium. https://kinder.rice.edu/sites/default/files/documents/Investigating%20Causal%20Effects%20of%20Arts%20Education%20Experiences%20Final_0.pdf

Briggs, S. (2014, November 1). *How empathy affects learning, and how to cultivate it in your students.* InformED. https://www.opencolleges.edu.au/informed/features/empathy-and-learning

Brinckloe, J. (1986) *Fireflies!* (J. Brinkloe, Illus.). Aladdin Books.

Caselman, D. T. (2007). *Teaching children empathy: The social emotion.* YouthLight.

Common Core State Standards Initiative. (2021). *How to read the standards.* National Governors Association Center for Best Practices and the Council of Chief State School Officers. www.corestandards.org/ELA-Literacy/introduction/how-to-read-the-standards

Covey, S. R. (1989). *The 7 habits of highly effective people*. Free Press.

Decety, J. (2005). Perspective taking as the royal avenue to empathy. In B. F. Malle & S. D. Hodges (Eds.), *Other minds: How humans bridge the divide between self and others* (pp. 143–157). Guildford Press.

Djikic, M., Oatley, K., & Moldoveanu, M. (2013). Reading other minds: Effects of literature on empathy. *Scientific Study of Literature, 3*(1), 28–47. https://doi.org/10.1075/ssol.3.1.06dji

Drayton, B. (2012, May 17). Empathy-based ethics: A strategic essential. *Forbes India.* https://www.forbesindia.com/article/third-anniversary-special/bill-drayton-empathybased-ethics-a-strategic-essential/32952/1

Durlak, J. A., Schellinger, K. B., Weissberg, R. P., Dymnicki, A. B., & Taylor, R. D. (2011). The impact of enhancing students' social and emotional learning: A meta-analysis of school-based universal interventions. *Child Development, 82*(1), 405–432.

Gordon, M. (2009). *Roots of empathy: Changing the world child by child* (1st US ed.). The Experiment.

Hammond, Z. L. (2014). *Culturally responsive teaching and the brain: Promoting authentic engagement and rigor among culturally and linguistically diverse students.* Corwin.

Hammond, Z. (2020). *A conversation about instructional equity with Zaretta Hammond, Part 1.* Collaborative Circle. https://www.collaborativeclassroom.org/blog/a-conversation-about-instructional-equity-with-zaretta-hammond-part-1

Hay, L. (2018, July 25). *A case for promoting empathy in schools.* Changemakers. https://medium.com/change-maker/a-case-for-promoting-empathy-in-schools-db1af5414a61

Jones, D. E., Greenberg, M., & Crowley, M. (2015, November). Early social–emotional functioning and public health: The relationship between kindergarten social competence and future wellness. *American Journal of Public Health, 105*(11), 2283–2290. https://doi.org/10.2105/AJPH.2015.302630

Kidd, D. C., & Castano, E. (2013, October 18). Reading literary fiction improves theory of mind. *Science, 342*(6156), 377–380. https://doi.org/10.1126/science.1239918

Knight, M. (2016). *Saving wonder.* Scholastic.

Krznaric, R. (2014). *Empathy: Why it matters and how to get it.* Penguin Random House.

Laminack, L., & Wadsworth, R. (2012). *Bullying hurts: Teaching kindness through read alouds and guided conversations.* Heinemann.

Lessne, D., & Harmalkar, S. (2013). *Student reports of bullying and cyber-bullying: Results from the 2011 School Crime Supplement to the National Crime Victimization Survey.* National Center for Education Statistics. https://nces.ed.gov/pubsearch/pubsinfo.asp?pubid=2013329

Lexico. (n.d.-a). Core. In *Oxford English dictionary.* Retrieved May 14, 2019, from https://www.lexico.com/definition/core

Lexico. (n.d.-b). Empathy. In *Oxford English dictionary.* Retrieved May 14, 2019, from https://www.lexico.com/definition/empathy

Maass, D. (2016). *The emotional craft of fiction: How to write the story below the surface*. Writer's Digest Books.

MacLachlan, P. (1980). *Through Grandpa's eyes* (D. Kogan Ray, Illus.). HarperCollins.

McKearney, M. (n.d.). *Empathy and stories*. EmpathyLab. https://www.empathylab.uk/empathy-and-stories

Merriam-Webster. (n.d.-a). Core. In *Merriam-Webster.com dictionary*. Retrieved May 14, 2019, from https://www.merriam-webster.com/dictionary/core

Merriam-Webster. (n.d.-b). Empathy. In *Merriam-Webster.com dictionary*. Retrieved May 14, 2019, from https://www.merriam-webster.com/dictionary/empathy

Miller, D. (2009). *The book whisperer: Awakening the inner reader in every child*. Jossey-Bass.

Morrison, V., & Wlodarczyk, L. (2009). Revisiting read-aloud: Instructional strategies that encourage students' engagement with text. *The Reading Teacher, 63*(2), 110–118. https://doi.org/10.1598/RT.63.2.2

Murphy, M. A. (2019, June 16). *Boundaries with Brené Brown* [Video]. YouTube. https://www.youtube.com/watch?v=5U3VcgUzqiI

National Governors Association & Council Chief State School Officers. (2010). *Common Core State Standards for English language arts & literacy in history/social studies, science, and technical subjects*. Common Core State Standards Initiative. http://www.corestandards.org/assets/CCSSI_ELA%20Standards.pdf

National Reading Panel. (2000). *Teaching children to read: An evidence-based assessment of the scientific research literature on reading and its implications for reading instruction*. National Institute of Child Health and Human Development, National Institutes of Health. https://www.nichd.nih.gov/sites/default/files/publications/pubs/nrp/Documents/report.pdf

Nikolajeva, M. (2013). Picture books and emotional literacy. *The Reading Teacher, 67*(4), 249–254. https://doi.org/10.1002/trtr.1229

Nussbaum, M. C. (1997). *Poetic justice: The literary imagination and public life*. Beacon Press.

Oatley, K. (2008, December 1). Changing our minds. *Greater Good Magazine*. https://greatergood.berkeley.edu/article/item/chaning_our_minds

O'Brien, K. (2010, October 17). The empathy deficit. *Boston Globe*. http://archive.boston.com/bostonglobe/ideas/articles/2010/10/17/the_empathy_deficit

Orloff, J. (2018). *The empath's survival guide: Life strategies for sensitive people*. Sounds True.

Paul, A. M. (2012, March 17). Your brain on fiction. *New York Times*. https://www.nytimes.com/2012/03/18/opinion/sunday/the-neuroscience-of-your-brain-on-fiction.html

Pinker, S. (2012). *The better angels of our nature: Why violence has declined*. Penguin Books.

Pinkney, A. D. (2010). *Sit-in: How four friends stood up by sitting down* (B. Pinkney, Illus.). Little, Brown and Company.

Poole, C., Miller, S. A., & Church, E. B. (2019). *Ages & stages: Empathy*. Early Childhood Today. https://www.scholastic.com/teachers/articles/teaching-content/ages-stages-empathy

Prose, F. (2007). *Reading like a writer: A guide for people who love books and for those who want to write them*. Harper Perennial.

Quindlen, A. (1998). *How reading changed my life*. Ballantine Publishing Group.

Riess, H. (2018). *The empathy effect: Seven neuroscience-based keys for transforming the way we live, love, work, and connect across differences*. Sounds True.

Rifkin, J. (2009). *The empathic civilization: The race to global consciousness in a world in crisis*. Tarcher.

Rosenblatt, L. M. (1995). *Literature as exploration*. Modern Language Association.

Rosenblatt, L. M. (2005). *Making meaning with texts: Selected essays*. Heinemann.

RSA. (2013, December 10). *Brené Brown on empathy* [Video]. YouTube. https://www.youtube.com/watch?v=1Evwgu369Jw

Scher, A. (2019, March 26). From Parkland to Sandy Hook, trauma of school shootings haunts survivors for decades. *Daily Beast*. https://www.thedailybeast.com/from-parkland-to-sandy-hook-trauma-of-school-shootings-haunts-survivors-for-decades

Schonert-Reichl, K. A., Smith, V., Zaidman-Zait, A., & Hertzman, C. (2012). Promoting children's prosocial behaviors in school: Impact of the roots of empathy program on the social and emotional competence of school-aged children. *School Mental Health*, 4(1), 1–21. https://doi.org/10.1007/s12310-011-9064-7

Segal, E. A., Gerdes, K. E., Lietz, C. A., Wagaman, A. A., & Geiger, J. M. (2017). *Assessing empathy*. Columbia University Press.

Siegel, D. J., & Bryson, T. P. (2018a, April 24). *How to raise a child who cares*. TED. https://ideas.ted.com/how-to-raise-a-child-who-cares

Siegel, D. J., & Bryson, T. P. (2018b). *The yes brain: How to cultivate courage, curiosity, and resilience in your child*. Bantam.

Simont, M. (2000). *The stray dog* (M. Simont, Illus.). HarperCollins.

Sims Bishop, R. (1990, Summer). Mirrors, windows, and sliding glass doors. *Perspectives: Choosing and Using Books for the Classroom*, 6(3), ix–xi. Retrieved May 14, 2019, from https://scenicregional.org/wp-content/uploads/2017/08/Mirrors-Windows-and-Sliding-Glass-Doors.pdf

Sipe, L. R. (2000). The construction of literary understanding by first and second graders in oral response to picture storybook read-alouds. *Reading Research Quarterly*, 35(2), 252–275. https://doi.org/10.1598/RRQ.35.2.4

Sipe, L., & Pantaleo, S. (2008). *Postmodern picturebooks: Play, parody, and self-referentiality*. Taylor & Francis.

Terada, Y. (2018, September 11). *Welcoming students with a smile*. Edutopia. https://www.edutopia.org/article/welcoming-students-smile

Thierry, K. (2014, September 21). Empathy and optimism research. *Momentous Institute*. https://momentousinstitute.org/blog/empathy-and-optimism-research

Tippett, K. (Host, Producer). (2020, August 6). Jane Goodall: What it means to be human [Audio podcast episode]. In *On Being with Krista Tippett*. The On Being Project. http://onbeing.org/jane-goodall-on-what-it-means-to-be-human

Turkle, S. (2016). *Reclaiming conversation: The power of talk in a digital age.* Penguin Books.

US Department of Health and Human Services. (2020). What we've learned about bullying. *Research on Bullying.* https://www.stopbullying.gov/resources/facts

van Hout, M. (2012). *Happy* (M. van Hout, Illus.). Lemniscaat.

Vega, J. (2016, January 21). *Boosting comprehension through empathy.* Edutopia. https://www.edutopia.org/discussion/boosting-comprehension-through-empathy

Willems, M. (2005). *Leonardo, the terrible monster* (M. Willems, Illus.). Hyperion Books for Children.

Willems, M. (2007). *My friend is sad* (M. Willems, Illus.). Hyperion Books for Children.

Woodson, J. (2018). *The day you begin* (R. López, Illus.). Penguin Random House.

Zaki, J. (2019). *The war for kindness: Building empathy in a fractured world.* Crown.

Zakrzewski, V. (2014, January 22). How to integrate social–emotional learning in the Common Core. *Greater Good Magazine.* https://greatergood.berkeley.edu/article/item/how_to_integrate_social_emotional_learning_into_common_core

Index

Authors

Christie McLean Kesler is a literacy specialist and professional developer in the Pacific Northwest. She supports teachers in expanding and deepening their instructional practice through facilitating inservice, presenting, and coaching. In addition to authoring literacy training materials, she is currently a senior instructor at Western Washington University, where she has been teaching and mentoring preservice teachers for more than two decades. She's the teacher that students describe as "inspiring," "enlightening," "effective," and "encouraging." Her love for teaching and learning began as an elementary classroom teacher. She's also the mother of two incredible young adults and an avid lover of the mountains and water. You can contact her at www.CoreEmpathy.com.

As an author of middle grade fiction, **Mary Knight** is a frequent presenter and writing workshop facilitator at schools and conferences around the country. Her novel *Saving Wonder* (2016) was the winner of the 2017 Green Earth Book Award (Children's Fiction), a Parents' Choice award, and was selected as a Notable Book for Social Studies by the Children's Book Council. Proving that it's never too late to go back to school, Mary earned her MFA in writing in 2013 at Spalding University in Louisville, Kentucky, where she is a frequent guest speaker. She is also a writing mentor at the Carnegie Center for Literacy and Learning in Lexington, Kentucky. Whether it's reading, writing, teaching, hanging out with friends and family, hiking, golf, or learning to play the ukulele, Mary enjoys all things "play." You can contact her at www.CoreEmpathy.com.

This book was typeset in TheMix and Palatino by Barbara Frazier.

Typefaces used on the cover include Poppl-Laudatio and SuperFly One.

The book was printed on 50-lb. White Offset paper by Seaway Printing Company, Inc.